HELMAND TO THE HIMALAYAS

OSPREY
PUBLISHING

HELMAND TO THE HIMALAYAS

ONE SOLDIER'S INSPIRATIONAL JOURNEY

DAVID WISEMAN

WITH NICK HARDING

First published in Great Britain in 2014 by Osprey Publishing,
PO Box 883, Oxford, OX1 9PL, UK
PO Box 3985, New York, NY 10185-3985, USA
E-mail: info@ospreypublishing.com

Osprey Publishing is part of the Osprey Group

A CIP catalogue record for this book is available from the British Library

David Wiseman and Nick Harding have asserted their rights under the Copyright, Designs and
Patents Act, 1988, to be identified as the Authors of this Work.

ISBN: 978 1 4728 0913 1
e-book ISBN: 978 1 4728 0915 5
PDF ISBN: 978 1 4728 0914 8

Index by Angela Hall
Cartography by Peter Bull Art Studio
Typeset in Garamond and Univers
Originated by PDQ Media, Bungay, UK
Printed in Spain through GraphyCems

14 15 16 17 18 10 9 8 7 6 5 4 3 2 1

Front cover: Sgt Rupert Frere, MOD/Crown Copyright, 2011
Back cover: Images courtesy of David Cheskin/PA Images and Petter Nyquist

Author's note: Some names and details have been changed to protect the privacy of individuals involved.

The following will help in converting measurements between metric and imperial:
1 mile = 1.6km
1 yard = 0.9m
1ft = 0.3m
1in = 15.4mm
1lb = 0.45kg

Osprey Publishing is supporting the Woodland Trust, the UK's leading woodland conservation charity, by
funding the dedication of trees.

www.ospreypublishing.com

INVICTUS

William Ernest Henley

Out of the night that covers me,
Black as the pit from pole to pole,
I thank whatever gods may be
For my unconquerable soul.

In the fell clutch of circumstance
I have not winced nor cried aloud.
Under the bludgeonings of chance
My head is bloody, but unbowed.

Beyond this place of wrath and tears
Looms but the horror of the shade,
And yet the menace of the years
Finds, and shall find, me unafraid.

It matters not how strait the gate,
How charged with punishments the scroll,
I am the master of my fate:

I am the captain of my soul.

DEDICATION

Dedicated to the boy I nearly never met, to the girl I nearly never made and to the woman who held all four of us together through all of this.

In memory of those who fell on 3 November 2009, Shin Kalay, Nad-e Ali district, Helmand Province, Afghanistan.

CONTENTS

PROLOGUE

The breath wouldn't come. The lung had collapsed in my chest, shredded and useless.

Moments before, the quiet of the morning had been shattered by the sound of multiple weapons on automatic fire opening up on the patrol. I'd assessed the situation, conducted my estimate and planned my counter-attack. We were under fire from a position to our front and right. I looked at the map and located a couple of compounds that were the likely staging points of the enemy attack.

I didn't know how many of them there were, so, crouching low, I inched forward to get a better fix on the situation. That's when I saw the Taliban spotter, or 'dicker'. He was standing there, 150 metres away, leaning against a compound wall, brazenly watching the firefight. He would have been relaying information about our numbers and position to the shooters. Bastard.

I could have killed him easily but I couldn't be totally sure that he was working for the enemy and this would have been against our rules of engagement, so I sent a warning shot into the ground next to him instead. That did the trick. He turned on his heels and ran. As soon as he fled, a second enemy position opened up directly to my front, likely drawn by my own firing at the dicker. The first round was so close I felt it whistle past my head; the second floored me. I had no time to react. It smashed into my shoulder like a sledgehammer, pulverising bone and tissue. It travelled through my chest, snapping my ribs like matchsticks and macerating a lung. I was picked up by the force and flung several metres through the air, spinning like a ragdoll.

I landed in a crumpled heap.

I tried to yell, but it came out as a rather pathetic sound.

'I'm shot… I'm shot… I'm shot, boys.'

The rounds were still coming as the sniper who nailed me tried to finish off the job. Survival instinct kicked in, and I slithered into the ditch by the side of the road for cover. In the fetid water I began to gasp for breath.

Dust, air and shitty ditch water sucked in through the angry hole in my shoulder as I tried to inhale. The exhalation sprayed blood and fluid bubbles from the wound in a disgusting cloud. The pain was indescribable and getting worse. I couldn't move my right side as I squirmed in the mud, blood and water, and my new paralysis combined with 35kg of kit and equipment resulted in me slipping under the surface.

I heard a call down the line of troops.

'Man down!'

All around me there was movement. A body crashed into the muck next to me.

It was my Fijian lance corporal.

'You're going to be alright, Boss,' he reassured me, as he dragged my body above the surface allowing me to breathe.

But we both knew that was a naïvely optimistic assessment of the situation. He set to work urgently, tugging and cutting away my kit and clothes in an effort to assess my injuries. Blood spurted in an arc from the bullet entry wound. It splashed on my face. The ditch water was tepid, but the blood was hot. I turned away as Manny joined us in the ditch and struggled to staunch the flow.

Further forward, the thunderous clatter of our GPMG sent a spray of deadly fire towards the bastards who had just hit me. Hopefully they were now experiencing the same level of pain and panic that was coursing through my body.

I tried to help my medic and remove some of the equipment I was carrying, but each movement sent a fresh wave of pain searing through my body. My arm wasn't working. My body refused to do what I wanted it to. I felt numb in some places and alive with burning agony in others. My right side felt as though all the nerves in it were being electrified and stung by bees at the same time. Nerve damage. The smashed bones in my shoulder, chest and back were in agony. I couldn't speak; I couldn't breathe. I was bleeding out and the blood was filling my chest cavity. I heard a weird sucking, gurgling sound and looked down to see the tiny round wound in my shoulder burbling with each difficult breath. The blood and air were filling my chest rapidly, and had started to prevent my good lung from opening.

'We need to get him out of here. NOW!' Manny yelled.

I was pulled and pushed out of the ditch and staggered back along the road we had been patrolling. Each step sent waves of pain through my broken torso. Each gulp for breath bought a fresh pulse of hurt.

I dropped in the dust. The air around me was alive with enemy fire. Too close for comfort. The ground vibrated as an RPG landed nearby. The pressure wave hit my chest and set off a fresh chain reaction of suffering. My useless lung convulsed in a chest cavity that was filling with air, blood and fluid. With all the space taken up by blood and air, my other lung struggled to inflate.

I was prone. I was a target. Manny dropped on top of me, a human shield against the threat of more hot rounds. We lay in that position for what seemed like ages while our guns sought out and neutralised the threats that were jeopardising my extraction from the scene. I knew my injuries were serious and that I needed to get to the hospital in Bastion where I'd have a fighting chance of survival. But while we were pinned down in a firefight it was unlikely a helicopter would be allowed to land and take me away.

'… and ye though I walk through the shadow of death, I shall fear no evil.' Manny's voice filled my ears. High pitched, breathless and panicking, he began to pray for us.

Damn, I really am in the shit, I thought. The medic is reciting the Psalms.

Then he started repeating the Lord's Prayer over and over again. I mouthed the words in time with his. I didn't have the air in me to speak them. We lay there in the maelstrom: me, dying; Manny, squaring it with the man upstairs. My breathing stopped. I tried, but I couldn't force any air into my chest. My lungs had given up. My eyes widened. I started to panic and point at my mouth. More than anything I wanted to live. I wanted to see my wife and unborn son. I wanted to see home. I didn't want my last memory to be a dusty Afghan street. Tears filled my eyes. My senses began to dull. The sounds of battle were becoming distant.

This is it. This is how I end, I told myself.

CHAPTER 1
BAGHDAD BLUES

I yawned and waited for the all-clear. Another insurgent had taken a mortar pot shot somewhere on the base. It happened at least twice a week and was more inconvenient than it was dangerous. The attacks inevitably took place at night. Each time they happened, the American early warning system screamed out and sent everyone diving for cover in the makeshift sheet metal shelters under their breeze block beds. We would all lie there in our little metal coffins, bollocks pressed tight against the cold floor.

It was exciting the first few times but after several months it became an annoyance. The Green Zone itself was pretty impenetrable, so the best the enemy could do was to lob something over the wall and hope it did some damage. It rarely did.

It was Baghdad, March 2009, and, despite the sporadic thrills, it's fair to say that Iraq wasn't what I'd hoped it would be. It was my first taste of the conflict arena and I'd been hoping to put into practice all that I had been trained to do, but I'd arrived late to the party. The old adage 'be careful what you wish for' would come home to haunt me just eight months later, but at that point in my military career I was royally pissed at having such an uneventful tour of duty.

Up to that point my hunger for the fight had been frustrated by my choice of regiment. I had been commissioned into The Yorkshire Regiment after a year at the Royal Military Academy, Sandhurst and a further three months at the Infantry Battle School in Brecon, South Wales.

I had done well at the academy and had a choice of two infantry regiments; The Royal Anglian Regiment and the Yorks. At the time the Royal Anglians were preparing to deploy to Afghanistan in the spring of 2007, but during 2006, when I was making my decisions, all the noise was about Iraq. Iraq was where the action was and Iraq was where I wanted to be.

The Yorkshire Regiment was formed when the British Army restructured in 2006 and consisted of The Prince of Wales' Own Regiment of Yorkshire, the Green Howards, The Duke of Wellington's Regiment and associated Reserve units. I was promised that if I joined 1 Yorks I would catch the tail end of a deployment and would therefore have my first medal within just a few months of commissioning. I didn't want to go to boring Afghanistan and sit in Kabul for six months doing the square root of naff all. I liked the idea of zipping around Basra or Najaf, fighting insurgents from a vehicle, so 1 Yorks it was.

The codename for the UK's military operations in Iraq was Operation *Telic*. The word 'telic' means a purposeful or defined action, but personnel joked that it stood for 'tell everyone leave is cancelled'. Apparently the MoD uses a computer to generate random names for military operations to avoid any embarrassing, overtly-political connotations. The US didn't get the memo, however, and called their equivalent deployment Operation *Iraqi Freedom*; the joke again was to change the word 'Freedom' to 'Liberation' to spell the word 'OIL'. Operation *Telic* lasted from the initial invasion in March 2003 until the withdrawal of the last UK troops in May 2011 and was split into 13 phases. I joined 1 Yorks at the tail end of the phase of operations known as *Telic 9,* which ran from November 2006 to June 2007, and hoped to join my colleagues on their tour. That eventuality never materialised, however. It took another two years before I eventually found myself in Iraq, and I welcomed the battalion home in the summer of 2007 looking a real chopper with my arm in a sling after sustaining a nasty injury in a rugby tournament that required reconstructive surgery on my collarbone. The irony was that most of the friends I trained with who went on to join my other choice of regiment, the Royal Anglians, returned from Afghanistan with war stories, having cut their teeth in the early days of the fighting in Helmand. They were among the second batch of battalions to enter the province which would play such a pivotal part in my life several years later and had a seriously punchy tour, fighting tooth and nail on a relatively conventional battlefield, before the advent of improvised explosive devices (IEDs) and other such nightmares. To make matters worse, their tour had been filmed by Ross Kemp for his *Ross Kemp in Afghanistan* series, so I had the ignominy of watching exactly what I had missed on the bastard television!

Stationed in Catterick, north Yorkshire, I took over 1 Platoon, A Company and became the commander of a unit that had suffered badly in *Telic* 9 when an IED struck their vehicles halfway through the tour. Private Luke Simpson was driving the lead vehicle in a convoy of three Snatch Land Rovers returning to base at Basra after a routine patrol to an Iraqi police station when the roadside bomb exploded as he passed. He died in the blast. My friend Lieutenant Ibi Ali, the vehicle's commander, had his right arm amputated, Private Paul Davey had shrapnel in both legs and underwent surgery and Private Christopher Herbert's right leg was removed just below the knee.

Even though the scars of war were so prevalent in my workplace, I still felt I had missed out on the chance to command a platoon of men on operations, which was everything I had trained to do and was the reason I had enlisted in the first place. I feared that I would be moved on to a different job before the next tour came about and would remain unproven in combat. I had a strong desire to test myself under the most extreme circumstances and to put my training and my skills to use in a firefight. I had trained in a range of environments but, like any serviceman, I had no idea of knowing how I would react under the pressure of a combat situation, and as long as those doubts remained, could I really class myself as a true soldier?

For the first six months after I joined 1 Yorks I lived in a single room in the Officers' Mess. I knew the living arrangements were temporary, as I was engaged to marry my childhood sweetheart, Lucy, at the end of September 2007. We had been together since school and she had stuck by me through university and throughout my training. Lucy was the sort of soul-mate some people look for all their lives and never find. It is not easy being with someone whose job is, by its very nature, unpredictable, unsociable and dangerous, but Lucy had been loyal and encouraging and our relationship had flourished where many others had floundered.

I proposed to her in December 2006 on the very day I finished my training at Sandhurst. We were walking to the 14 Platoon end of course party prior to the big Commissioning Ball, and I dropped on one knee in my dress uniform at the bottom of the polo fields beside the lake, with the iconic columns of Old College lit up in the background. I had a bottle of Bollinger in one hand and a ring in the other. Of course, she said yes.

We were married the following September in her local village church. Half the congregation was in uniform, with medals and swords glistening all over the place – a great combination when you had huge amounts of alcohol later on. In fact, it's traditional for the groom to buy the guard of honour a bottle of port, so between seven of us we had drunk a bottle of fortified wine on top of a few glasses of champagne before I even made it into the church. Lucy swore she wouldn't marry me if I stank of booze when she turned up, but, after a heavy session the night before and the few glasses before the service, I doubt I smelt wholly sober – she was bluffing. A lot of people said we were quite young to be getting married at 26 years old, but we had been together for so long that it was just the right time.

In the church, as the vicar asked 'Is there anyone here with any lawful reason why these two should not be wed?' the six big blokes who I had chosen to be my guard of honour stood up with great drama (and not a little noise) at the back of the church. The whole congregation turned around to see the boys with their swords half-drawn in a threat to anyone who thought they had a reason, lawful or not!

Marriage entitled us to a married quarter, and we moved into a relatively decent four-bedroom semi on the edge of Catterick Garrison, close to the Dales and the idyllic market town of Richmond with its Norman castle and cobbled streets. Living away from the mess had its benefits and allowed Lucy and I normality and refuge from the army and work. When it came to practical jokes I had always been a ringleader (or as Lucy described me more accurately, a bad influence), and I admit I missed out on some of the camaraderie of living in close proximity with my work colleagues and I worried I would no longer be seen as one of the boys. But in our new home I could slob out in front of the telly and do what I wanted.

The returning troops adjusted quickly to life on base following the tour, and for the next two years we trained hard to prepare for the next deployment as the insurgency in Iraq continued and the situation in parts of Afghanistan became progressively more dangerous. The highlight of this period was a two-month exercise to the southern tip of the Kalahari Desert in South Africa, where I was given fairly free rein to plan, organise and execute an exercise that would develop and test my platoon. I was lucky enough to have some experience in difficult environments, as, during my training at the Infantry Battle School, I had spent several weeks in Kenya and was prepared for the hardships that the heat, dust and Bastard Bushes would bring. There must be a proper horticultural name for a Bastard Bush, but I've never heard it called anything different. It is the name given to any clump of flora with an inordinate amount of thorns that is practically invisible in the darkness. If you are unfortunate enough to stumble into one of these spiky shrubs, it is impossible to extract yourself silently, without help and without uttering the word 'bastard' – hence the name.

Despite the discomfort, I loved being out in those conditions. The previous year I'd spent five weeks in the punishing heat of Kenya, training in the middle of a nature reserve called Oli Naishu. There, before we set off into the *bundu*, one of the reserve's rangers came to tell us about the animals in the park. He spoke in a deep, heavily-accented voice and obviously loved a bit of the theatrics.

'There are three animals here in the reserve that will trouble you. Number three is the lion.'

At this point he held his hands out as claws and roared. Sixty newly commissioned officers sat there, stunned by the comedic delivery of the guy, not entirely sure if he was joking or not. He was deadpan serious.

'The lion will always let you know if you are too close.' He let out another roar. 'I advise you to back away very slowly.'

'The second is the elephant.' He swung his arm like a trunk in the air and trumpeted. Several of us began to laugh behind our hands.

'Again, the elephant will let you know if you are too close. But the most dangerous animal in the whole park is the buffalo!'

The big ranger put his fingers up to his head like a pair of horns and danced around mooing. By that point there was no one who wasn't clutching their belly and shaking silently with laughter.

He dropped a couple of decibels and warned: 'The buffalo, she will wait oh so very quietly and let you get so very close before BOOM! She jumps out of the grass and you are dead.'

We all thought this guy was brilliant, and he went on to tell us about snakes and spiders and all the other deadly threats we'd encounter. We left his chat thinking that if any of us survived the exercise without being eaten, crushed, poisoned or contracting the shits so badly we turned ourselves inside out, then we'd be lucky.

Two weeks later we were lying in a night ambush looking over a dry river bed, or wadi. We had been there for hours, and even though we all had night vision sights attached to our weapons, we couldn't see anything; it was so dark. The directing staff were all sitting up on the hill behind us, making sure the serial ran as it should and watching how we would react to whatever they threw at us. We had been in position for about seven hours, lying prone in the long grass, so they were probably also making sure we weren't asleep.

All of a sudden I heard someone moving through the wadi below us. This was a blank firing exercise and we were expecting a group of Gurkhas to come along at some point and act as the enemy. Hearing the noise, we all assumed that our long wait was over. I looked again through my night vision but could see nothing. The noise got closer until it went right past me in the black ravine below. Then I heard it moving up the grassy bank just 5 metres to my right before stopping. I heard it pass. Silence hung in the dark African night until the very panicky voice of my friend Redders broke it with a half-whisper, half shout:

'FUCK OFF!'

The noise crashed off back down the bank into the wadi and up the other side at great speed, running off into the night. The instructor, Captain Mike Willis, also from The Yorkshire Regiment, came sprinting down from his vantage point on the hill.

'Wisey, you alright?' he asked.

'Fine. It wasn't me, it was Redders – that way.' I pointed to the guys to my right and Mike bolted over to them.

'What happened?' I shouted after him in the darkness.

'It was a bloody buffalo and its calf, came right up the wadi!'

Talking to a rather shaken Redders the next morning, he said it was so dark he hadn't seen the buffalo until he was literally nose to nose with the thing (most likely he'd been dossing and only woke up when the bugger was right over him), and at that moment the only thing he could think of was to tell it to fuck off with all the aggression he could muster. It obviously worked as he wasn't trampled to death. Maybe the ranger needed to change his brief to include the vital survival technique of verbal abuse.

The South Africa exercise was less eventful in terms of fauna; however, that's not to say we didn't bump into some unusual and unexpected creatures, from flesh-eating crickets with bulbous eyes that stank like shit to wondrous sea creatures. The sea creatures were probably the most unexpected thing to see on a trip to the southern tip of the Kalahari, and it was only due to the fact that we were being flown to South Africa by the RAF that we came across these amazing creatures.

We were sitting in the terminal at RAF Brize Norton for hours waiting for our plane. When it arrived, we were told we'd have to wait for another plane to land so that a part could be cannibalised from it to fix the jet we were about to board – not hugely reassuring, and even less so when we saw RAF technicians fixing something to the wing with cable ties as we boarded!

Mack, the company sergeant major, stood at the front of the cabin and everyone stopped talking.

'Right, you lot. Stick up your hands if you think we are going to be in South Africa later today.'

A few of the younger lads put up their hands to a chorus of jeers of 'Red Arse! Put your hand down, crow bag!'

'Alright, who thinks we'll be in South Africa tomorrow?'

No hands went up, and I looked up at Mack, wondering where he was going with his line of questioning.

'Well, I've just been speaking to this here RAF officer who doesn't even seem to know where he's going. Says we're off to Dakka, then Ascension and then finally South Africa sometime in the next few days!'

A new chorus filled the cabin of 'Fookin Crab Air!'

'Mr Wiseman?' shouted Mack in my direction. 'Two questions. Did you know about this, and where the hell is Dakka?'

'Not at all Sergeant Major, I've only got the clothes I'm wearing, and Dakka is the capital of Senegal on the western coast of Africa.'

Mack sat down next to me and jabbed me in the ribs.

'Typical bloody officer: smart arse but a fat lot of use!'

Ascension Island, in the middle of the southern Atlantic, was a true paradise. We spent the afternoon on the beach; me and the other young officers started Operation *Bronze* whilst the lads dug pits for crabs to fight in (actual crabs, not honking RAF types).

That night most of the lads stayed in the NAAFI bar and got annihilated, while around five of us booked the only taxi on the island for a crawl around each of the island's bars. There were only around five or six. The first was halfway up the volcano that had formed the island in the first place and the last stop backed onto a wide, sandy beach.

As the driver pulled up, he said, 'As soon as you've got your beer, head out on to the sand and see what you see.'

It was well into the night by this point, but the full moon bathed the beach in a silvery glow and the sound of the surf gently crashing against the sand was magical. As we walked a little way onto the beach we were met by hundreds and hundreds of shapes moving slowly and arduously up the beach. Turtles as far as the eye could see, each one of them enormous and crawling up to lay her eggs.

I have never seen a sight like it in my life, and probably never will again.

We finally got to South Africa and got stuck into the long-anticipated exercise. We had very few close encounters of the animal kind, except for at notably arduous points of the exercise when a number of the less robust members of the company claimed they had been bitten by snakes and were taken in for the day to be checked out.

There were plenty of snakes kicking around; in fact, before the exercise started proper, we spent a day with the South African Special Forces who were specialists in survival and living off the land. They taught us how to make traps and rub sticks together to make fire, and fed us bushtucker-style snacks such as grubs, snakes and ground squirrels. At one point they gathered everyone together around a box that the chief instructor was tapping with a stick.

'All of you, come close and do not move. This is to show you that most of the animals that live here mean you no harm, and if you don't bother them, they will not bother you,' he explained.

At that point he lifted the box off the ground, and a long fat puff adder hissed angrily and started to move around the tiny circle of troops. It slithered across the toes of my boots, but bit no one.

The day culminated with us being stripped of any kit other than a pair of boots, a pair of trousers, a t-shirt, a water bottle and a chicken egg, before being loaded up onto a rickety truck and dropped off at intervals all around the park. I spent hours gathering firewood and just before dusk I got it to light using the skills I'd learned earlier. I had no time to make a trap, so instead I buried my egg under the fire and poured some water around it in the hope that the egg would cook – it didn't, and instead it cracked under the ground.

Hungry, alone and more than a little bit scared, I settled down for an amazing night under the most incredible night sky I've ever seen. Hundreds of miles away from any settlement that could affect the stars with light pollution, the night sky was worth every second of discomfort. I curled up in the dust as close to the fire as I dared and had a rather uncomfortable sleep on the bare earth.

During the two months that followed, my platoon worked tirelessly and my sections responded effectively to commands; I hoped that I had proved to them that I was both a capable soldier and commander. I also had the privilege of building up a great rapport with my right hand man, Sergeant Jas Friend, who left the army after 23 years and remains a true ally to this day. By the end of the exercise I knew that I could proudly and confidently take the lads on tour.

Within months of our return from Africa the battalion moved en masse to Munster in north-west Germany and went straight into pre-deployment training (PDT), as in the winter of 2008, we were to deploy to Iraq once more. I can't lie. The prospect excited me.

Both Lucy and I were looking forward to moving to Germany; seeing as though we had only been married for less than a year, we were keen to have a bit of an adventure together. We packed what few belongings we had and ferried them across the channel. The army had provided us with a furnished home in Catterick and did so in Germany too; most of our furniture was army issue – we didn't even own our bed.

The quarters in Germany are renowned for being massive, but when we were shown our quarter in Munster, neither of us could believe our eyes. The size of the building was astonishing, with five bedrooms, two bathrooms, a cellar, an attic and a lawn on which you could have played a small game of cricket. It really was too much. There were rooms we barely went into. However, despite the lovely home, Lucy was far away from her family and we were all gearing up for an operational tour, which meant that while she had the support of the other wives and partners, she missed her parents while I was involved in the time-consuming tasks of preparing for tour.

PDT involved a great deal of time away from home on various exercises and training courses. It is an extremely busy time for a battalion, and the wives always say that a tour is ten months long rather than the standard six to seven because they don't see their husbands and partners in the months before deployment. Along with the physical training there is also a psychological element to the process. In the months leading up to operations, there is a subtle shift in attitude as soldiers focus on the job at hand and mentally prepare for whatever may lay ahead.

I was eager about the prospect of finally getting the opportunity to see action but was also slightly disappointed by the operational tasking I was handed. The deployment was to be split. Two rifle companies would spend their tour in Basra, and my company was to spend seven months in Baghdad. While the situation in the nation's capital was far from pedestrian, the guys in Basra were potentially doing a far more interesting job: they would be part of the Military Transition Team, or MiTT, which meant integrating with the Iraqi forces in an attempt to develop them through a process of mentoring. Meanwhile, up north in Baghdad, we were tasked with providing security for the Senior British Military Representative in Iraq (SBMRI), at that time Lieutenant General John Cooper, who lived in a small but beautiful riverside palace that had once belonged to Saddam Hussein's eldest son, Uday. The area around it had been built up into a small fortress by the British Army with a series of reinforced portable cabins, high fences and elevated sentry positions, or Sangers in military parlance. The complex was known as Maude House and was in one tiny corner of the city that had become the fortified headquarters of the allied forces. Officially it was the International Zone, but everyone called it the Green Zone, as opposed to the potentially hostile rest of the city, which was the Red Zone. It would be our home for the duration of the deployment and was a relatively safe area. Every entrance was heavily guarded by a series of checkpoints that were manned by a combination of American forces and well paid private security personnel who were all former military. Every vehicle was thoroughly searched, and attacks inside the Green Zone were extremely rare. The only real threat we would face inside those protective walls was indirect fire or IDF: the acronym used to describe any ordnance that an assailant lobs in a high angle trajectory and does not require line of sight in order to fire, such as rockets and mortars as opposed to bullets.

With this in mind I wasn't unduly worried about my safety, and in September 2008 I said goodbye to Lucy after she dropped me and my considerable luggage off at A Company lines in Oxford Barracks, Munster, just a mile away from our quarter.

We flew into Qatar, then changed at Kuwait onto a smaller Hercules four-engine propeller plane. The C130 Hercules is the work horse of the British Armed Forces as a cargo and personnel carrying aircraft, and a trusted and valuable work horse it may be, but it's hugely uncomfortable and damned noisy. The Hercules took us up to Baghdad with a short stop in Basra to drop off some equipment.

We flew into Baghdad International Airport (known as the BIAP) and after a bit of hanging around (which always happens when the RAF are involved) we were shuttled into the International Zone by a couple of Puma helicopters, flying ultra-low level across the sprawling city, seemingly just above the rooftops to avoid any chancer with an RPG getting enough time to take a bead and loose off a lucky round. It was then just a short drive round to Maude House, and after what felt like an age of travelling in all sorts of different modes of transport, we were finally in the place where we would be stationed for the next seven months.

The IDF warning alarm became a part of regular camp life and began almost from the first night. Thankfully, the Americans had several early warning systems in place around the Green Zone that could detect and track fast moving objects through the air, and once or twice a week sirens would scream around every camp in the Green Zone to warn us of incoming rounds. Our beds had been built up off the ground on breezeblocks and metal sheeting, which created a little bed-sized shelter underneath in which we would scurry, slightly disorientated and half asleep as the alarm would invariably sound in the middle of the night. Inevitably, I would be stark naked with my bollocks painfully pressed on the frigidly cold metal plate that formed the base of my shelter.

Apart from the sporadic excitement of dodging mortars, my days in Iraq were uneventful. In between the infrequent patrols, I spent time either watching DVD box sets or training in the gym. I was keen on the punch bag and the rowing machine. Throughout the tour I became friendly with the young officer who commanded the Signals detachment at Maude House, and both of us were fairly handy on the indoor rower. Every few days one of us would beat the other's record for the 2,000 metres by a couple of seconds, and the rest of the week would be spent trying to squeeze a little bit of extra speed out of our bodies, so the record would never stand for long. I eventually got my time down to 6:39 but have never been able to recreate it.

We ventured out into the Red Zone two or three times a week. Our platoon-strength patrols were conducted in crappy vehicles called Vectors that were brought out to replace the controversial armoured Snatch Land Rovers. The Vector was equally as poor as the Snatch and offered pretty much the same level of protection. Most of us would have preferred to have had the Snatch back, as the Vector was not mechanically reliable and accelerated like a fat bastard in treacle. However, the Snatch had received a lot of bad press. It was criticised for not offering adequate protection against roadside bombs and had been labelled the 'mobile coffin'. With this in mind, the army would have sent us out in Ford Mondeos before it brought back the Snatch. The Vector became a running joke. When we parked up in the American camps, the Yanks would point and laugh at our funny little vehicles. Many of them asked if they could take photos and all of them were astounded that we frequented the Red Zone with such little protection.

Our vehicles had two hatches in the roof out of which two guys would stand brandishing their personal weapons – either the standard SA80 assault rifle or the 5.56mm light machine gun (LMG). We also had two pintle-mounted general purpose machine guns (GPMG, often called a Gympy or simply The General), which are beautifully crafted weapons that replaced the Bren Gun in the 1960s and have been used by British soldiers ever since. The lads loved them despite their crazy weight because in a firefight they are a pure force multiplier. They spew forth hundreds of 7.62mm rounds a minute in a cone of fire, with enough force to smash through a brick wall with just a few bursts.

In an attempt to discourage trouble, we tried to make ourselves look harder than we actually were by mimicking one of the standard operating procedures (SOPs) of the Americans. Most of their vehicles bristled with .50cal heavy machine guns (HMG). These were huge weapons that took mammoth half-inch rounds which smashed through pretty much anything. When a .50cal was used, cover was notional. Each HMG was equipped with green laser aimer, and the US practice was to flash this as a warning to any possible threats seconds before firing if the threat didn't (quickly) back down. Ninety-nine times out of 100 the perceived danger was an innocent motorist who had just got a bit close to the patrol, rather than a suicide bomber on a martyrdom mission to explode himself and his car and cause maximum damage to the Americans. All the civvies in Baghdad recognised the green laser warning and soon slammed on the brakes if the interior of their car suddenly lit up like a trance club. We didn't have HMGs, but we did have $2 green laser pens, which we bought from the jingly stalls and used to fool potential insurgents into believing that we had itchy trigger fingers and the propensity to deliver swathes of death. We didn't, but in the darkness it didn't matter; the cheap trinkets had the desired effect.

In addition to commanding men in operations, I also felt an obligation of pastoral care towards my men which was tested halfway through the tour when one of my blokes, Stevo, developed a problem. He was one of my favourite lads. Even Stevo would acknowledge that he didn't always think things through, but his loyalty was unshakable and he tried his utmost at any task he was given. Stevo's problem was both medical and moral. He'd returned from R&R with warts around his arse. Apparently his girlfriend had been adventurous with a dildo, using it on herself as a delightful show for her brave boyfriend returning from the perils of Baghdad before bending him over and smashing it up his ring. I wasn't sure about the latter part of the act, but hey, different strokes for different blokes as they say.

I found out about Stevo and his problem when I was grabbed by one of the platoon on my way to the gym.

'You probably want to see this, Boss,' he beckoned.

I chased after him and followed him into the lads' accommodation, where Stevo was on a bed with his knees tucked under his body and his rancid bare arse pointing up in the air in a rough approximation of the Downward Facing Dog position that would put even the most ardent yoga fans off their exercise for a while. A small crowd of blokes had gathered round and were laughing, cheering and pointing at Stevo's bumpy ringpiece, as another lad, Kel, parted his cheeks.

'Are you sure this is going to work?' asked Stevo nervously.

''Course it is, mate. You just hold still while I get the laser out,' replied Kel, stifling a laugh.

'Make sure you laser them all off; I don't want them coming back.' Stevo looked round and saw me standing there.

'Oh, hello, Boss.'

I couldn't help but burst into fits of laughter when I figured out what the silly fuckers were trying to do.

'Stevo, I'm pretty sure you can't burn off warts with a laser pen! Even if you could, would you really want Kel to do it?'

Stevo sat up and thought about it for a few seconds.

'Yeah, 'course,' he sniffed, before assuming the position again.

Bemused, I shook my head and left them to their amateur STD clinic.

I love soldiers. I love working with them and I have forgotten 90 per cent of the things they have had me in stitches over. They trust each other implicitly – God only knows why, as they are always setting each other up for a piss-take. Sometimes I felt a bit like I was looking after Peter Pan's Lost Boys – a really great bunch of enthusiastic guys who would do anything for you and just lived for the moment. They were impulsive and had little concept of cause and effect, which sometimes got them into trouble but invariably made their lives more interesting and staved off maturity.

There were two main objectives to our patrols into the Red Zone. The first was to add muscle to the close protection teams escorting VIPs to various political meetings around the city. If General Cooper had an appointment in one of the government ministry buildings, he would normally fly. However, if the weather was crap or the visibility was reduced by either a thick cloud of dust or a sand storm that frequently threw a blanket over Baghdad, he would go by road, and we would take him.

The main bulk of our patrols, however, were routine logistical re-supplies to BIAP which took us down the notorious Baghdad Airport Road, or Route Irish as it was more commonly known. The road was a 12 kilometre stretch of highway that linked the Green Zone to the airport. Because of its strategic importance and heavy military and VIP use, it became a magnet for insurgent booby-trappers, suicide bombers, snipers and drive-by shooters after the invasion. For several years it was like shooting fish in a barrel for the insurgents, as convoy after convoy was channelled along it. Civilians would pay private security companies thousands of pounds for a one-way ticket, and it soon developed a reputation as the most dangerous road in the world. Once or twice a week we would find ourselves on this deserted motorway in the middle of the night, but by the time we arrived, Route Irish was considered to be relatively secure, and we never had any bother. In fact, that was the tone of the whole tour. Things were going pop all over the city, and the Americans were getting hammered with IEDs and grenade attacks, but we didn't get a sniff of action. It was dull, and the last couple of months I spent in Iraq became even duller when a new red-arsed officer was flown across for the last section of the tour and I was promoted to second in command of the company (Coy 2iC). It was not a welcome promotion as it meant that I would have to let go of the command of my platoon which I had led since the spring of 2007. It was a sad day for me as it would be unlikely that I would directly command a body of men for another ten years until I had reached the rank of Major and would be lucky enough to be given a Rifle Company. That was too long to conceive, and I was staring down the barrel of a series of staff officer jobs in HQ.

As Coy 2iC, I worked more closely with the Officer Commanding (OC) A Company and helped to plan and coordinate patrols throughout Baghdad. When a patrol was ongoing, my job was to sit in the American Ops room situated in one of Saddam's palaces inside the Green Zone and watch and direct as the men on the ground carried out their detail. From a literal ivory tower, I would help to direct any assistance in the form of American troops to the patrol if the shit hit the fan. The fan remained poo-free for the whole tour, and I reached new levels of boredom sitting for hour after hour staring at the big ops screen and monitoring the net. It was video games without the fun, and when the time came to finish deployment and return to base, I was glad to see the back of Iraq.

CHAPTER 2
THE ROAD TO AFGHANISTAN

Before Iraq, Lucy and I had discussed starting a family. We both wanted to have kids while we were young, and after a month of me getting home she was pregnant. We were both overjoyed, and the news acted as a happy counter-balance to the professional dissatisfaction I felt on my return to Germany. My ambitions were unfulfilled, and I began to carefully consider my next move. I made it quite clear to my chain of command that I wanted new challenges. I voiced my desire to do some proper soldiering and signed up to take the Jungle Warfare Instructors Course held in Belize. Each year 3,000 troops were exercised at the British Army Training Support Unit Belize (BATSUB), including a few dozen that were put through their paces on the specialist Instructors Course. The facility had been in operation since the small Central American country gained independence in 1981. The BATSUB training area gave British troops some of the most testing exercises in the world with access to 8,000 square kilometres of primary jungle provided by the Belize government.

I was looking forward to getting into the jungle; one of the most hostile environments on the planet. Jungle warriors are afforded a certain reverence in the British Army. They say if you can soldier there then you can soldier anywhere, and I wanted to push myself and develop the skills

I'd already learned. I'd missed my chance at combat in Iraq but maybe I could find challenges elsewhere in the army.

Lucy had, and still does, put up with a great deal. I had dragged her out to Germany in the summer of 2008, and she had pretty much lived there on her own up to that point, while I had either been preparing for deployment or on deployment. Then, almost as soon as I got back, I smashed myself onto a long course in the jungle and started talking about how I was thinking about attempting to move my career into a more challenging direction that would put more demands on our time as a couple. Lucy is a hugely devoted wife and offered me nothing but support in all of my endeavours. She didn't once try to dissuade me, as she could see that it was something I just had to do. If I didn't scratch the itch for combat and the desire to keep pushing myself, she knew I would never be happy.

As things turned out, fate intervened and my plan never reached fruition. On 15 September 2009 I was working in my office. It was a bright evening, and I was looking forward to finishing the mountain of work I had and going out for a run. A door, always open, connected my office to Phil's, the OC of A Company. He popped his head round the door with a smile.

'David, I just got off the phone to the Colonel Jonny. He wants a word with you.'

'Well, from the look on your face I can tell I'm not about to get a bollocking, so what's going on?' I asked.

'He wants to tell you, but I know it's what you want: something about Afghan.'

Suddenly I was really interested. My stomach lurched and I started to get excited. I pulled my beret over my head and straightened out my uniform before half-running over to battalion HQ.

The long corridor to the commanding officer's (CO's) office was flanked on each side by pictures and citations of all the regiment's Victoria Cross recipients and huge paintings of cavalry charges being repulsed by squares of infantrymen brandishing deadly bayonets. I was always a little nervous when I went to see the CO, but this time I was more nervous than usual as I tapped on his open door.

'David, come on in,' he beckoned.

The colonel was a short, broad-shouldered man in his mid-forties. He rarely smiled when sober but was the life and soul of the party after a couple of beers. The infantry was his life, and he could beat anyone in the battalion at physical tasks due to his dedication to personal strength and fitness. He was a straight talking man's man who oozed aggression and accepted no nonsense. His speech was punctuated with swears, and one was never in doubt that he was in charge. In short, Colonel Jonny was the epitome of the alpha male and he was deeply respected by the Officers' Mess and loved by the boys.

'The Second Battalion are looking for a captain for *Herrick 11*, and I've called you in to see if you want me to put you forward as the First Battalion's nomination.'

I had no hesitation. I didn't need to think. It was exactly what I had been hoping for and suddenly it was happening.

'Definitely, Sir!'

'Hang on. I haven't even told you what the fucking job is yet. Anyway I don't want you to tell me now, I know your family situation, so come and see me after you have spoken to Lucy.'

At four months Luce was just starting to 'show', and we were getting really excited about the prospect of becoming parents.

'You can tell her that 2 Yorks have agreed to release you at the end of January so you'll be home in time for the birth,' continued the CO. 'They want you to command an OMLT so it'll be a fairly crunchy job.'

Operational Mentor and Liaison Teams were attached to Afghan National Army (ANA) units and worked alongside them providing training and operational support in the fight against the Taliban. The job would involve commanding a unit of men attached to an Afghan Company in Helmand Province.

'Timelines are pretty tight. In fact, you'll be leaving in nine days.'

If he told me I was leaving that night it wouldn't have made a difference. I was going and that was that.

'That's mega, Sir. I'll go home now and speak to Luce, but, trust me, it'll be a "yes" from me tomorrow,' I said.

I banged up a salute, spun on my heel and headed straight out the door in order to get home as fast as possible to break the news to Lucy.

I didn't plan on telling her how much of the decision was my own and that I'd been practically begging for something like this to come along for the past few months.

It's fair to say Lucy didn't view the opportunity with as much enthusiasm as I did. There were tears. I was sitting on the kitchen work surface with my wife's sobbing body between my legs. Her body shook against my chest as I held her close.

I tried to reassure her.

'It'll be fine. I'll be the commander. I'll be surrounded by my soldiers and in the middle of lots of cover. I'll be the one telling my soldiers to go and do the actual dangerous stuff.'

Lucy nodded bravely. She wanted to believe the lie, but we both watched the news every night. Allied forces first entered Afghanistan in 2001 and then moved dramatically into Helmand in 2006. By 2009 the fighting had reached its fiercest, and it had already been the bloodiest year on record, with the highest numbers of British casualties since boots first got dusty. In the summer of 2009, a large operation called *Panther's Claw* had been executed across Helmand, resulting in large numbers of allied casualties. During *Panther's Claw,* a friend of mine, Harry Parker, was terribly wounded in an IED strike. He lost both his legs above the knee; one up to the hip. God knows how he survived such horrific injuries, but if some good has come out of this conflict it's the advancements we have seen in medicine, specifically trauma care and surgery. I didn't know it at the time, but his uncle Ed Parker would also become a good friend of mine in the years to come. When Harry lost his legs, Ed was having a mid-life review (bit rude and inaccurate to call it a crisis) and was planning to walk to the North Pole with his friend Simon Daglish. When he heard of his nephew's injury, Ed decided to undertake the feat in support of our nation's wounded service personnel, and the charity Walking With The Wounded (WWTW) was born.

Panther's Claw had been conducted throughout the summer 'fighting season' (Easter until September), and the vast majority of deaths and injuries were sustained in horrific blasts from IEDs. A number of my friends had already lost limbs that summer. We didn't know it at the time, but that year the traditional fighting season was to extend well into the winter of 2009/10 in retaliation for *Panther's Claw*.

With the situation in Afghanistan so critical, it was a tough, emotionally draining evening as Lucy and I discussed my deployment, especially when I told her that I would be leaving in just over a week's time.

The following morning I told the CO that everything was squared at home, and the rest of the week was spent frantically trying to get everything sorted. I needed the right kit issued; I needed all the right forms filled out and all the correct injections shoved into my body.

I hated the Medical Reception Station (MRS). I tried to make my trips there as brief as possible.

'I'm sorry, Sir. There is no time to have all of your hepatitis jabs; the third one is three weeks after the second. Will you be in contact with blood or unsanitary conditions at all?'

'I'll be fine, don't worry,' I replied as I rolled up my sleeve and exited the med centre as soon as possible. It is a natural reaction for any soldier to want to leave the med centre. It's perceived as the home of the weak, the malingerer and the skiver. I wanted to spend as little time as possible in that facility, so I certainly wasn't going to hang around discussing what vaccinations they did or did not have. If they had it, I took it; if they didn't, I didn't give a damn. As a young infantryman I was obviously immune to minor annoyances such as hepatitis and yellow fever. Malaria tablets? No thanks, they give me mood swings, and as an infantryman I could probably shake off a bout of malaria in a few days.

This is honestly how my comrades and I felt. The sick were weak. We tortured those at Sandhurst who fell by the wayside with twisted knees and sore backs. They were not robust; they didn't have the mettle. The infantry thrives on this kind of attitude, so much so that when I developed an inguinal hernia during training I kept it quiet for weeks until it was unavoidable, and even then I refused to go sick and had it operated on during the next period of leave instead.

Little did I know how much time I would be spending in med centres over the coming months and the repercussions that our collective attitudes would have on my sense of identity. David Wiseman, a malingerer? No fucking way, Sir!

The nine days leading up to my departure flew by in a whirlwind of logistics, planning and high emotion. My overriding feeling had been excitement. I remember running around the beautiful pedestrianized avenue that runs around the inner city of Munster with my best mate Alf and chattering away about Afghanistan all the way round.

'When do you reckon my first contact will be, mate? Could even be next week, don't you reckon?'

For me it was still a game. I knew it would be dangerous. I knew colleagues who had been killed and injured in Iraq and Afghanistan, so I knew the risks, but at that point I was not calculating them. It crossed my mind that I could be wounded or killed, but I knew, I just knew that it wouldn't happen to me. I was far more worried about messing up and getting one of my boys hurt through incompetence than I was about myself.

I felt like Christmas was just around the corner and I was counting the 'sleeps' until I would wake up on that special morning, but instead of presents under the tree, my gift would be my own body of men and a deadly game of cat and mouse with the Taliban.

In the last week of September Lucy dropped me off at the airport. I had around 50–60kg of kit spread out amongst my grip, day-sack and Bergan, and eyebrows were raised as I dumped them at the check-in desk. Lucy was at my side, keeping very quiet.

'Sir, you will have to pay £450 in excess baggage,' the pretty girl behind the counter explained in the cool, polite but authoritative way only Germans can pull off.

It was my turn to raise my eyebrows.

'Surely there is some mistake. The movements clerk must have booked excess baggage for me,' I insisted.

'No, Sir.'

'Do I look like I'm off on my holidays?' I pointed at my kit, unzipped the grip and showed her my desert camouflage Kevlar helmet and body armour.

'It's not as if I've over packed the hair straighteners and sun cream!'

The girl nodded.

'Oh, I see. Let me see what I can do, Sir.'

She picked up the phone and spoke rapidly in German to the person on the other end of the line. I glanced across at Lucy. She had held it together pretty well in the car as we made painfully strained conversation, avoiding any reference to my imminent departure. But the altercation at the check-in desk had been the final straw, and the cracks began to show as silent tears crept down her cheeks. She looked away in a vain attempt to hide her emotions from me.

'My manager says she can waive half of the excess baggage fee,' the girl said, replacing the receiver.

I wasn't going to argue any further. I would just have to claim it back when I got back off tour. I couldn't help feeling bloody angry though. What if I was a private who didn't have the odd surplus £200 in the bank to cover such oversights? Most would pay the money, go into their overdrafts and incur six months of bank charges without giving it any thought until they got back. Soldiers seem to get themselves into dramas like that all the time.

Lucy and I walked away from the check-in desk. There was no point in her hanging around waiting for me to fly off, so we just said our goodbyes in the large open check-in hall while the rest of the world moved around us. I held her close for a long time and told her that the time would fly by; I felt her crying into me and I too began to feel an ache inside. I looked up and saw a couple of middle-aged ladies looking at us. They gave me a sympathetic smile.

There are different kinds of goodbyes. If you watch people at airports or railway stations, you will see a whole spectrum of them. From the quick 'see you tomorrow', through to the 'I will miss you'. But this was right at the end of the spectrum: it was a 'this could be the last time I ever hold you' kind of goodbye. Those ladies could tell that just by looking us how precious those moments were.

I stroked Lucy's tear-streaked cheek with my thumb and then turned to make my way to the escalator. I looked back as the stairs carried me up to the departures floor and watched Lucy walk away. At that point my emotions nearly got the better of me and I rubbed a tear away from my eye.

I flew first to the UK for a whistle-stop, two-day course on the dos and don'ts of fighting in Afghanistan at a horrible camp on the Kentish south coast called Lydd. I felt like a character from George Orwell's *1984* as we sat in a huge darkened room being force fed information by a never-ending Power Point projected on the big screen. It was the most basic of courses that covered everything from Afghan history, an introduction to important Afghan phrases and a look at some of the new technology that we would be likely to experience in theatre, including specialist kit used to detect IEDs. The most useful couple of hours spent in the whole weekend was a lesson on cultural awareness including the fundamental differences between the many ethnic groups that are found in Afghanistan.

The ANA, with whom I would be working, were drawn only from the northern parts of the country and included groups such as Uzbeks, Turkmens and Hazaari. Their language, Dari, was based on Persian, as they had belonged to the Persian Empire thousands of years ago. The Hazaari looked very different from the rest of the population with oriental features. They descended from the Mongol Hordes that controlled the region in the time of the Khanates. The population of Helmand were from an ethnic group called Pashtu, whose language is more akin to Sanskrit. The Pashtun culture was more akin to Pakistani, and they based their lives allied to both the teachings of Mohammed and also a code of laws called Pashtunwali.

I felt that understanding even the basics about the people with whom I would be working for the following months would be vital.

Following the crash course in Central Asian warfare, I made the long drive up to Weeton Barracks, the home of 2nd Battalion, The Yorkshire Regiment. The garrison is a concrete jungle just outside Blackpool – great for the lads in terms of smashing out on the piss, not so great for the officers who have to clear up the mess that inevitably follows.

The vast majority of personnel were already in theatre when I arrived, so the barracks were pretty much deserted. It felt like a ghost town as I wandered round, trying to find someone who could direct me to where I needed to be. I was in the last tranche of guys to be lifted out so I spent the evening alone with my thoughts and a couple of books.

Early the following morning I stood amongst a group of soldiers on a cold, black parade ground, waiting for a coach to turn up and take us to RAF Brize Norton in Oxfordshire. It was starting to drizzle as the vehicle arrived. I knew none of the men I was with, and everyone else had mothers, wives and kids to see them off. I felt terribly alone as I climbed aboard, and it was starting to dawn on me what I was about to embark on. I was about to go to war with a bunch of guys I had never met in an environment I had no experience of. However, I had been training for this moment for years. I might not have known the mission specific details of fighting in Helmand Province, but as an infantryman I knew I would be dynamic and flexible enough to adapt to the situation and the challenges it presented very quickly. I was also confident about working with guys I had never met before, as I have always considered myself to be a soldier's officer. Some officers struggle to make relationships with the men they lead and prefer to keep a distance between them and their men. To me they appear uncomfortable in command, but there are many various styles of leadership and different things work for different people. I much prefer to get stuck in with the blokes, have a laugh and a joke with them and forge relationships and a respect that is not entirely based on rank. Other people may look at the way I do business and say that I get too close, but I've never had a problem with discipline.

Bastion is a huge city which stretches for square mile after square mile. The airstrip is at its core and must be one of the most heavily protected landing sites on the planet. Still, we had to don helmets and body armour before we touched down on its tarmac. The aircraft made an incredibly steep and fast descent in order to reduce the chance of being shot down on approach. I always enjoyed getting off a plane in a new country; each destination has its own particular smell, and in Bastion the air was warm and thick with dust and foreign scents.

I disembarked in darkness and immediately felt like I was on a big conveyor belt being processed through a system, being told to go to one place, report to another desk, pick up kit from another room, before being loaded onto the back of a truck and driven off into the night. Hulks of equipment were silhouetted against the night sky as we drove slowly through checkpoint after checkpoint; armoured vehicles, ISO containers and watchtowers passed by as we carried on our slow journey. I was absolutely knackered after such a long trip but I was also extremely excited to be nearing the end when I would meet my troops and get stuck into some real war fighting.

I was taken to a huge white tent where I was shown a bed space that was just wide enough to fit a standard issue collapsible bed frame (which is of course a lot smaller than the standard issue soldier). There were around 50 of us in the digs. I dug around in my kit bag for my sleeping bag before unfurling it on my carry cot. I unsuccessfully tried to shove all my kit under the 'bed' to keep it contained within my tiny allotted space. Then I crawled into my doss bag and fell into a deep sleep.

The following morning I met Captain Mike Willis who was the adjutant of the 2nd Battalion. The adjutant was the senior captain in the battalion and worked directly to the CO. Mike had been an instructor when I was in training at the Infantry Battle School in Wales (the same guy that had bounded down the hill after the close encounter with the buffalo in Kenya) and had also hosted me on a couple of visits to his Battalion before I enlisted and had been deciding which regiment to join. I don't know anyone who doesn't like Mike. A diminutive figure at only around 5'6' but he totally makes up for that with his affable nature and his easy confident manner.

Mike told me that I was to hang around in Bastion for a few days to conduct final training and last minute, essential administration that included zeroing my rifle, being issued specialist equipment from the stores and, morbidly, having a photo taken in front of the regiment colours in case the worst happened and an image of me was needed to release to the media.

The training was good fun and extremely informative. Over the next three days I spent time on the ranges zeroing my rifle and being trained up on some very gnarly weapon systems including grenade machine guns (GMG) that fire 40mm high explosive (HE) over half a kilometre, and the HMG, a beast of a weapon that rapidly fires shells half an inch across and can penetrate even the thickest walls. I was introduced to specialist equipment used for detecting IEDs and trained in how to find them, what to do when one was discovered and what to do if one went off. I also honed my battlefield first aid skills during a series of lessons and cleverly-run scenarios; these would prove to be vital in the coming weeks.

Mike's was not the only familiar face I saw during my brief spell at Bastion. I met both my colour sergeant and my OC from my time at Sandhurst. Colour Sergeant 'Nobby' Clark had picked up the next rank of WO2 since I had last seen him and was the company sergeant major for one of The Mercian Regiment companies that was lifting off the ground. It was strange to see him out of the training environment. I felt like I knew him very well after spending so much time with him at Sandhurst. He had taught me a great deal and I was very pleased to see him. However, he really didn't seem himself. He had lost a lot of weight – even from his characteristically chubby cheeks for which he had gained the nickname Nobby's Nuts – and appeared tired right down to his core.

I also saw an officer I knew from the 3rd Battalion, The Yorkshire Regiment. He nodded at me from across the cookhouse one afternoon. His hair was long and unkempt and he had a couple of days' growth on his face. One could read both a deep fatigue and an unbridled aggression in his eyes, and he looked as though he couldn't really believe he was off the ground, that he had to keep his guard up despite his obvious tired disposition. I remember thinking one word – 'grizzly' – and stupidly I hoped to gain that level of grizz during my tour. I was an idiot to hope that the next time I saw acquaintances it would be obvious to them that I had seen action just from my appearance. At that time I didn't appreciate what it took to attain such a grizzled appearance. Those men had paid a deep price to look the way they did. Back then I called it grizz; today I would call it haunted.

The time soon came to leave the relative safety of Bastion and move to the front line. I was heading to an area bang in the middle of Helmand called Nad-e Ali. Nowhere in Helmand was deemed to be quiet at the time, but I didn't care where I was headed, as long as it wasn't Sangin. The name Sangin carried with it an air of dread, as the winding streets and alleyways were chocked full of IEDs and had seen the death and maiming of the majority of British casualties. It was the dead of night, and I was sitting in a pen marked off with white mine tape at the edge of the airfield. Masses of kit in Bergans, grip bags and day sacks were lined up with soldiers sitting on them inhaling cigarette after cigarette. My throat was dry as the air was heavy with dust, churned up by a hundred soldiers, passing pick-up trucks and the steady stream of Chinook helicopters that were relaying us all to the front line.

When my turn came I queued up with around 30 other blokes at the back of a Chinook. The blades were not turning so we were saved the blast of hot air that usually welcomes you as you board one of these huge, twin-rotor machines. We squeezed up as much as we could on parallel, inward facing benches before being told we would have to squeeze up some more. We were already stifled by the closeness of each other, with our kit shoved wherever it would fit and our rifles, loaded but not cocked, pointing downwards between our legs. All remaining space in the central aisle of the helicopter was filled with freight until each of us had our faces pressed up against a towering central wall of provisions and equipment. Despite our protestations of lack of space they kept on filling the helicopter with load after load. The soldier next to me could barely move his head.

'If this fucking thing goes down, Sir, we're fucked. How are we expected to debus and fight?' he muttered.

I didn't have an answer for him.

Considering the altitude of Helmand Province and therefore the thinness of the air, God only knows how that Chinook was able to take off with so much weight, but it did, and with every bank and turn the freight tipped from one side of the aircraft to the other. As boxes were flung around, curses and shouts echoed through the fuselage. It was ridiculous, but as we flew at extremely low level and high speeds above the ground, I couldn't help but be thrilled by the whole experience. The door gunner to the rear of the aircraft swung his machine gun left and right as he studied the blackness below for threats, and I (figuratively speaking, due to being wedged in place) sat on the edge of my seat, just waiting to see an arc of red light as enemy fire streaked up through the night sky.

The rounds never came, and after around 20 minutes we banked steeply and started our rapid descent towards Forward Operating Base Shawqat (FOB SQT) in the Nad-e Ali district, right at the heart of Helmand Province.

CHAPTER 3
HELMAND

The Chinook swooped down onto the dusty landing site with all the grace it could muster, given its size and weight. The pilot didn't bother to turn off the engines. He wasn't staying. The ramp at the rear of the helicopter ratcheted open and a brown cloud of Afghan crap billowed in. Pushing aside some of the freight that had fallen on me during the flight, I got up from the cramped bench and disembarked with the rest of the personnel. Outside, through the choking dust clouds, I saw a couple of quad bikes racing around with the cargo from the chopper on their trailers. The noise of the rotor blades was deafening. A soldier ran over, gave me the thumbs up and beckoned for me to follow him. Shielding my eyes, I followed him behind a low mud wall, where we crouched as the helicopter blades changed pitch. The wall afforded us some protection from the rocks and stones that were being launched towards us by the downdraft as the chopper took off on its journey back to Bastion.

As the dust settled, a strange calm fell over the evening. The small wall behind which we sheltered was part of a much larger structure. I would not appreciate its size until the sun came up the next day, but essentially the modern-day FOB was built around an old British fort that had been constructed during the Afghan Wars of the mid-nineteenth century. It was completely dilapidated, and therefore none of our modern day equipment or buildings were found within the fort itself, but it was amazing to think that soldiers from nearly 200 years ago had been on the very spot I found myself on, probably experiencing the same mix of emotions that I was at that point – anticipation, excitement and trepidation.

The man crouching with me stood up. He thrust his hand in my direction. I shook it firmly as he introduced himself.

'You must be Captain Wiseman, Sir? I'm Sergeant Major Chuck.'

He looked like the stereotypical sergeant major you see in the movies: older, barrel-chested and stocky with salt-and-pepper hair. He led me round the helicopter landing site (HLS) past a number of parked armoured vehicles to a row of around half a dozen tents that would be my home for the remainder of the tour.

Inside he introduced me to the OC, Major Al, who was a tall, thin man with an air of studied intelligence. He spoke with a clipped BBC accent but did not come across as stuffy. His 2iC was Ed, who also made me feel welcome. We had been at Sandhurst at around the same time and had the usual discussion about who we know from such-and-such regiment. Exchanging acquaintances is always customary when officers meet.

After I'd spent some time chatting to the senior officers, Chuck then led me back along the row of tents to introduce me to my team. There was no ceremony or a squad formed up ready for my inspection. It was real life on an operational base. My team were a bunch of guys milling around their tent. A few were sorting out kit; others crawled out of mosquito nets where they had been watching a movie. A tall bloke in his mid-to-late twenties with black hair strode over and held out his hand.

'Alright, Boss, I'm Sergeant Coops.'

Coops spoke with a nasal north-east accent, probably because of the prominent pointy beak that stuck out from his grid. He was well built, and over the next few weeks his spare time was spent working out. He prided himself on keeping fit. He loved boxing and was obsessed with Manchester United football club. He seemed pretty young for a sergeant, so I was confident that he was progressing up the ranks quickly. He had an aptitude for soldiering that would prove itself in the following weeks. I later found out that he had recently been promoted specifically to fulfil the post on tour. He was obviously respected and valued by his peers, as, just before he deployed, he had been voted Best Corporal by the Corporals' Mess. Coops introduced me to Barney, an older corporal in his mid-thirties and obviously Coops' partner in crime. He was short but broad with fair hair and the beginnings of a tan. The lines on his face told me he had been a soldier from a young age. He was confident and mischievous, and as the older man in the team I immediately recognised him as an important ally. On his wrist he wore a brightly coloured bangle of beads like something you would get at Mardi Gras or a Pride March. I thought it odd but didn't get a close look at it. I asked him about it later and he gave me a look. On each bead was a different letter spelling out the word 'DADDY' all the way round. It was the last thing his daughter had put in his hand when he left on what was his second tour of Helmand, and he said wouldn't take it off until he was back home with his family.

I recognised two of my men; Tag and Fiji. Both were Commonwealth soldiers whom had attended a course that I had run two years previously and so had only known me as a hard-arsed instructor who had made their lives difficult for ten weeks. Coops and Barney explained to me later that when Tag and Fiji heard I was coming to command them for the tour their faces sank and they were expecting the same treatment they had suffered at my hands in the past. At that point they hadn't served long enough to understand one of the army's secrets: that instructors on courses are playing an act and it is a soldier's job as a candidate to play along. When someone is screaming in your face at five in the morning because your mess tin hasn't been scrubbed clean, is he really that excited? Does he really think you a worthless piece of scum that he wouldn't lead into combat if you were the last soldier in the billet? It is mostly an act to get the best results from the individual.

As we got to work as a unit, Tag and Fiji were pleasantly surprised (I hope) to realise that I adopt my command and leadership style depending on the situation and actually very rarely get too excited with my men at all.

The next soldier I met was Cowhead, a young man of around 20, so called because of his long face and dopey appearance. Despite his looks, he was genuinely a very reliable guy who would crack on with the task in hand without complaint. Cowhead was to be the gunner for the tour and so on every patrol he carried the GPMG in the ironically named 'light role' (i.e. without its tripod) and a great deal of ammunition. He didn't come across as a guy with a great deal of ambition to become the next regimental sergeant major, but was happy with a heavy load on his back, as long as he had a steady stream of Lambert and Butlers from the UK.

He was joined at the hip with Endo, a rapid-talking, short-haired 20-year-old who fancied himself as a hard case. He was gobby from the start, but after spending years around soldiers you get to know the type. Underneath the bullshit he was just an insecure young lad who thought he had to play the hard man in the world of men. He was obviously thought of as capable with honed soldiering ability, as he had been selected to be a sniper within the Support Weapons Company.

Tucked away quietly in the corner was a young man called Clarky; he was 20 but looked much younger. This was his first tour, and he was desperately trying to grow a moustache. Clarky was a bright young man who mainly kept himself to himself and never gave much away.

Finally, Humph was the fall guy of the team. He seemed to be the butt of most of the jokes. He was around 6'3' and weighty to boot. He was pretty intelligent but had little street smarts and so often led with his chin. However, he was an extremely loyal soldier and was the front man searching for IEDs for the vast majority of our patrols, demonstrating a quiet but undeniable level of courage.

After the introductions I went to grab some food from the mess tent with Coops and Barney, and we talked about the team, the week that they had already spent in theatre, the couple of quiet patrols they had conducted and the company of Afghan National Army with whom we would be working and who I would meet the following morning.

We set off in a two-vehicle convoy after breakfast on the short 3.2-kilometre trip to the ANA checkpoint where 3 Company were stationed. I was in the front vehicle, a WMIK with a pintle-mounted GPMG pulled close into my chest.

That morning I amassed all the kit and equipment that I would be using for the remainder of the tour. In my trouser pockets I carried tourniquets, morphine and highly absorbent field dressings. The tourniquets were already half-fastened in case I got injured and had to apply it to myself.

Our Osprey body armour consisted of two large Kevlar plates that protected chest and back and slotted into a heavy T-shirt. Within the elastic loops of my body armour, I pushed a paint brush. Everyone was issued with one and all wore it in the same place. The brush was used whenever a suspected IED was found. The Taliban's bomb-making techniques had evolved and they had started placing anti-tamper devices on their bombs, so when the top-soil was scraped away, the device would detonate. This is where the paint brushes came in. With them we could remove loose dust and debris much more delicately and gently, making a very dangerous operation a bit safer.

I wore a Mark 6a helmet that fitted comfortably and on my back hoisted a large pack containing food, water, clothing, smoke and strobes for marking helicopter landing sites and various communication equipment and radios.

I carried the standard assault rifle of the British Army, the semi-automatic SA80. When in automatic mode it continues to fire its entire 30 round magazine as long as the trigger is depressed. It fires a bullet that is 5.56mm in diameter and is typically used for engagements up to 300 metres. Attached to the rifle I carried an under-slung grenade launcher (UGL), a beautifully crude weapon that is essentially a tube with a firing pin that fires either a HE or White Phosphorus 40mm grenade over hundreds of metres. Both detonate on impact. The HE grenade obliterates everything within a 5 metre radius and sends shards of plastic in a devastating pressure wave a lot further. The phoss grenade produces a near instant plume of thick smoke that can be used for cover and screening; however, if the smoke comes into contact with skin it results in horrific burns, so horrific in fact that it is against the rules of war to use it as a weapon. The first aid for someone who has phosphorus on their skin is to cut out the affected flesh with a knife, as the chemical will continue to burn as long as it's in contact with oxygen and cannot be doused by water. I also carried normal smoke grenades for providing a screen.

My pistol was the excellent Sig Sauer 9mm, a beautiful side arm which produces very little recoil and is therefore very accurate, and my final weapon was a bayonet: 8 inches of glinting, blunt steel designed to separate the rib cage and disembowel. The bayonet has a special place in the infantry as it naturally spreads fear in the hearts of the enemy. Every infantryman knows what it means to affix a bayonet to a rifle and we are conditioned through training to respect the weapon for the crude and unforgiving piece of equipment that it is. As recruits we are beasted to within an inch of our limits, soaking wet from crawling through stinking rivers, chanting 'KILL KILL KILL' until our throats burn and then we are urged to channel all that aggression into the point of the bayonet and destroy the simulated enemy dummies. The practice hones the mind for the moment when a soldier may have to drive steel into a man's chest and keep pushing until the life ebbs from the enemy in a slick of blood and entrails. It is one thing to pull a trigger and watch a man drop 200 metres away, quite another to get your hands wet as your enemy dies in front of your face. The bayonet is the symbol of the British infantry. It captures in a single piece of equipment what it is to be an infantryman and what you are prepared to do for your country when engaging the enemy at close quarters.

My main vehicle was the WMIK, a pimped up, aggressive Land Rover. It is completely open to the elements with no windows, roof or windscreen and doesn't have any doors. Instead we used elastic bungee ropes to fit a Kevlar panel where a door should have been to provide some protection to our legs. As we left the compound for our meeting with the ANA I had a pintle-mounted GPMG in front of me in the passenger seat, and we had another mounted GPMG in the back, from which our rear gunner could stand in an elevated position and provide suppressive fire.

The GPMG is an awesome medium-sized machine gun that has been in service for around 50 years and shows no sign of being replaced due to its reliability, effectiveness and the genuine love of it shown by all ranks. It is a belt-fed weapon firing a 7.62mm round up to around 1,800 metres, depending on its mount. It is heavy but portable and has a voracious appetite for ammo. It is a suppressive area weapon, which means it is not supposed to be terribly accurate. It is most effective when it is spitting out a cone of fire at and around the enemy, who, caught in the middle, are given the very real impression that if they move anywhere they are going to cop the good news. The GPMG fixes and suppresses the enemy, allowing infantrymen to close in, engage and destroy him at a closer and therefore more definite range. Job done.

My gloved hand was wrapped around the pistol grip of my own pintle-mounted Gympy as we exited FOB SQT for the first time. My other hand rested lazily on top of the gun, ready to pull it round and engage any threat that might appear. All our weapon systems were loaded and made ready as we pulled out of the camp, and I was thrilled to be leaving its safe walls with my own troops.

We bounced along a dirt road with deep, water-filled ditches on each side. As we passed sporadic compounds, children would run up alongside the vehicles waving and screeching 'Chocaleet! Chocaleet!' with outstretched hands. The buildings were all built from mud. The locals wore long robes, beards and turbans. The landscape was medieval. The settlement was small, and beyond it the landscape was open field after open field, cut by irrigation ditches and wadis. The tall maize crop had thankfully been harvested, so the fields were either ploughed or filled with low plants like peanuts or potatoes – a fact that made our lives easier by giving us much better fields of view. The 7-foot tall maize crops had provided the Taliban with a convenient shield of cover, allowing them to sneak up regularly on our comrades who had fought them the previous summer.

After a short drive we arrived at the ANA checkpoint where my company of ANA warriors was stationed. We turned left off the main road onto a narrow track. A group of children and a wizened old man poked their heads out of a tiny building at the junction that was being used as a Madrassa, or Islamic school. The checkpoint gate was a thin tree trunk resting on a frame that was lifted to allow us in.

As we crept into the small courtyard of the checkpoint, I had a look around at where these men had been living. To my left, facing north towards FOB SQT was an elevated Sanger position. Our engineers had obviously built it, as it was constructed out of Hesco (wire mesh boxes containing a bag filled with rubble or sand which can be piled on top of each other to make a blast-proof wall). Millions upon millions were shipped out to Afghanistan and Iraq and must have made their inventor a bucket-load of cash. There was obviously not enough Hesco for this checkpoint, however, as large sections of the perimeter only had a single roll of razor wire as a barrier. Just behind one segment of razor wire on the north-east corner of the checkpoint, the commander had placed a sandbag gun nest facing east.

The main building stood in front of us as we drove in. It was a two-storey construction and like pretty much everything in Helmand it was made from baked mud. I could see another Sanger position on its roof facing south-west and proudly sporting a DShK, a seriously punchy ex-soviet machine gun that spews out rounds a half-inch across that can stop a car and rip a man in half.

The courtyard narrowed to our right into a passageway to other outbuildings, on top of which was the last defensive position facing south. It was a small area to house around 60 men, maybe 30 metres across by 15 metres deep. They must have been living right on top of each other.

The company commander, Captain Imam, was a man in his mid-to-late thirties with a short thick black beard that covered his face. He was tall and thin, with crow's feet etched from each eye from years in the harsh sun which were accentuated by his beaming smile. He had baby twins waiting for him at home whom he had never seen. He ran a tight ship and frowned upon other commanders who allowed their soldiers to take drugs. As a result, he was well respected by his men and his company was the best outfit I worked with in my time in Afghanistan.

Despite the higher levels of discipline, Imam's men still looked like a rag-tag bunch. Imam always wore the uniform of the ANA, dark green disrupted patterned material, but through necessity and scarcity of kit and equipment, many of his warriors wore a hotch-potch mix of uniform: plain t-shirts or Premiership football shirts (perhaps donated by previous British OMLTs). They wore sandals or light trainers and carried just a couple of ammunition pouches with a few magazines of 5.56mm rounds for their American M16 assault rifles. They complained bitterly about the rifles they had been given because they were unreliable and they had to clean them daily to make sure they worked. The warriors laughed at the amount of kit we carried and the weight of our protective body armour and helmets. It was a game for them to try on our kit and run around the courtyard, laughing at the silly British who had to lug it all around in the hot sun and then fight the Taliban.

The ANA preferred to be referred to as 'warriors' rather than soldiers, to highlight their nature as fighting men. We happily obliged, and after a few days it didn't sound weird at all and served as a useful distinction when talking about British and Afghan troops.

During that first visit to Imam's company, I talked to him about our Area of Operations (AO), where the enemy were concentrated, the attitudes of the people living in the small villages dotted around the vicinity and what their patrolling schedule had been over the previous months. It turned out that the area south of Shawqat was quieter than the north. There were a few areas where they were contacted 75 per cent of the time when they patrolled and a number of roads that were marked with IED, but on the whole the people were chiefly on-side. I was happy to take the lead from Imam, and we drew up a patrol schedule for the next week with a matrix showing the rough areas that we would be covering and the rough timings. It was wise not to talk in too much detail about where we were going to be and at what time. As much as I liked Imam, no one could be sure how much information would get into the wrong hands, either through mistake or malice.

Imam and I also discussed training. My men could provide short practical lessons in areas such as first aid, IED confirmation and actions on finding a device. Imam was happy to plan these sessions, but, in practice, over the following days and weeks, it became apparent that the warriors resented attending them as they had received similar training and had no concept of revision. Instead they were insulted at the assumption that they did not understand basic soldiering skills. We assured them that we also practised the most simple of lessons or techniques again and again on a regular basis.

I was frustrated as our AO seemed so quiet compared with the area to the north. Every time those guys went out they ended up in a fight, whereas we just seemed to be going on a series of really hot and dusty walks around the Helmand countryside carrying shit loads of heavy kit. I should have been thankful that things were so quiet. The patrols we mounted were important as they showed the enemy that we had control of the area and that we were a constant presence. Besides, enemy fighters had their hands full further north where the Grenadier Guards Battle Group (including a company of soldiers from The Duke of Lancaster's Regiment [Lancs]) were conducting a big old battle in an attempt to push the forward line of enemy troops (FLET) from 300 metres to around 1,200 metres. The FLET is what most people would understand to be 'the front line', although a front line would be difficult to define in that type of warfare. It was the point beyond which the enemy have relative freedom of movement and action aside from that which is hampered by raids, air assault operations or air strikes. The Guards and the Lancs were supported by two companies of ANA; unfortunately, my ANA company was not one of them. In the down time between our patrols we listened to the series of firefights just a few hundred metres up the road.

While we waited to be invited to the party, there were plenty of other, mundane duties to be getting on with, such as maintaining weapons and equipment. None of these tasks were considered as bone as shit bag duty, carried out by the ingloriously titled Shit Bag Man. FOB SQT was still a relatively austere place to live at the start of *Herrick 11*. There were no permanent buildings to speak of and there were no showers and no toilets. We left bags of water out in the sun all day so that we could wash in warm water and we shat in bags. For a while we had special 'wag' bags that were specially designed for the purpose and contained chemicals to dry the waste and reduce the smell. MDF stalls had been erected in one corner of the FOB with crude seats inside – essentially a hole cut in a wooden board through which one could push their wag bag, sit on the edges to stop it falling through and take a dump. After a few weeks all the wag bags were gone, and we were issued one bin liner a day. You know things are pretty dire when they have to ration bags for shit and you pray that you don't need to go more than once a day!

All this waste had to be burnt in a pit just outside the camp gate: a stinking hole in the ground 5 metres out of the back gate. And there was one unlucky Royal Logistics Corps private whose job it was to collect all the shit bags and get them burnt. God only knows how he managed to get himself chosen for such a mega job, but I hear the selection process was fairly demanding! The infantry often unfairly look down on the other corps who conduct the supporting tasks which mean that the job of soldiering can be done to a high standard. In any organisation you are going to get the people who are delivering the final product, but behind that there are several layers of support who work tirelessly to ensure the people at the coal face have exactly what they need. In this case it was food, clothing, clean water, ammunition and serviceable vehicles. However, that does not stop the banter, and most of these people fell under the banner of

REMF (Rear Echelon Mother Fucker). I'm afraid that as important a task as Shit Bag Man was fulfilling, he was still a massive turbo REMF, but even uber REMFs have to be careful in Helmand…

During the first day of the advance to the north, our callsign were feeling pretty REMFy themselves. We were sitting with our shirts off back at FOB SQT, cleaning our weapons outside our tent and listening to rounds whizzing high above our heads (which was a pretty strange situation in which to top up your tan), when Endo came striding over with a stupid grin on his face.

'Guess who's been shot?'

I gave him a serious look.

'This had better be good, Endo. First of all, is he okay?'

As a soldier you soon learn to develop a dark sense of humour as a coping mechanism against some of the things you face. Even so, casualties are no laughing matter.

'Yeah, yeah, he'll be okay. Took a round in the leg. Are you not gonna guess?'

We all looked at each other; no one had any idea.

'Shit Bag Man!' he exclaimed.

'No fucking way! How the hell has he been hit?' I asked.

Endo explained that the shit bag man had been just outside the gate stoking his pit into a faecal inferno when a stray round from the battle up the road had come whistling in much lower than all the others and smashed him in the leg. It wasn't funny really, as he had some really nasty shattered bones in his leg, but we couldn't help but laugh at the irony that the biggest honking REMF in the whole FOB was getting more action than us!

Black humour descended on the team after the news about Shit Bag Man, and banter flew back and forth as we continued with our weapons. Things must have been hotting up, as an Apache Gunship crept into the airspace directly above us. We watched the impressive silhouette of the helicopter, bristling with missiles, rockets and a deadly 30mm cannon, moving very slowly high above us.

All of a sudden the helicopter began opening up on some unseen enemy a kilometre or so to our north. The 30mm cannon was spewing forth hundreds of enormous rounds that were winging their way to rain death on some insurgent in a ditch just up the road.

I looked at Coops for a second and realised he was coming to the same conclusion as me. Over the loud crackling noise of the weapon system high above us, I shouted, 'I tell you what, I don't fancy catching a 30mm case on the grid. Get in the tent!'

Seconds after the chopper let rip its weapons, a soft 'tink-tink' sound could be heard as a weird rain of scorching hot empty shells of brass fell onto the rocks around us. We legged it to the nearest tent and must have looked hilarious, giggling as we scrambled over one another to be the first to dive through the narrow flaps and into safety.

The Apache moved forward out of range, and while we managed to dodge its spent cartridges, our ANA chums were no so lucky. Minutes later we saw two Afghans striding over to the sergeant major's tent; one of them looked worse for wear and the other looked pissed off as hell. Chuck told me later that he had caught five minutes of uninterrupted hell off one of the ANA NCOs, without the benefit of an interpreter, because one of the ANA warriors had been knocked out and burnt by the Apache's ejected cartridges and for some reason the Afghan thought that Chuck was responsible for the gunship opening up above the FOB.

The next day the push in the north continued as we prepared to head out on a bog standard patrol to the south of the FOB. We were not expecting trouble as any bugger with an AK was involved in the scrap up north. I pulled on my body armour and helmet and placed my weapon in the foot well of my WMIK, before heading off to the Ops room to book out.

The atmosphere was buzzing. Several radios on loudspeaker were transmitting information from the battle to the Watch Keepers and signallers who oversaw and directed troops. The Ops room was the nerve centre of the battle where informed and balanced decisions could be made in a comparatively calm environment.

The Lancs Company 2iC looked up as I walked into the room.

'Hang on, Wisey, we might have a situation developing here.'

He continued to exchange information over the net as I tried to strain an ear in order to get a grip on what I might momentarily be asked to do. I started to write my patrol's details on the white 'panic' board in the corner of the room that held a record of personnel on the ground, their whereabouts and what vehicles they have. It is a handy quick reference guide for the guys in the Ops room to see what resources are where and who is in the best position to respond if the shit hits the fan.

After a couple of seconds of urgent conversation, the 2iC spoke across the busy room to me.

'Wisey, forget that patrol for now. I need you to push north to a casualty exchange point here,' he said, pointing to a compound on the huge map nailed to a table in the centre of the room.

'What have we got?' I asked him.

'British Soldier, gunshot wound to the head. It'll be quicker and safer to get him back here to our HLS rather than faffing about clearing a hasty HLS under contact and getting the chopper brassed up. The Medical Emergency Response Team [MERT] won't even land in that shit.'

The MERT was a precious commodity: a Chinook filled with paramedics and medical equipment so that any wounded personnel got the best treatment possible as soon as possible in a large high speed flying ambulance. Unfortunately, they were also a prime and easy target for any insurgent to bring down, and so the MERTs were reluctant to land if a situation was still active.

I nodded, then looked at the map. The route was easy; the casualty exchange point was a compound just off the main road. The 2iC started pointing at the map again.

'The road has been cleared up to this junction, so you'll have to leave the wagons and go on foot once you get here. IEDs have been found in and around this compound and this compound,' he said, jabbing at a couple of points on the map. 'So obviously avoid them.'

'Roger that. Anything else I need to know?' I asked.

'No, that's it. Just hurry up and get there.'

I was already out the door, running back to the tent to get my men. By the time I had reached my WMIK and spread my map on the bonnet, they were all around me looking in.

'CASEVAC lads. One of ours has been shot in the head so it's not going to be nice. Prepare yourselves for that now. We're leaving the wagons here at this junction, and, Barney, you'll stay with them on the gun with Tag and Endo to secure the vehicles and just in case we come under contact once we get this bloke and need the Gympy to support the extraction.'

Barney understood. He was an utterly dependable NCO and that was all the brief he needed.

'The rest of you are coming with me to pick up this lad. I call the route as I see it on the ground, but stay away from these compounds here and here as they are riddled with IED. We'll carry this guy back to the wagons and straight back here for a Helo CASEVAC.'

There were no questions, and we were out the gate 20 seconds later.

We pushed the vehicles hard, and a dust cloud billowed out the back of our little convoy. Within a couple of minutes we were at the limit of the safe route, so we left the vehicles at the side of the track. The guys quickly debussed and spread out along the deep ditch to the right hand side, which we followed for less than 50 metres before wading through the water up to our balls and up the steep bank on the other side. As I fought through the thick bulrushes at the top, I kept thinking, how the hell are we going to carry this bloke back across this terrain?

We took turns to sprint across a piece of open ground to another ditch behind the two booby-trapped compounds. We were close to the battle, and the sounds of automatic and rapid fire filled the air as rounds cracked and whistled above us. It was exciting; adrenaline surged through my veins, and my stomach churned when it was my turn to race across the open ground with gritted teeth and heavy breathing under the weight of our patrol kit, before crashing into cover after the short dash. This is it, my first real taste of war, I thought, and then immediately felt bad as I remembered what I was doing here.

Listening to my radio, I waited for a gap in the information being relayed about the fight across the net before announcing that I was in position and ready to pick up the casualty.

The thick vegetation across the track in front of me began to rustle like a scene from Jurassic Park, and I could see shapes moving through.

'These must be our lads but just make sure,' I told my small team above the noise of firing, as I watched intensely and prepared myself to fire if what came out of the bushes was not what I was expecting.

The rushes parted, and out ran a couple of British soldiers looking absolutely spent. Sweat poured from their faces and they were gulping huge lungfuls of air. They crashed into the ditch beside me.

'Where's the casualty, lads?' I asked.

'He's coming now, Boss.' They pointed back to the vegetation, where, one by one, half a dozen more soldiers emerged.

Finally a pair of blokes came through; one had the other by the elbow, as he was staggering about all over the place like a drunk. I couldn't believe what I was seeing at first. This guy was cutting about the battlefield like a pissed up tramp; he was carrying no kit, he had his helmet in his hand and a single drop of blood was trickling from his hairline to his left eyebrow.

I grabbed the young man by his other elbow as he slumped into the shallow ditch next to me. I lent close to his ear and shouted over the noise of gunfire.

'Are you the casualty?'

He looked at me with a dazed expression.

'Erm, yes Boss.'

'Have you been shot in the head?'

A huge Cheshire cat grin spread across his grid.

'Yeah!'

I looked at him in amazement as he lifted up his helmet to show me a hole at the front where the round had entered right in the middle just above the eyes and another larger crack at the back where it had exited.

The helmet is designed with a core of extra hard material surrounded by an outer coating of Kevlar. When the round hit this boy's helmet, it penetrated the outer covering and followed the line of the hard inner core all the way to the back of the helmet, where it fired out. This was exactly how it had been designed, and it was reassuring to see that, at a time when the papers were full of articles reporting how badly equipped our forces were, when some of it was put to the test it passed with flying colours.

'You lucky bastard!' I shouted, before dragging him to his feet and helping him back to my vehicles and back to the chopper waiting at FOB SQT.

I hadn't fired a round; I hadn't seen the enemy; I had only been there for a really short time and had only given a minor contribution to the action, but this taste of what it felt like to be involved in a fight was exhilarating, and I wanted more.

CHAPTER 4
SHIN KALAY

I had been in theatre for about three weeks when my callsign, Amber 13, was tasked to deploy alongside our ANA counterparts into a small town a couple of miles to the west of the FOB. International Security Assistance Force (ISAF) troops had not been into the town at all in recent memory, certainly with no permanent presence, and so my team was sent in to obtain some ground truth. What was the general feeling in the town? Were the Taliban firmly established, and if so how much resistance would we experience?

Shin Kalay was a town of just a couple of thousand souls, 500 metres wide by 800 metres long in a near perfect rectangle. The streets were evenly spaced and laid out in a grid of streets running north to south and east to west. With one main street running straight through the middle it was like something a five-year-old would create in the Afghan version of The Sims video game.

Shin Kalay 'high street' was wide enough to fit two cars down side by side and was always busy, mostly with people and animals. All the other streets were barely wide enough to fit a vehicle down and every hundred metres or so were criss-crossed by narrow alleys running between buildings. The streets were lined with imposing walls, 6–10 feet high, making the whole town an insurgent's paradise of hemmed-in rat runs. The enemy could easily track your progress and lie in wait to throw a grenade over a wall or snipe you from the other end of a long narrow street.

SHIN KALAY DISTRICT

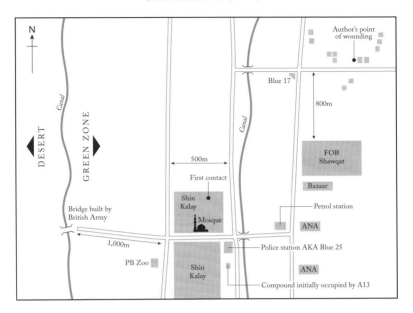

At the very centre there was the mosque, which proved a gift for navigation as I led my team around the disorientating town. Its bright blue minaret provided the only splash of colour in a town otherwise stained the standard Afghanistan dusty brown.

The eastern boundary of the town was marked by a 5-metre wide steep-banked canal which ran north to south and from which the local farmers irrigated their fields of cotton and peanuts and watered their goats and cattle. Unfortunately, it also provided the sewage system and the water supply for the whole town. At the very eastern edge of the town, the point at which a Spartan concrete bridge crossed the canal and ran into the high street, we found the only government building in Shin Kalay. The police station was unusual in that the main structure and the high walls that surrounded it were made from brick, plaster and concrete, as opposed to the mud brick walls that were found everywhere else in the region. The once white walls were pock-marked and cracked with the intense gun-fire that had been directed towards them and the people inside.

We planned to build a small platoon base (PB) in Shin Kalay to be occupied for just a couple of days, with a view to building a more permanent PB in the near future depending on our finding. For that we needed equipment. Luckily I had a pal in Shawqat who had the key to the stores. Jamie Craggs was a good friend from my platoon back in Sandhurst who had joined the Royal Engineers and was the Battle Group Engineer Officer. He lived in Shawqat HQ and advised the head shed (powers that be) on all matters engineering. He had all the equipment, materials and, most importantly, the skilled workforce required to build pretty much anything in theatre. However, like the rest of the British Army, he did not have enough equipment, materials and manpower to do what Head Shed asked him to achieve. But because he was a good friend he took me round to his stores the night before I deployed and let me raid it for sandbags, razor wire, shovels and anything else I needed.

The following morning we loaded up the WMIK and Vector and drove the short distance to Shin Kalay. I wanted to establish a compound just outside of the town with good all-round visibility. If we had established ourselves right in the centre of town we would have been surrounded by unknown quantities at close range with a difficult extraction route. We found a small, disused compound on the eastern edge of the town, around 150 metres south of the police station, which was ideal. As soon as we had checked the area for IEDs, I started to site our Sanger positions, three in total all on top of the compound roofs. The first looked across two fields and into the town approximately 300 metres away – handy, as this was the effective range of our small arms. The second looked back toward Shawqat to our east over a wide canal with deep embankments that ran alongside the road down from the police station to our compound. Our final position looked south down the road and overlooked another compound around 200 metres away that the police later told me was often used as a staging post to launch attacks on their police station. We also planned a vehicle checkpoint a little further down the road to prevent un-cleared cars, motorbikes and people getting close to our compound, thereby reducing the risk of suicide, IED and grenade attack.

Each Sanger needed to be built up with sandbags. We always carried some in our kit just in case we had to hole up somewhere for a while and defend ourselves unexpectedly. However, as we planned to stay we had a couple of hundred in the vehicles.

When I was happy that things were running smoothly at the compound, I left Coops in charge and suggested to Imam that we had a chat with the local Afghan National Police (ANP); it was only polite. We had rocked straight into their AO without warning, as we didn't want anyone to know we were coming.

I took a small contingent of Imam's warriors and strolled up to the police station. Imam was grumbling to me on the way. He hated the ANP, as did all the ANA. He told me they were not to be trusted and that there had been history of fighting between the ANP and the ANA. However, once we entered their compound walls, he was all smiles and hugs: a good actor!

The police station itself had obviously seen a lot of action. The walls were scarred by thousands of rounds, and large black smudges showed where RPGs had struck. Coils of razor wire ran along the tops of the walls and policemen in the blue-grey uniforms studied us from sandbag Sanger positions on the roof as we approached.

They waved and let us in. Inside the outer walls there were several buildings and we were directed towards the main one, which was concrete. Good job really, considering the amount of incoming fire it had received. A rug was laid out at the entrance to the building: a double door at the top of five steps, which was quite a grand entrance by Afghan standards. We sat on it with a couple of the older policemen.

It was difficult to judge the ages of people in Helmand. Everyone over the age of 30 looked about 50, and anyone over 40 looked bloody ancient! But I reckoned the two blokes we were with were in their thirties. Two teenagers, not wearing uniform, served us chai and brought out sultanas and seeds for us to nibble on.

We went through the usual small talk that preceded any conversation in Afghanistan. I was not in a rush and so enjoyed this cultural nuance. In our culture, and this is massively exaggerated in the army, we always try to cut to the chase straight away. You are deemed a waffler or a time waster if you are not concise. But in Afghanistan it is rude to avoid conversational foreplay.

I asked the policemen about the Taliban in Shin Kalay. Apparently they were very prolific. The enemy patrolled the streets every day and most of the civilian populace were Taliban sympathisers. This did not look good for us.

I explained that we had established ourselves in the compound to their south. We discussed tactical points such as firing arcs and actions on contact from the south. The basic message I wanted to get across was do not brass us up; we would deal with it, and if it looked like we were getting over-run, we would extract back to the police station and fight the enemy together. They liked the idea of fighting together, so I pushed a bit further. How about some combined patrolling? Imam barely flickered at this, but I could sense him bristling. He certainly did not want to patrol with these cowboys. However, our counterinsurgency doctrine highlighted the importance of police supremacy and of power being advocated to police forces rather than the military where possible. It was my job as an OMLT Comd to get this point across to Imam, but I would do that later back at our own compound over dinner.

We agreed to go and see them again in the afternoon and take five of their men out on a joint patrol. However, we did not give them any specific timings or routes or any other information that may have been used against us.

Back at the compound I explained my actions to Imam, and as usual he was pretty relaxed about the whole thing. He didn't like it, and neither did I, but as we were sharing the same AO it would benefit us all if we cooperated. I was fairly sure they could provide us with useful information regarding ground truth in Shin Kalay. However, I decided that we would go out on our own first and get a general idea of the area before we went out blind with an unproven ally.

While we had been at the police station the boys had been working hard, and defensively the compound was looking good. Coops and I sat down and went through what had been discussed.

'We'll work with them up to a point, but they look like some of the dodgiest bastards I had ever come across. Better the devil you know!' I explained.

Coops rallied the blokes, and after a brief set of orders from me we kitted up and headed out into Shin Kalay.

We entered the town through the south-east corner. The street was lined with over-arching trees and metre-deep ditches. As we cautiously pushed north, civilians started to appear in doorways to the left and right. They did not seem to be the shifty Taliban sympathisers that the police had warned us about. They waited patiently at their doors and as we passed they stepped out to shake our hands and talk to us. They were especially happy to see the ANA.

I asked them about the Taliban and they confirmed what the police had told us: that they had full control of the town. They patrolled daily on motorbikes and extracted money from the locals, who did not seem all that bothered as the Taliban offered security and they had lived a pretty peaceful existence. What they were bothered about was the presence of the ANP, who were hated with a passion. The locals accused them of not only wrongfully arresting folk and beating them to a pulp, but also of taking their children. My mind immediately went back to the young boys I had seen earlier that day, and I felt sick. Later on a group of kids came to chat to us and asked for chocolate. One of them told me he always ran away when the police were coming, in case they 'found him handsome'.

It became apparent that the boys were being used as slaves by the police, both for domestic chores and to satisfy their own sick gratification. It was abhorrent. I did not want to believe what I was hearing and I felt helpless. Every instinct told me to use some of the firepower at my disposal to let the ANP know that the practice was unacceptable, but that would have been way beyond my remit. What was I supposed to do? Storm the police station, kill them all and return the two teenage boys to their homes? The political maelstrom such illegal actions would cause would make the Afghan situation a million times worse than it already was. So I did nothing. And I am not proud.

I was battling with my own feelings of helplessness about the situation when I noticed that the street we were in had gone very quiet. In training we had been warned this was an indicator that trouble could be brewing, and I certainly noticed a distinct tension in the air, as if we were being watched.

I chirped up on the Personal Role Radio (PRR). 'Stay focused, boys, the street's gone quiet.'

I scanned the tops of the compound walls on the right and could see the point man to the front and left of me doing the same on his left. It would have been easy for the enemy to lob grenades over the wall into the middle of our patrol.

Suddenly the world around me erupted in a cloud of dust, noise and a hail of bullets. Everything seemed to happen at once. Explosions of dust popped up on the road all around me as I cut left and jumped into the stinking water of the ditch to my right for cover. I could hear that the rounds were coming from in front but I couldn't tell exactly where. We were only around 30 metres from the end of the road, which ended in a walled T-junction. I realised there could only be a small number of places that the bastard could be.

The firing stopped, and I tentatively raised my head from cover. Whoever had fired had obviously sprayed out his whole magazine and was either reloading or bugging out. Either way, now was my chance to do something.

I had no idea where he was. I knew he had to be close. In training, whenever I had a close enemy I had always taken the view that rolling over the fuckers in a fast aggressive move is always the best option.

'FORWARD! FORWARD! FORWARD!' I bellowed as I pulled myself out of the ditch at what seemed to be the slowest speed a human can move without going backwards. The kit was heavy, my trousers were sodden and my boots were filled with water and stuck to the bottom of the shitty ditch. I charged forward between 5 and 10 metres, passing Humph, my point man, on my left. I knew he was covering me as I ran out in the open. I trusted him wholeheartedly, as he trusted me a few seconds later, when I dived into cover and covered him as he made his way past me.

Within seconds we reached the end of the road, and I directed Humph to the left edge of the junction and my third man, Henderson, to the right whilst I tried to get a handle on the situation. The firing had stopped, but I still didn't know where the firing point was; it could start again, and next time we may not be so lucky.

I took the opportunity to look down the street where we had just been contacted. It was only around 3 metres wide at the very most. The insurgent had emptied his entire 30 round magazine in that small area at around 20 men. The air had been thick with 'angry wasps', and I had seen the dust dance as 7.62mm bullets struck the ground around my feet. But no one had been hit. We had been lucky. Very lucky.

We secured the junction, and I took the opportunity to radio back to Shawqat the sentence that all infantry commanders are dying to send over the net:

'Contact. Wait. Out.'

Corporal Fiji called me over to check something out. There was a small hole in the wall facing the T-junction around two inches across. The insurgent had seen us coming up the long narrow street, chipped a small hole in the wall and waited for us to get close. He had stuck his rifle muzzle through the hole and let rip blindly down the road, then had run as fast as he could from the firing point before a platoon of angry infantrymen stuck him full of bayonets.

We waited in position for a few minutes to ensure there was no follow up, but I did not want to sit there for too long providing a target for the enemy. So we pushed off, finished the patrol and ended up back at our compound. And that was it; we had broken our clear run. We had been contacted and we had come out unscathed. It was nothing really; it had only lasted the time it takes to empty a magazine – around five seconds – but I was happy. I knew I wasn't going to leave another theatre having not come across the enemy.

After our first contact in the street with the 'spray and pray' tactic shown by our assailant, we had no further contact with the enemy during our brief foray into Shin Kalay. However, we came back to Shawqat with some good information about the general atmosphere in the town and the state of play between the civilians, the Taliban and the police. It was judged that Shin Kalay, being the most populace settlement in the immediate vicinity of FOB SQT, deserved more attention and that the population could perhaps be won over if a popular project was undertaken.

It was decided that a bridge was to be built across another wide canal that also ran north to south but was 2.5 kilometres to the west of the town. The project would connect Shin Kalay with a better road that ran south to the main route leading east to Lashkar Gah and south to the district of Marjah. In short, the people of Shin Kalay would be much better connected with larger towns and therefore the travelling time to substantial market places would be greatly reduced.

The operation would be called *Tor Sara 1*, and my part in it was to establish a semi-permanent platoon base in Shin Kalay from which we could disrupt enemy activity within the town and provide security to the logistical patrols that would have to run down the high street in order to reach the bridge site. We were to be partnered with a different company of ANA, and Imam would return with his men to his southern AO. I didn't know it at that point, but the new group of warriors would be rougher around the edges and would provide a great deal of colour to the coming weeks.

Tor Sara 2 would also see the establishment of a permanent PB in Shin Kalay. It was to be built by the Royal Engineers with permanent defences and enough room for up to 40 people to live and operate. We would also be tasked with providing a screen of protection for this venture, behind which the engineers could do their business.

Initially, however, we needed a compound that we could occupy for a few days whilst the bridge build got underway. It needed to be in an elevated position with a good view up and down the main street so we could provide overwatch and protection for the large number of vehicles that would be bringing men, equipment and materials to the bridge site over the following weeks.

We needed somewhere with a couple of escape routes if the shit hit the fan and narrow side streets around it which we could block off with razor wire to stop some keen bastard from walking up to our door and posting a grenade or blowing himself up. I also planned to erect a screen to cover our moves out and was going to stick some Claymores out on the perimeter just in case it went all Rorke's Drift on us.

Our patrols had given me a couple of ideas about where we could base ourselves, but because the thick undergrowth that ran along the ditches at the sides of the roads obscured views, the only way we could truly find out what vantage points these possibilities offered was to get inside the compounds and up onto the roofs and check our arcs of fire. The first place we looked in was just opposite the mosque. The family who lived there were happy for us to have a look around, and I gave them a couple of minutes to move all the women into one room out of the way, in respect of their custom.

I borrowed the owner's ladder and put it against the side of the building. I had a couple of my own guys with me inside the compound for protection, and the rest were outside forming an outer ring of defence. A few of the ANA were inside chatting to the locals and reassuring them; the warriors were trusted, as the people knew they were on their side.

As I looked over the top of the flat roof, I started laughing.

'Coops, you'll never guess what's up here!' I shouted down.

'What you got, Boss?' he replied, interested to know what I found so funny on the top of some Afghan's roof.

'There's a bloody unexploded RPG sitting on the roof!'

I realised immediately the thing had been fired off and wasn't being stashed. The compound owner was as surprised as I was, and also about as bothered. If it had been in the middle of a small town in the UK, the whole area would have been evacuated, but he shrugged his shoulders. Ordnance was part of everyday life. I promised him we would get it removed as soon as possible. The bomb boys were very busy getting rid of IEDs, so the RPG was classed as a 'routine clearance' and would be dealt with when the disposal teams had a bit of slack time.

We moved on to the next compound. I had a good feeling about it. The roof was higher and had better eyes on the road. Coops climbed up with Captain Imam and we all agreed it would be a workable compound to live in. There were areas inside the compound walls where we could park the vehicles and a couple of fallback positions if the Taliban decided to get a bit 'Black Hawk Down-ish' on us.

Imam started to speak to the owner, who looked at least 100 due to the extra years Afghanistan seemed to put on everyone's faces, but was probably only around 50. He had a long, white beard down to his waist and was bent over a stick. He had few teeth left but his eyes were kind. Tears formed in them as Imam said over and over 'Babba, Babba, lutfan,' or 'Old man, please'.

I got on the net to ask my OC what sort of powers we had to chuck people out of their homes. I knew by law we could commandeer any compound we needed. Owners did not need to be reimbursed, but I carried hundreds of dollars' worth of Afghanis on my person to smooth the way whenever we caused damage or had to take over compounds for tactical reasons.

I was told that the town elders had agreed that we were able to take any compound we deemed suitable but that we were not to get physical unless absolutely necessary.

I looked back at Imam talking to Babba. He had his hand on his shoulder and was talking soothingly to the old man.

He came over to speak to me.

'David,' he said, speaking through my interpreter, 'he has nowhere to go. I have told him you will give him money, but what will an old man do with money? His family are far away, too far for him to get to before nightfall.'

I tried to keep my tactical head on. We were running out of time; we needed to be secure before nightfall. We had spent too long messing around, and it was time to be decisive. It was either one old bloke upset or my whole unit staying out in danger for longer until we found another compound to use.

'Go talk to him again, Imam. Tell him we are taking his compound and I will give him money for his trouble.'

Imam went back to the old man. More tears fell through the wrinkles on the poor man's face. I tried to stay focused, but as Imam talked to the man he looked back at me, looked me in the eye and started pleading with me. I didn't need a terp. 'Please don't make me do this to the old man,' he was saying.

I cracked. The old man was someone's father. How would I feel if a bunch of soldiers back home rocked up to my Dad's house, told him he had 20 minutes to leave, made him cry then stuffed some money in his back pocket as they booted him out the door? I couldn't do it.

'We're off somewhere else, boys, I'm not kicking a bloke as ancient as that onto the streets,' I decided.

Coops walked by to round up the blokes and gave me a smile. I knew then that he agreed with me and I was glad. It didn't stop him giving me a nudge and calling me a 'soft bastard' though. As we walked out on to the road I nudged him back, trying to get him in the stinking ditch, but he kept his footing and carried on down the road.

Imam knew we were running out of time and came up with a suggestion.

'What about the mosque?' he offered.

I thought he was joking.

'You're not serious?'

'Yes.' He was emphatic. 'My men can occupy the minaret and can see all the way up and down the road. Your men can defend the compound using the outer buildings.'

Tactically it made sense, but the devil would be going to work on ice-skates long before I would be the commander of a British unit that occupied a mosque, provoked a riot and became the dumbest officer in the army.

Imam did not appreciate this and demanded we took a look. It would have been disrespectful to go against him, so we went, we looked, and I thankfully talked him out of his idea.

Finally we came across a compound that had great arcs, was easily defendable and offered a couple of escape routes. I decided it would be our home for a few days and was not going to take no for an answer.

Imam explained this to the compound owner, who wasn't best pleased but agreed to take our money and move in with his brother temporarily. It was all cordial until his brother and some of his cohorts turned up from the fields outside, shouting and throwing clumps of soil in his frustration. I wanted them to understand this was an Afghan situation with an Afghan resolving it, so I let Imam deal with the group, but made sure they could see there was a bloke with a rifle nearby who would have no qualms dropping them if his mate was threatened.

Four blokes surrounded Imam, and the compound owner seemed to have changed his mind too, or more likely did not want to appear weak in front of his peers.

The brother squared up to Imam, who held up his hands to show he did not want to get physical, and then bent down and threw another piece of soil in his direction.

Imam flipped. His wiry arms swung, and in an instant the antagoniser was sent reeling back as a couple of well-aimed blows caught him in the face. The other men stood back as rifles, including mine, were re-cocked and aimed at them. All our rifles were obviously cocked before this, but noisily cocking your weapon is a very good visual and audio statement of intent to anyone nearby that they are a finger squeeze from death.

The brother stood up silently. Imam's face was rock hard. The creases that were usually smile lines were emphasised by his frown and turned his face into a mask of pure rage. He pointed at the compound owner and said something quietly but with force before he walked back to where I was standing. I lowered my rifle. The small group of men dispersed.

I put my hand on Imam's shoulder as he stood in front of me rubbing his bony knuckles. He could see the concern in my eyes as I asked him if he was okay. His hard face softened immediately and he smiled broadly. He chuckled and patted me, laughing at my concern.

The compound owner quickly gathered up some rugs, blankets and sleeping equipment for his family: a wife and four children between the ages of around four and ten. He sat with me inside the compound as I counted out his money and made him put his mark on my receipt (like many Afghans, he could not write). He apologised for his brother and made it clear he wished us no harm. I told him he could come back to collect more of his belongings, and he was grateful. As I handed him a wad of notes he suddenly looked very worried and darted glances between my interpreter, Rayes, and myself.

'Please do not tell anyone that I took money. Promise me you will not; they will come back tonight and take my children's feet.' he said. I was shocked and looked open-mouthed at Rayes, who nodded solemnly at the gravity of the statement he'd just translated.

He explained that the Taliban had told everyone in the town that anybody helping ISAF, including their family, would be mutilated, and I imagined that was at the very least. He said that a lot of the aggro had been an act. If he had given up his compound without trouble, it would be obvious to the Taliban that he had taken the infidel's money.

Even though I had paid the man a handsome some of money ($300: quite a lot when you consider that the average daily wage in Helmand was $4), I felt like a royal shit. I just couldn't help feeling sorry for these people that lived in a country where soldiers could throw you out of your home, beat you if you resisted and if you didn't resist other armed men would cut off your hands.

That day I had walked away from a family in a building with a potential time bomb on the roof, threatened an old man with eviction until he wept and helped forcibly evict a farmer and his family from their home just before nightfall. It was one of the least proud days I had ever had. But we had finally established PB Zoo.

CHAPTER 5
CONTACT

We called our little base PB Zoo. It didn't have an official name.

Our new team of around 20 ANA were far less disciplined than Imam's lot. They openly smoked marijuana, refused to patrol at night and had a very relaxed attitude to discharging their weapons when either on patrol or on sentry duty (stag), probably as a result of what they were smoking. Everything was a negotiation, whether it was how long before a patrol they had to abstain from taking drugs, how many Sangers they would occupy or whether or not I would give them night vision (I was reluctant because they seemed to be unable to make it through the night without chewing through the rubber eye pieces). The commander was an aggressive short sergeant called Faraz with fairly long hair flicked over in a big fringed side-parting. He had a high-pitched, effeminate giggle and loved to mess around. But what Faraz loved most of all was his animals.

PB Zoo was so named because of the number of creatures we had stationed with us in the compound. Faraz arrived in a pick-up truck with crates of various types of birds – including fighting cocks and large partridges – a couple of cats and two dogs; one gave birth to a litter after a week and the other was training to fight.

Faraz was always up for a joke and adored being the centre of attention. He was a showman, an extrovert and a diva with short fuse. After a few days we had a stand-off over his animals. I was not keen on the dogs being in the compound; the bitch especially was very aggressive and was constantly having a go at my men. There were also hygiene issues around living in such close proximity to so many animals. I would not back down, and eventually Faraz moved with his dogs to a small outer building joined to the compound, where he was quite happy.

Faraz's younger dog was a frisky hound that he often liked to take out on patrol. It was quite bothersome, especially when the front man was attempting to confirm an IED and the dog would come over and start sniffing, treading its big paws all over potential pressure plates. However, it was quite nice sometimes to go out for a patrol with the pooch trotting alongside, as if we were just taking him for a walk around the park.

The dog was going to be a monster. He was only a pup and was massive with paws that easily filled my palm and a shoulder that reached my knees. He was a very happy animal with a lovely blue-grey, silvery coat, big eyes and a nice temperament – too soft for fighting in my book, but what did I know about dog-fights? He would always come and shove his snout into an armpit or crotch when we were sitting around for the evening and he wanted his shaggy neck ruffled.

Sadly, however, he fell victim to not-so-friendly fire when the sergeant and his team were patrolling with a different team outside of our usual AO. The patrol they were with had an American sniffer dog attached to it. These dogs were highly sought after, highly-trained and highly regarded. They could only be 'on task' for short periods before their senses got overloaded and they had to rest. Their handlers were extremely defensive, as was the case when Faraz's pup repeatedly tried to mount and hump the US sniffer dog. So far as the US soldier in charge of the hound was concerned, our dog was a random mutt that was endangering the lives of the patrol by interfering with his professionally trained and highly valuable animal. So he did what many Americans would do: he pulled out his pistol and shot the poor thing in the head.

Faraz went from nought to angry in a way that I have only ever seen Afghans do. He and his friends immediately ran towards the confused Yank with weapons in the shoulder, ripping the fronts of their T-Shirts like the Incredible Hulk and yelling. To save the American who had no idea of what had just happened or why his life was so clearly being threatened, the British soldiers stood in their way and allowed the Yank time to sprint into the back of a nearby Mastiff (ironic that he sought refuge inside a vehicle named after a big dog).

The Afghans were baying for his blood and demanded that he be handed over for execution. The British commander tried to calm the situation and stated that he was never going to hand the American over but that he could make him apologise.

'Apologise! The only way he could show me he was sorry was by coming out here and kissing my dead dog!' screamed Faraz. He didn't think for a minute that any real man would perform such a base action. But that's what happened. The offer was translated to the American dog handler through the door of the armoured vehicle, held slightly ajar. The American was incredulous and took some convincing to leave the safety of the 24 tonne hulk, but eventually he gingerly stepped out of the vehicle and made his way across to the broken body of the dog, took a look around at the damning eyes of his supposed allies, knelt down and kissed the fallen hound on the snout.

As I heard it, the Afghans erupted in laughter, patting each other on the backs and wiping tears from their eyes, whilst pointing at the infidel that had lowered himself and forfeited his dignity so quickly. This was not a man in their eyes – not an individual that could possibly challenge a proud warrior's honour – and therefore not worth killing, in fact, not worth being angry with, as he was lower than whale crap.

The Afghans got angry very quickly and had sharper tempers than I could ever have believed existed but they cooled their jets equally as fast and the dog handler also got a slap on the back. Honour was restored and all was forgiven.

To add to the mix of the interesting menagerie we had in our PB, two Americans were attached to our merry band for a few days. They were part of a 'combat camera crew' and produced a few short films on their time with us.

Word of our arrival in Shin Kalay must have spread because within a few days we were getting attacked every day, and I was getting sick of it. PB Zoo was a bullet magnet. It was only a couple of quick bursts followed by some pot shots and after the first few contacts it became routine. But it was a declaration of intent, and a lucky pot shot is just as deadly as a sniper's well aimed round. Something needed to be done. I could hardly say that we as a callsign were doing our utmost for the security of the area if we did nothing about a couple of Taliban punters who took pleasure in hosing down our compound every day.

They always attacked from the same spot and usually in the late afternoon. The firing point was the roof of a compound 250 metres to our south that was being regularly commandeered as a staging post. I spoke to the guy who lived there. He was not happy with the situation but what else could he do? If he resisted, he would be tortured or killed. I tried to highlight the dangers and explained we would have to return fire. I told him to get himself and his family out of there as soon as the Taliban turned up, but he explained that they wouldn't let him. He was being used as a human shield.

I decided enough was enough and formulated a plan. The next time rounds came down range from the compound, we would pop smoke out our front door to give us cover, sprint over the road and down the alleyway heading west, then flank the enemy, hopefully cutting them off in the open ground to the south of the town before they got away. My two guys on the roof would control the ANA fire support so we didn't get brassed up by over-zealous Afghans.

As predicted, the rounds rained down the next day. The guys jumped onto their feet and pulled on their kit. I was first at the door – fuck the smoke, no time. I dashed across the dirt road with Cowhead and the GPMG right behind me, followed by the others, and within seconds we were in the snicket.

It was roasting hot, and even though it was only a few hundred metres, the blokes were blowing as we turned south. Killing the enemy would be the reward for the hard work. It was the first time I felt I was taking the enemy on instead of reacting in a fog of war, and I wanted to see the look on their faces and feel their panic as they saw a section of British infantrymen pile round the corner and punish them for daring to take us on. It might sound bloodthirsty and un-officer like, but I was glad I had no doubts over what I was potentially about to do. As soon as a man decides to be infantry he must realise he is at the pointy end of British politics, and if he does not relish all that entails and if he doubts his own mettle then maybe he should reconsider.

We reached the end of the town boundaries and were about to cross into open ground. I stuck my head round the corner and took a look at the compound where the firing was coming from. Nothing. Humph legged it across the road and straight into cover. Crossing the dirt track, about 4 metres wide and about 150 metres from the fire point, he ran straight into the ditch on the other side. He drew no fire, so we followed in pairs whilst being covered by our buddies on either side of the open ground.

We took up position around a derelict building. Coops pushed forward and left of my position on an embankment with a fire team and tried to get eyes on the enemy. Everything was quiet.

We remained in position for a while but it was evident that the bastards had got away. They must have either been warned we were coming by lookouts or 'dickers', or cut and run quickly. Hopefully we had given them a scare and they realised we meant business. The trap would only work once, however, as next time an ambush or an IED would certainly be waiting for us in one of the narrow alleyways.

Disappointed, we patrolled carefully back to PB Zoo, where, as per standard operating procedures, fags were brought out and the kettle was put on. The Yanks came and sat with us and looked very pleased with themselves. Both of them grabbed me by the hand and pumped it up and down.

'Thank you very much, Sir!'

'What for?' I asked, puzzled.

'Due to that action we will now be entitled to the Combat Badge.'

I had seen this badge on a number of US troops and was aware of its significance. The proud owner displays a badge of a horizontal bayonet across his chest on pretty much all his uniforms, including working dress. It looks pretty ally and tells everyone that this is a bloke that has mixed it with the enemy. I didn't realise that what we had just done would qualify, but the Yanks assured me it did. Fair enough, I thought, these two chaps have bravely followed a British Army officer through the streets of Shin Kalay in an attempt to smash the Taliban at close quarters. Even if the enemy had scarpered before we got there, these guys were willing to launch into a very hostile situation with someone they didn't know in order to produce media that would benefit the morale of the allied force.

As the weeks went on we became increasingly integrated with the ANA. We got to know their personalities and their customs, one of which was dog fighting. It seemed that all the men in the area loved dog fighting; it was like their national sport. The ANA welcomed the locals to fights outside of our platoon house where everyone would bring their prized beasts. I wasn't too pleased that it was becoming a social hub in the dog-fighting calendar, not only due to the obvious barbarity, but also due to the security risk of having so many people gathered very close to our compound. However, on the plus side, my ANA troops were gaining the trust, respect and friendship of the locals by inviting them over a couple of nights a week to use the field to the side of our compound. If that friendship translated into a tip-off for even just one IED location then it would be worth having to put up with an hour or so of barking and snarling in my back garden.

The dogs were huge beasts of questionable pedigree with their ears and tails cut off (these were removed when the animals were puppies). The two owners would stand in front of each other with their dogs gripped at their scruffs. The dogs would be held just inches apart and would be wound up by the owners and the crowd. They were prodded and jabbed and handled roughly, and after a while each dog would be up on his hind legs before being released into a clash of teeth, flying fur and pure aggression. The fights did not last long enough to allow the animals to be seriously wounded; instead, once it was obvious that one animal had the better of the other, the owners would somehow get a grip on their dogs and pull them apart. It wasn't pleasant to witness; dog fighting is barbaric and belongs in the Middle Ages.

At night these huge aggressive dogs own the streets. Larger males roam around on their own and the smaller ones group together in packs, barking constantly at all hours through the night. I had to shoot a couple during my time in Nad-e Ali. The first was an enormous beast that went for Rayes as we were conducting a patrol through the narrow alleyways of Shin Kalay and this bear of a dog stood at the entrance to a compound barking away. When I stopped to talk to the owner, the beast went straight for the terp. It must have weighed nearly 10 stone, and I thought he was done for as he was down on one knee and would have been bowled straight over. I fired two quick shots into the front of the hound. It didn't drop as the small 5.56mm rounds just went straight through. However, it was enough to stop it attacking, and the animal turned on a sixpence and hobbled as fast as it could back into the compound.

I apologised to the owner when I next saw him a few days later for having shot his dog and was astounded to hear that it was okay. He found it quite funny that I was bothered and even more funny that I would pay for any vet bills. He had no concept of what a vet was and gave a huge belly laugh when I explained it was like a doctor for animals.

'It's only a dog!' he shrugged, still laughing at the idea that in a country where they barely have doctors for humans, people might want to give medical assistance to animals.

The second dog I shot had a less happy ending.

We were patrolling in the countryside to the south of town. There were a number of small compounds standing alone surrounded by fields. As we passed one, there was a miserable looking hound lying in our path. It seemed very lethargic, and, as we got closer, it struggled to lift its head and gave a sorry bark in our direction. There was something wrong in its eyes; it didn't look right and it sent my spider sense a-twitching.

'Give this old bastard dog a wide berth, lads. Looks like it has rabies or something,' I broadcasted over the PRR.

Later that same day we were relaxing in the compound when Rayes caught something on the Icom which suggested there was enemy movement in the area. The Taliban had unsecured radio communications, and a lot of Rayes' time was spent flicking through frequencies on a piece of equipment called Icom listening in to what they were transmitting. Unfortunately, the enemy knew we had that ability and often transmitted false information or messages intended to intimidate us. However, in that instance we thought the information was valid, so we grabbed our kit and headed back out in a show of strength. Our patrol took us back to the farm with the mangy dog. He was still there but was much more alert and came staggering over to us barking his head off and wobbling from side to side like a bad actor in a zombie movie. He didn't look like he was going to stop. Corporal Fiji, the on point man fired the first shot, and I was quick to join in. As I kept squeezing I saw splashes of red on the dog's body.

The strong little beast must have taken ten rounds before he fell and a further five on the ground until he was dead. This worried me slightly as it showed the stopping power of my weapon. If it took ten rounds to stop a dog, how many to drop a man?

By that point any Taliban in the area would have heard us, so we needed to get into cover. We pushed forward into the small group of three compounds that made up a farm where I could plan the next move. The farmer came to speak to me. I immediately apologised for the dog and explained I was worried it was sick and I didn't want a sick dog biting my men. He told me he was not bothered about the dog, but he was bothered about the cow. I looked up, and he showed me a lovely, large, milky-white calf with four or five pinpoints of blood bleeding streaks of claret down its flanks. The poor thing had been caught by a number of rounds that had ricocheted off the rocky ground, and he was taking it inside to kill it in accordance to Halal.

I explained that we never intended to shoot the cow and we were very sorry, but that I could offer some sort of recompense. I carried a chart which stated the appropriate prices of all farm animals so that we wouldn't get shafted by locals in case of such eventualities as had just happened.

I dipped into my wad of Afghanis and offered the appropriate fee: around $100. The farmer made a big scene about it not being enough and asked for $500. I almost laughed, and he soon realised he was only going to get the fair price from me and took my original offer.

CHAPTER 6
IED

Inevitably, the roads leading up to PB Zoo became targets for enemy IEDs. A small mud bridge over an irrigation and sewerage ditch which ran between fields on either side of the street provided a classic 'vulnerable point', which we always made sure got extra attention before crossing.

ANA troops on stag spotted a couple of men hovering around the area in the middle of the night and came to get me. I wanted to get a closer view of what they were up to so I quietly left the compound with Coops through the front door and made my way to the middle of the road, where we lay down and looked through the Common Weapon Sight, or CWS, which was a night vision sight system that fits onto the weapon. It amplifies ambient light from the moon, stars or any other source to create a green flickering world that allows the viewer to see in the dark. The image was a green blur, but the two bright green blobs I saw hanging around at the bridge were obvious.

'What do you reckon, Boss?'

Coops was looking through his own night vision equipment. I really wasn't sure. I couldn't see them digging or bending down or carrying anything, but it was very suspicious. I had not been in theatre for very long and I really didn't want to brass up a couple of farmers working in their fields at night – as some did in order to avoid the heat of the day.

I made a decision to take a small team for a closer look. Along with two guys I ventured down the right of the track, keeping the compounds to the south in between us and the diggers for as long as possible, while Coops and another couple of blokes followed closely on the left side of the track, keeping low in the ditch.

The air was cold, but we were already quite warm as we made our way across the ploughed ground. Heavy sods clumped around our boots as we quickly but silently pushed on through the darkness. Minutes passed in the pitch-black night with no artificial lights glowing in the whole of Shin Kalay. It was a thrill to be there under the stars with the potential of a fight on our hands. We were primed, ready and in strong positions of cover with a half decent withdrawal route and plenty of depth and reserve. My tiny team went firm, and I looked across my shoulder to check on Coops.

His team silently drifted past to my left. I whispered my location over my PRR and gave a quick wave so he knew exactly where I was. His team moved, weapons in the shoulder, towards the bridge. They paused in dense cover to allow us to continue our advance. We reached the compound wall just 100 metres to the south of PB Zoo, and I whispered through the PRR to make sure Coops was making the correct progress.

'I've got you, Boss. I can see you up against the wall there. We'll go firm as you move around out of cover but we'll lose sight of you when you get to the other side of the compound. Give me a couple of pips when you want me to move up.'

Tapping the pressel switch on the radio was a signal when you weren't able to talk due to close proximity to the enemy. Depressing the switch without speaking sent a clearly audible pip of white noise across the net.

My two boys were right up with me, shoulder to shoulder. Humph hugged into the corner of the compound with just his rifle and his eyes poking round the edge to look for any potential danger when we moved off. Clarky crouched next to me with his back against the rough mud wall. I tapped them both on the shoulder and started on what I thought would be our last bound before we got a good view of what were either innocent farmers digging a ditch or insurgents bent on tearing our limbs apart with a device. I looked over Humph's shoulder and noted a treeline to the rear and right of where the tiny bridge sat, and considered it as a likely depth position, a point at which any enemy commander might place a couple of troops to give protection to the guys digging.

I moved passed Humph, who remained in position until both Clarky and I overtook him. As we did, sharp cracks filled the air. There weren't rounds coming at us from either the bridge or the treeline. They were fired from behind us. A long spray of automatic fire arced high over our heads from PB Zoo. In the confusion we stopped still and hit the deck, crawling back to the last safe position at the corner of the building.

Silence was restored for a few seconds. There was no more firing, but a motorbike started up and raced away into the night. I got on my feet and raced forward to the south-western corner of the compound where I could see the bridge.

I scanned the area with my CWS and saw nothing. I whispered into my radio:

'Anything Coops?'

'Nothing Boss,' he whispered back.

Whoever had been there had gone.

We returned back to the PB in the same fashion, keeping one bloke static as the rest moved so that he could return fire immediately if we were surprised.

The ANA were known for being trigger-happy and for not liking the dark. They would commonly shoot at shadows in the night, and that was exactly what had happened as we edged towards our target. It was difficult working with people who didn't speak the same language, and, perhaps due to the speed at which we had to react to the threat, the gravitas of the situation hadn't been fully explained to our Afghan friends. I was pissed off, but I couldn't wholly blame them. They probably thought they were protecting us. We used it as a learning point and decided that whenever we did any action ahead of an ANA fire support position, we would always have a British soldier sitting with them to calm trigger fingers and direct any potentially wayward fire.

The next morning we set out on our first patrol of the day and I decided to pass the bridge where we had disrupted the diggers the previous night. It was just a matter of a few hundred metres away from our front door: a tiny structure that took only about three steps to cross. I was amazed when I saw something yellow poking out of the ditch under it.

I didn't want to get too close so I had a good look through my Advanced Combat Optical Gunsight (A-COG). It was clearly a pressure plate that had been tossed to the side of the road in a hurry. On closer inspection I could see that it was not attached to anything, so once the area had had a good sweep with the Vallon detector I went to get a closer look.

Sure enough, it was a strip of foam which held apart two strips of metal like the filling in a sandwich. Holes had been punched through the foam to allow strips of metal attached to each face to touch once weight was place on the item, thus forming a circuit and allowing current to pass to the ignition and then activate a device.

The plate was evidence, and I handled it wearing gloves as it may have contained valuable prints. I planned to stick it in one of the evidence bags we carried before dropping it off at Shawqat on a later patrol in the hope that some information could be gained from it about who was operating in the area. I had been told bomb makers had signature *modus operandi* that provided clues to a trained eye, and therefore significant intelligence could be gained from bomb parts. I turned to speak to one of my men briefly and when I turned back around I saw that someone had moved the pressure plate. Rayes was holding it up to his face to get a really good look at it.

'Put it down, you moron!' I shouted.

He looked hurt at my tone but did as I said.

'You just put prints all over that. You could have wiped away evidence and you have certainly contaminated it with your own. We're going to have to get someone to come down and take your prints in order to eliminate them from the evidence,' I scolded.

Rayes apologised. He didn't know, he wasn't 'forensically aware', as we called it, and was rather sheepish for the next couple of days. I didn't want a grumpy terp following me around for the next few days with a face like a slapped arse, so we had to make up. The Afghans were childish in that way and were prone to sulks, but everything had been forgotten a few days later when Rayes sidled up to me one morning when I was having my usual breakfast of a fag and a brew.

'Good morning, David!' he grinned.

'Morning, Rayes. How can I help you, mate?'

I could tell he wanted something, but it is not the Afghan way to get straight down to business, especially during the first conversation of the day, so we spent a few minutes discussing weather, my sleep and other nonsense before he came out with a simple request. He pointed at our standard issue green string washing line.

'The warriors would like some string, please.'

I could see our makeshift washing line hanging up outside with stinking clothes covered in crust that was left when the ditch water dried, and naturally thought that they wanted to put up a washing line of their own.

'Not a problem, mate,' I nodded.

Barney was listening in and rummaged around in our makeshift store before pulling out a whole ball of string and throwing it to Rayes, who wandered off.

Within the hour all my lads were up, dressed, fed and ready for the day's work – a few patrols for an hour or two each spread out throughout the day and covering most of the town and the rural outskirts. We pushed out of the compound for the first time that day and turned left up the road towards the crossroads that sat around 250 metres away. Around ten warriors were milling about outside and as soon as they saw us they started shouting and waving.

'Hey, Rayes, what are they shouting about?' I asked.

'They have found something and want to show you. They are very proud and excited for you to see,' he answered.

I realised he was talking about an IED.

'They've got a device? Why the fuck didn't you tell me, Rayes? For fuck's sake!'

I broke into a jog and was up close to the crossroads moments later. I knew I would have to handle the situation delicately because a) there was a device that I knew fuck all about and b) the Afghans are annoyingly sensitive and if I went in blazing about proper IED SOPs I would lose a lot of their respect.

I stopped about 25 metres away from the warriors and shouted across.

'What you guys got there?'

They pointed excitedly and clapped their hands, happy that I was there to see their triumph.

'Mi-ine! Mi-ine!' (the word they use for bomb).

'Sais, sais. Hobass askar!' (right, right. Great soldiers!) I replied.

I gave them a thumbs-up and turned to Rayes to help me translate.

'OK, boys, that's absolutely great. Well done for finding it! I think you should probably get well away from it now.'

They tried to tell me how they used their superior skills with the Vallon to find the device, but as it turned out later one of the locals had pointed it out to them. To my outrage, instead of backing away from the device, they were now trying to prove to me and each other how brave they were by walking right up to the bomb and having a look. The crazy sergeant beckoned for me to go and have a look – he was testing my mettle to see if I was as 'brave' as his boys – but I wasn't that stupid. Instead, I gave him my camera and asked him to take a couple of pictures which would be helpful for the Brimstone callsign (bomb disposal boys from the Royal Engineers or Royal Logistics Corps) when they arrived to clear it.

Whilst he was taking photos, I grabbed a few of his men and ordered them to move to the other side of the IED through the back alleys and to redirect any traffic coming down the main road. I didn't want anyone else to come close to this bomb.

Faraz was back shortly with my camera and I regarded the snaps that he had taken for me. I was shocked to see how much of the IED they had uncovered. I could clearly see a portion of a yellow plastic container sticking out through a hole several inches across. We were trained only to uncover the smallest amount of a device possible, just enough to confirm that we were actually dealing with a bomb and not just some other rubbish that was strewn by the road.

I told the sergeant to pull his men right back as I didn't know how unstable the device had become. He marched over to the small group who were still milling about on the crossroads and started emphatically pointing and shouting. I was glad to see they all obeyed instantly and I started planning my next move and compiling my radio message to request the bomb disposal team ASAP. However, my gladness soon turned to horror when I saw what was going on. Faraz retired only around 10 metres before bending over and picking something up from the dust. I couldn't believe my eyes. It was the green string I'd handed out that morning. It had been attached to the bomb and the crazy Afghan was tugging it.

I turned round to my men and pointed to the ditch.

'DOWN! All of you now! DOWN!'

I turned back to the sergeant and grabbed Rayes.

'Tell that silly bastard he's just making the bomb angry; he's making it unstable for the disposal team which is en route now!'

The sergeant looked at me and grinned as he tugged away.

'No need for the disposal team. I'll do it. Done it hundreds of times.'

Stupid Afghan bravado and pride would not let him walk away, but thankfully after a couple of seconds something snapped and he stumbled backwards. As it turned out, it wasn't the string that snapped, but a pair of wires that had been connected to the device. It was hard-wired to a battery pack in a nearby compound, ready to be activated later. If the insurgent had been in the area all he would have needed to have done was touch the wires to the battery, and everyone in the vicinity would have been blown to pieces.

The bomb disposal squad turned up a bit later. I stood at the back of their Mastiff, smoking cigarettes with the staff sergeant who was to go down and do the actual disarming. It was a hell of a job, but I was glad someone was doing it. He smoked about three bines before heading off, and just before he left I said, 'Hey, d'you reckon I can blow the thing up when you dig it out?'

'Yeah, no worries, Boss,' he replied.

Then off he went. As he got closer he popped a couple of smoke grenades and let them swirl around the area of the device before he disappeared into the cloud and got to work. He told me after the smoke was to prevent anyone seeing what specialist tools and techniques he was using, as well as to prevent any sharp shooter getting a bead on him.

The staff sergeant eventually came back and I couldn't believe the size of thing he was carrying. It was a huge yellow plastic container about the size of a suitcase.

'25kg, Boss. I reckon about enough to pick up this Mastiff and throw it in that ditch.'

We carried the bomb to the field next to the compound, plonked it down in the middle and packed plastic explosives all around it. The staff sergeant lay down next to me in a ditch around 150 metres away from the bomb.

'Right, Boss, just push that button.'

I had a huge grin on my face as I anticipated the enormous explosion I was about to unleash on the world. It was going to be mega with dust and shrapnel flying everywhere and a mushroom cloud rising overhead as 25kg of homemade explosives and 10kg of plastic vaporized.

I pushed the button and immediately the most disappointing boom erupted from the middle of the field. I turned to the staffy and uttered the words no man wants to hear after he's just expected to make the earth move.

'Was that it?'

We lifted our heads above the ditch and could still see the yellow container as bold as a bulldog's bollocks sitting in the field.

'Reckon we need more PE, Staff.'

'Yeah, thanks, Boss.' He gave me one of those funny looks that senior NCOs often give young officers that basically say, 'Shut up, Sir ... and by Sir I mean Dickhead!' I smiled back, helpfully.

'Have you made it angry now?'

'Oh, yes!' he replied as he crawled out of the ditch and across the field. He returned a few minutes later.

'Try again now, Boss. I've put double the amount of PE on the device so it'll definitely go this time.'

I confidently pushed the button and with great satisfaction unleashed the biggest explosion I had ever experienced. I felt the shock wave in my guts and the wind in my hair as the air all around the bomb was pushed away with unimaginable violence. Lumps of field were launched hundreds of feet in the air and continued to rain down on our ditch for a minute after the event. The noise was outrageous, and the pleasure I got from the knowledge that I'd made that happen was immense.

I was glad those ANA boys found it and we were able to blow it up in a safe and controlled manner rather than it going off under one of our vehicles.

IED security became like a game of cat and mouse with the enemy; it was hard to tell who was the cat and who was the mouse.

On another hot and dusty day, my callsign had been tasked with securing the road running through the middle of the town in order to allow a logistics convoy to reach the bridge building site 3 kilometres up the road.

We had to maintain security of the route for around seven hours to allow the transports time to get to the new bridge site, unload, go back to Shawqat and repeat the process several times. We had already done it a number of times. It became more and more dangerous as everyone got completely and utterly bored with the situation. It was a battle to keep the blokes motivated and watching their arcs in what was a completely bone task.

The guys did their best, but even the most professional soldier would flag in the heat, with kit on, looking down the same street for hours on end. I tried to rotate the guys to keep them fresh. There was a small shop down the road, which was a room at the front of one of the local's compounds. The only way you knew it was a shop was by the fact the owner pinned empty packets of cigarettes and sweet wrappers to his outside wall advertising the brands he had in stock. Every now and again I would send one of the red-arses down to the shop with a $5 note to buy everyone cans of 'Pebsi'.

Rayes provided entertainment too. He wandered up and down the street chatting to the locals – by being friendly he occasionally got some decent information. He also had the deepest pockets in the world. They were like Mary Poppins' handbag! No matter how long we had been out for, he always seemed capable of pulling out another bit of food.

After several hours on task, Rayes came over to me with a couple of the local kids.

'David, there are two Taliban doing a patrol in the third street on the right,' he exclaimed excitedly.

He pointed down the road. I didn't have time to rally the guys; the enemy would slip away, and by calling all the men in I would leave the rest of the 450 metres strip of road that we were protecting open to allow the enemy to lay IED or an ambush.

I made a snap decision. Looking back now it was probably the wrong one, but to combine a cliché and a paraphrase 'hindsight is always 20/20' and an 'average plan enacted aggressively now is better than a great plan carried out too late'.

My decision was to jump on the back of the WMIK and to grab hold of the Gympy. Barney piled into the front and revved hard, slamming the vehicle into reverse – no time for three point turns, we were just going to go straight backwards at full pelt. At the last minute Clarky ran and joined us in the passenger seat, and then we set off, racing in reverse towards who knew what.

BANG!

The sound made us all jump. What have I stirred up here? I thought, as I held tight to the pistol grip of the machine gun.

'Contact left!' screamed Barney, and I swung the gun round on its pintle but saw and heard nothing.

He kept the vehicle moving backwards and forwards to make us a harder target for the enemy. I felt dangerously exposed standing up on the back of the open-top vehicle as Clarky and I scanned possible fire points. Where the hell did that noise come from?

To me it sounded like a mini-flare firing: a cross between a bang and a loud pop.

'Anyone see anything?' I shouted above the roar of the WMIK.

'Smoke. Range 150, right behind the wall,' Barney replied.

'Didn't sound like a gunshot to me, Barndog. What the fuck was it?'

It didn't make sense. Firing one shot then legging it just wasn't the Taliban's style. I didn't like it. I knew something was amiss and I certainly wasn't going to hang around waiting for whatever it was to come and bite me on the arse.

'Let's get back to the boys, Barney, and we'll do this in a more controlled fashion. We're not achieving anything here other than being a target.'

Barney drove back up the street, forwards this time, and I told Coops what had gone on. I took a small group of blokes back down to where we heard the noise and investigated the possible firing point where Barney had seen the smoke. Then we checked out the street.

Barney spotted something in the thick vegetation which fringed the stinking ditch that ran alongside the road. It was yellow IED with a thick black stripe around the middle, which I thought was a bit odd as it stuck out like a turd on a pool table. It was cylindrical in shape and around 1 foot long by 6 inches wide and it was wrapped in clear plastic. We had obviously disturbed the bastards as it clearly hadn't been laid with precision: just dumped in the hedgerow pointing at the road and the exact spot that my vehicle had been sitting in when we heard the pop.

After clearing and cordoning off the area, I called in the Explosive Ordnance Disposal (EOD) boys. A big chap with an outrageous 'tache arrived and cleared the bomb in minutes. He brought it over to show us.

'Someone's been proper lucky here, Boss!' he told me as he handed over the 10kg device.

'Yeah, that was probably me.'

He told us that the device was a command wire pull. A very simple trigger that uses a battery and something like a common spring-loaded garden peg with tin foil wrapped around the ends that touch. These ends are kept apart with another piece of wood attached to a bit of string that you can pull in order to release the wood, allowing the peg to close, the tin foil to touch and the circuit to be made. This gives a spark that then fires a detonator which is embedded in the main propellant, be that fertiliser or plastic explosive. The detonator provides enough energy to ignite the main charge, and BOOM! Off goes the IED. The bomb which we'd dodged was also packed with about 5 kilos of spark plugs which would have shredded anyone in its blast radius and the only reason it didn't blow was because the detonator wasn't properly set in the main charge. Instead of giving it the energy required to explode, it gave just enough to set it on fire and the explosives burnt harmlessly away.

My rash decision to race off down the road might have saved our lives as the enemy didn't get enough time to set up the device. We had been seriously close to being torn apart by spark plugs and hit by a blast wave that would have picked up our bodies and thrown them like rag dolls to crash into the wall behind us. A little more time on that bomb, just pushing the detonator in a fraction more would have been the end of the tour for Barney, Clarky and for me.

CHAPTER 7
DAMAGE

We were sitting in PB Zoo having just completed another patrol around Shin Kalay. Smokes were being handed out. The brand of choice was Pine. Even at the bargain price of $5 for 200, the ANA warriors still laughed at us for being ripped off. I got used to the harsh cigarettes that advertised 'American Taste' on the packet, whatever that meant.

Pretty much everyone smoked out there. I'm not a big smoker myself back home and will probably only have one or two a week if I'm having a particularly bad time. However, I was on 20 a day out there. It was part of the routine. Finish a patrol, have a chai and smoke a couple of bines.

My usual vice, a beer, wasn't an option on tour, so I needed that hit of nicotine to chill out. And as you were on edge a lot of the time, you really did need to relax whenever you could. I didn't come across a bomb disposal guy out there who didn't smoke, and all the Afghans smoked. When you asked one for a cigarette they would give you a whole packet. It was a demonstration of their generosity.

That particular afternoon my post-patrol ciggie was abruptly interrupted. The explosion came out of nowhere. It was loud and it was close.

'STAND TO! STAND TO!'

I was yelling at the lads to get their kit on and to man the loopholes we'd cut in compound walls. At this point I had no idea what was happening, and everyone needed to be ready to react. It sounded like an IED, but for all I knew the Taliban were trying to hit us with RPG.

The lads got in position and I rocked up into our Sanger position. Cowhead was on stag and he pointed out where he had seen the explosion. It was on the edge of a compound about 350 metres to our south. I couldn't make out what was happening, as there was thick cover around the explosion site.

Details came over the net. A unit had been hit. They had a casualty and needed a MERT at an emergency HLS. The chap on the net was calm and concise, but you could hear the tension through the radio waves. I wanted to jump on and let them know we were available to help, but I knew I needed to wait for a break as it was imperative for the poor guy that had been hit that the callsign and Zero swapped as much information as possible.

As soon as there was a pause, I jumped on.

'Amber 13. We are platoon strength currently 350 metres to your north and available to help if required. I can see where you are setting up your HLS. I suggest we can push onto your western flank at the road and secure that for you. Over.'

'Roger, many thanks. Over,' came the reply.

'We'll be there in under five minutes and will signal our position with mini-flare. Out.'

The guys had stood to and were ready to move immediately. I quickly briefed them on what had happened. A British soldier and a couple of Afghans were hurt and the MERT was inbound. We would take the WMIK so the GMPG was on a platform and we would take the Vector as well just in case the MERT couldn't come in and we needed to move the guys by road back to Shawqat to be lifted from there.

We were out of the door within a minute and headed down the road. I stopped short with the men and vehicles in cover behind a compound just before the rendezvous point and pushed forward into a ditch. I figured that the guys on the ground would be a bit jumpy after seeing one of their mates get hit and I didn't want any of my blokes to be caught in friendly fire due to confusion.

Once in cover I launched a couple of mini-flares into the air to signal our position and immediately regretted it. The sound of a mini-flare going off could be mistaken for a gunshot. It wasn't a problem as it got no incoming from the Tiger Team, but I logged it as a lesson for the future.

I called the team forward. I had brought seven of my own men and about the same number of warriors. I spread them out either side of the road with the Afghan medium machine gun (MMG) up on a compound roof to the right hand side. Coops went up with the gun and had good eyes on over the ground.

I broke the ground down for the guys. This is a process by which different parts of an area being operated in get referenced. So the road running south became our axis, and I named each of the compounds in our arcs and in range and, most importantly, I gave a no fire line to our right where I could see the friendly troops working on the injured soldiers and clearing an HLS.

I was well aware that the Taliban knew a soldier had been injured and would therefore know a helicopter was inbound.

'Lads, MERT inbound, five mins,' I broadcast.

I was being stupid. Instead of tucking myself in cover, I was in a position that screamed 'officer'. My map was spread across the bonnet of the WMIK and my rifle was laid across it to stop it blowing around in the hot breeze that was stirring the dust around my boots.

Without warning I heard the whizzing and cracking of bullets around my head.

'Fucking hell! Contact! Contact!'

I dived to the ground and crawled into a ditch. The rounds were close. I found out later that a round had taken out the top of one the antennae on the WMIK, around a foot or two over my head at the time. I saw Endo in front and we both laughed at the sight of me sprawling unceremoniously in the ditch. I hadn't even thought about it. I just hit the ground and crawled into cover on instinct and so quickly that I had left my rifle acting as a paperweight on the bonnet of the WMIK.

I leopard-crawled out of the ditch with my arse as low as I could get it. It was a long 3 metres to the wagon. At the last minute I jumped up, grabbed my weapon and map off the bonnet and dived back on to the dusty track before crawling back into the ditch.

I scanned the ground in front of me, looking for muzzle flashes from the enemy. We needed to win this firefight quickly and effectively if the MERT was coming in.

The air was alive with bullets flying over our heads. Most of us were in pretty good cover from fire in the ditches and obscured from sight by the thin trees that ran along them. But I was worried about Coops and the gun group up on the roof.

'ENEMY! 250 right hand edge of compound, one fist left of axis!'

Endo had spotted the enemy and shouted at the top of his voice to bring everyone's fire onto that spot. I shouted up to Coops with the guns to pass on the message but added 'watch my strike!' before popping a UGL accurately right onto the enemy position: 40mm of HE landed on his head and chunks of compound flew as we opened up.

Through the dust and debris I saw a figure move. I pulled my rifle in tight before taking up the slack on the trigger. The weapon kicked slightly and the figure dropped. In a firefight like that when there are rounds flying about all over the place and there are kills, no one can be too sure that it was them who made that kill, but if I did get the target, I have no remorse. It was him or me and my men.

The enemy was either dead, badly wounded or had decided that after the response we gave he was going to retire to fight another day as it went very quiet. However, for all we knew they could have been manoeuvring to another fire position or sitting tight with an RPG waiting for the chopper to come in. We stayed where we were, ready to repel any future attack. It didn't come. The MERT arrived and three guys were loaded onto the back. I didn't know it at the time, but I would see one of those men just a few weeks later.

In the meantime, we continued our job. Several days later Amber 13 was pushing north out of Shin Kalay. We had been shot at the day before from an area to the north-west of the village, and my intention was to patrol in a semi-circle to dominate the ground and show the enemy that we were a force that was not to be intimidated.

We were patrolling in staggered file formation: two ranks of men, one either side of the road with the left rank scanning the left flank for potential dangers and visa-versa.

We were just a few hundred metres out of the town when a white Toyota Corolla (apparently the only car and colour available in Afghanistan) was forced to stop by the lead Afghan section. The patrol came to a halt, and my men checked the area around them before taking cover in the ditches either side of the track. I took the time to look forward, straight down the middle of my two columns, and could see a man get out the vehicle and pull something from the back seat. I immediately trained my rifle on the man, partly to be able to react to anything dangerous he was taking from his back seat and partly so I could use my scope to get a better view of the situation.

The bundle he was carrying in his arms was clearly a small child. The man was led by one of my Afghan soldiers down the middle of the track to my location. I lowered my rifle to show I was no threat.

The man was in his thirties, clearly a Pashtun, and his beard was starting to thicken as opposed to the sorry wispy affairs that the 20-year-old males sported. He was wearing traditional sandy brown clothing and his head was uncovered, showing his jet black hair. The child was wrapped in a white sheet, and he held it close to his body. I could see concern and fear in his eyes as he approached. It is likely that he had never spoken to a westerner before, but his face was a picture of desperation.

Rayes was on my shoulder as the man began to talk. As he spoke, he unravelled the white sheet to show me the pathetic body of his poor little boy. He must have been around a year old, barely moving and his eyes rolled in his head. He lay motionless in his father's arms: a dead weight.

The toddler's body was a mass of angry, bright red burns from head to toe. As he breathed in, the skin on his chest tightened painfully around the blisters and loose rags of skin hung from open sores. The poor thing began to shiver despite the intense heat of mid-afternoon in central Helmand.

'Jesus Christ, what's happened, Rayes?'

'He says the boy pulled a pan of boiling water over himself and he wants us to help.'

I didn't hesitate.

'Of course, of course. Tell him I can't do anything to help here but I'm radioing back to Shawqat now. The doctor there will see him. He must drive there now!'

I grabbed the radio and pushed in the button to transmit my request to send this guy to our med centre back at camp only 3 kilometres away.

The man was talking to my warriors. I had another look at his son and something just didn't look right.

'When did this happen, Rayes?'

A flow of Pashto filled the air.

'Three days ago,' Rayes replied.

'Jesus Christ!' I knew those burns did not look fresh and I felt anger rise. How could a father leave his son in that state for three days before going for help? What kind of culture was it where life was so cheap and pain so normal that a little boy could be left writhing in agony for days and near death? I couldn't even look at the guy. I couldn't even comprehend it.

He took the child back to the car, gunned the engine and drove past towards base. His wife was in the car which was rammed with around six other kids. I never did find out what happened to that boy but I know the medics would have done all they could to help him.

Another few days passed and we began to wonder how long the detail would last. I kept telling my guys it wouldn't be long. The mission had changed. Initially we went in to have a presence in Shin Kalay and disrupt the Taliban's activity through patrolling, picking fights, information gathering and hearts and minds. Then the decision was made to build the bridge, and we were required to provide security for the convoys and logistics.

Conditions were far from ideal, and it felt like the operation was stringing on for longer than we had been told. The ANA couldn't understand it either. I tried to explain how the situation was changing and we were important in the over-arching security plan in Shin Kalay, and they shrugged their shoulders and cracked on.

The guy I felt sorry for the most was the poor bloke whose compound we had commandeered. He kept coming back to see if we were shifting. Every time he came he brought one of his many kids to help him shift some more of what we considered junk but were actually the bloke's possessions. One time he left a 4-foot long stick covered in what looked like big manky lamb chops. They were all dried up in the sun and covered in flies. I should have got someone to shift it as it was without doubt a serious source of infection. Five days later the owner came back and asked again to grab some of his kit. After a quick search to check for weapons we let him in. He made a beeline for the stick of E-Coli and tucked it under his arm. With an old carpet under the other, away he went, presumably to cook his dinner.

It never ceased to amaze me what the Afghans could eat and drink. They must have had Kevlar stomachs! The ditches beside every road, track and field were used as toilets, drains and rubbish tips. It broke my heart to see kids every day with yellow plastic drums collecting water from the ditches to take back for the families' daily drink. I ate with the ANA very often and always enjoyed it, but I tended to stick to the rice and tried not to think too much about what it had been cooked in.

We had been there a while with no post and could not understand why none came with the resupplies that we received every three days or so. Every night on the net I requested mail along with all the other important consumable supplies we needed. Always top of the list was more water; post was a close second.

For some reason, after a week or so HQ relented and we got a big load of letters and parcels in one trip. It had been Clarky's 21st birthday, and Barney had turned 37 or something (he was so old he had stopped counting, the ancient bastard). It was my 27th birthday the next day, so it was party time!

We bought some tiny, shrivelled potatoes with some sunflower oil from a local shop. Those who weren't busy sat on the sand bags and ammo tins that we used as furniture and peeled and chipped the spuds with bayonets. One of the empty ammo tins became our deep fat fryer, and we found an old frying pan amongst the owner's clobber. WO2 (company sergeant major) 'Chuck' Berry had kindly grabbed a few steaks from the cookhouse and chucked them in a cooler box, so they went in the pan.

In the midst of the madness it felt great to sit around a fire in the middle of Helmand tucking into steak and chips cooked tenderly over the hexi stove by the best cook amongst us, Corporal Fiji.

The morale was high as hell that night. We all ate our fill and drank a few brews. We had had a couple of contacts, we felt our task was important and we were all still there without a scratch. Happy times!

Along with the post and steaks, the company sergeant major had dropped off a 'sound commander' to be used at the bridge opening ceremony. I'll admit that when I heard over the net he was delivering a sound commander, I honestly believed (as did the rest of the blokes to be fair) that some guy from the Sigs was joining us to for a few days to conduct a psy-ops / propaganda task, and was surprised when a heavy day-sack was dropped off containing a huge speaker and a Britney Spears-type microphone that fastened at the ear with a thin wire bent round to the wearer's mouth. Trust the army to think of a completely bone term like 'sound commander' to name what is essentially a big speaker in a bag.

The following morning I was chatting to the Afghan NCOs in their room about the day's patrolling schedule (actually I was trying to get the buggers out of bed so we could start the day's patrolling schedule), when I heard a couple of the boys shouting outside.

'Boss … Boss, check this out!'

As I stuck my head out of the doorway, I saw them all gathered round and noticed Barney wearing the sound commander. They all pressed their faces close to Barney's – and therefore the microphone – and sang me the best and most heart-warming (and slightly out of tune) rendition of 'Happy Birthday' I have ever had and expect I ever will have.

For the rest of the day Rayes wore the audio kit on all our patrols to announce to the whole town that the 'Friendship Bridge' was opening with a grand ceremony. In the UK no one would have bothered to walk miles to see some British colonel and the mayor declare a bridge joining one dust track to another dust track open. However, in Afghan it was a big deal, and the locals went in their droves to see this wonder – a metal bridge over the canal. At that point, with so much goodwill on display, I could almost have believed things were improving in the war-torn province.

CHAPTER 8
POLICE STATION

We took the short trip back into Shawqat. We had to drop Endo off, so that he could catch the next chopper out to go on his R&R. I also wanted to grab some information about the next stage of *Tor Sara*. This could be done over the radio, but in ten minutes of face-to-face you can achieve so much more than in a protracted radio conversation.

I had left Clarky and Humph back at PB Zoo with the Afghans. This was normal practice; we always left two guys back at the ranch whenever we went on patrol so they could still operate the Sanger and snatch some rest in between stags. They were also to man the radio and relay back to Shawqat when we were out of range.

I liaised with the commander of the neighbouring platoon and caught up on his intent, then gave him some details about what we had been up to and any intelligence that might be useful to the other callsigns. I then sat for a half an hour with the Tiger Team OMLT Comd. He was moving to the south-west of our AO for the next stage of *Tor Sara* (which involved pushing out yet another cordon of infantry, allowing the engineers space and protection to build a permanent PB on the edge of Shin Kalay. I explained the ground and my assessment on the enemy, and we discussed boundaries and no fire lines to avoid potential blue-on-blues, as our forces were operating closely on the ground.

I folded up my map and shook the guy's hand. It had been a good meeting, and we had got a lot sorted that would make the next few days run smoothly. I was glad to have the Tiger Team on our flank. They had a good reputation and would hopefully act as a good example to the rest of the ANA in the coming years.

As we were walking away from the table, still chatting about the weather or something else equally insignificant, both the company sergeant major and Coops shouted over to me.

'Boss, kit on. We need to move!'

I could see all my lads charging about the tent chucking their kit on the WMIK and pulling their Osprey over their heads. Anyone could see they were cutting about like they meant it; Coops and Barney were getting amongst them and making sure that nothing was forgotten and they were good to go in the shortest possible time.

I legged it over to CSM 'Chuck' Berry.

'Sergeant Major, what's going on?'

'All we know, Sir, is that something has kicked off at the police station. We got a radio message through a couple of minutes ago. We know there's probably a couple of Brit casualties but no further int, sorry.'

'What did the message say?

'Pretty incoherent. Just shouting "Get some fucking help here now!"'

We left quickly. Whatever had happened was a big deal.

The ride into Shin Kalay was fast. We meant business. The weapons-ready Land Rover I was in raced out of FOB SQT and onto the main connecting road between the two settlements. Coops and his team followed in the Vector. We were motoring hard, spewing clouds of choking dust behind us that hung in the dry, stinking Afghan air. We were going in with a bare minimum of intelligence. We knew there had been some kind of incident and we knew there were casualties. Sergeant Major Chuck's description of the SOS call echoed in my head. 'Pretty incoherent. Just shouting "Get some fucking help here now!"' Whatever was unfolding in the bullet-scarred police compound was serious.

We had left all essential kit on the wagons. That is how we always operated, so that we could move with a moment's notice for exactly this type of situation. Within a minute of talking to Chuck, I was kitted up and sitting in the front of the WMIK, plugging in to my radio and sending a check in to Zero.

POLICE STATION

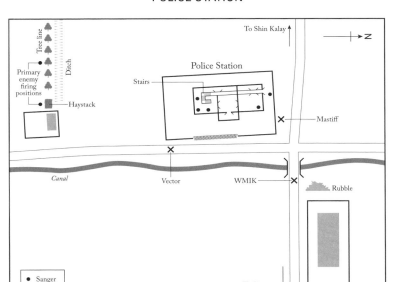

I briefed the lads over the PRR. I didn't have a lot of info, but it was my job to steady the ship and ensure we rocked in there with some semblance of a plan.

'Boys, looks like we have a couple of British casualties at the police station. Unknown status. We don't know what has happened, but we can assume the enemy are still in the area. Therefore we are not going to charge into this.'

Whatever temptation there was to roll in with all guns blazing was easily outweighed by the need for calm assessment. Gung-ho attitudes cost lives.

We turned right at the petrol station and Shin Kalay came into sight: a shitty smear of shitty buildings on a shitty landscape. When we were around 400 metres away from the police station, I stopped us short and stood up in my seat. Bringing my rifle to bear, I looked through the sight. I could see two of our guys up on the roof; their weapons were trained to the north, sporadic muzzle flashes issued from them and I could hear shots cracking through the air. The gunfire was not sustained, however.

I turned round to my unit and told them the plan.

'Right, looks like they have been contacted from the north. They are not in the middle of a blazing firefight, but there seems to be enemy nearby. We will advance with caution and stop 50 metres short of the canal. From there we will be in cover from view and any fire from the direction of contact. Move now!'

I could hear Coops giving arcs to the top gunners to ensure we had all-round protection as we cautiously advanced. Of course the lads already knew what they were doing, but it was his job to make sure they were gripped and on the ball. Coops' control of the peripheral aspects of any operation we were involved in was vital. His command of the small things gave me the freedom to take a strategic overview and analyse the bigger picture: exactly what a commander needs from his NCOs.

We pulled up before the bridge that spanned the wide canal running along the flank of the police station and stopped the vehicles. The two guys on the roof were still bearing arms to the north but as soon as they saw us they began shouting and waving.

'MAN DOWN! MAN DOWN! GET THE FUCK OVER HERE NOW!'

I knew I couldn't rush into the situation without a proper assessment, but it was obvious we had to get a shifty on. Whoever was in there was obviously in a bad way, and our medic, Manny, needed to get amongst them.

I was still convinced there was enemy to the north, and it was a 100 metre dash across open ground to get to the entrance of the compound. The gateway into the police station was narrow, and the angle of approach would prevent us driving straight in. We were in open-top vehicles, and manoeuvring into the tight turning would have left us vulnerable. I decided the safest option was to go in on foot.

As I jumped out of the vehicle, I looked behind me and could see Coops and Manny getting out of their Vector and running up to me. I waved at them back. I figured we were the three most important blokes on the ground at that minute and I didn't want an enemy RPG in that mix.

I waved Barney forward instead.

'See that pile of rubble on the side of the canal? Get yourself behind it, face north and tell me what you can see.'

Barney was a reliable, steady hand. I knew he would give me an accurate and concise view of the battlefield. The sporadic firing had stopped, but that did not mean the enemy had gone.

Low and fast, he sprinted the 50 metres to the vantage point I had directed him to. His voice came over the radio.

'Can't see anything, Boss. There is nothing incoming.'

Even a soldier with relatively little experience (Barney had experience in spades) can tell the direction and distance from which a round is fired. When a bullet passes close, you hear a crack, exactly the same as the noise when you snap a belt or crack a whip. It's the sound of the missile breaking the sound barrier as it goes over your head. This is followed soon after by a bang: the sound of the rifle going off. The time difference between the crack and the bang tells a soldier how far away the shooter is.

The blokes on the roof were still desperately shouting, and I knew that now was the time to act.

'Barney, stay where you are. Tag, you bring the WMIK forward so we can bring the Gympy to bear to the north. I'm going to leg it across the canal and into the police station. Clarky, you follow up with the Vector. I want it on the track past the police station with a Minimi on top facing south. Manny, you're with me.'

Manny was a Commonwealth soldier from Ghana and a deeply religious young man. He had only been with us for two days and this was his second ever patrol. All of us did first aid, but Manny was a Royal Army Medical Corps medic. He was trained to a higher standard than we were and could, for example, intubate and do more complex procedures than any of us. He'd done military training, but fighting was not his strong point and wasn't his reason for being in theatre, for example on his first introduction to PB Zoo I put him on a stag roster, and on his first stag I went up in the Sanger with him. He looked at the Gympy blankly and explained that he didn't know how to use it. I knew then that his strong points were elsewhere and I was so glad to have him with me as we ran into the police station that afternoon.

With my men tasked and moving, I took a deep breath and began to sprint. I knew the enemy were near but figured if I broke cover quickly and unexpectedly, I would have the element of surprise on my side and be able to dodge anything they decided to chuck at me. I had no idea what I was going to see behind the compound walls but my focus at that moment was to get me and Manny across the open ground safely. I'd deal with anything else when I reached the target.

I ran as hard as a man can with around 25kg on his back. I crossed the bridge and could see the long straight road that led into Shin Kalay town centre. It was normally a bustling thoroughfare, packed with motorbikes, trucks and goats herded by men who looked like they'd stepped off the pages of the Bible. Today it was empty. A few metres in front of me, parked along the north wall of the police compound, was the imposing figure of a Mastiff. I could see a guy with a moustache in the turret waving me on into the compound.

I rounded the corner. Manny was a few yards behind me, and just behind him I could hear Coops telling him to run faster. I guess he thought the best place for him was inside the compound, ready to support me.

Despite the caution, I was told later that it had taken us only seven minutes to get to the gates of the police station from when we first received the order to move. I am proud of that. My men were well-prepped, well-trained and did exactly what they needed to do. However, no amount of training could have prepared us for what was waiting on the other side of the mud walls. Normally there was a roll of razor wire acting as a make-shift barrier across the entrance to the compound. But today it lay strewn to one side; I ran straight through into the compound courtyard.

Directly in front of me a British soldier was slumped against the steps of the main building. He had been shot several times and had injuries to his limbs and head, and his trousers were shredded where the rounds had cut through his limbs. He was barely conscious and groaning with pain. I ran straight to him. It was obvious from his injuries that he needed assistance quickly.

'Mate, you're going to be okay. Can you hear me?'

He grunted a reply. Manny was right behind me and knelt down next to me in the dust to start assessing the injured soldier. After a few seconds

I left Manny to it and tried to compute what had happened. Initially it appeared to me that the Taliban must have driven past on a motorbike and sprayed bullets through the open gateway before speeding off. The plan was simple. HLS, no drama, nice open ground to the west, range 75 metres. Enemy seems to have gone. MERT will be here in less than 20mins and we'll get him away.

Then a thought occurred to me. Where was everyone else? I had been chatting to this callsign only yesterday. There was one guy down, two on the roof and one out the front in the Mastiff. I knew there were around 15 Brits stationed there, plus around the same number of Afghan police officers. These British soldiers, a mix of Grenadier Guards and Military Police had been recently stationed at the police station to fulfil a mentoring role with the ANP, similar to my tasking with the ANA. They had not been there when we had initially met with the ANP but we'd kept close comms with them since they had deployed a week or so previously.

I walked cautiously across the courtyard and rounded the northern edge of the building. The horror of the sight that confronted me has burnt itself into my memory and is something that will haunt my dreams for the rest of my life.

Three bodies lay to the left of an open doorway. Two men lay atop a third who was obscured from my view. The two men I could see were pale and still, they had both received multiple gunshot wounds and had obviously died very quickly from their injuries.

Just inside the open doorway to the right of the bodies, a small fire flickered. It was producing the most acrid smoke I had ever smelt, catching the back of my throat and making me gag as the smell of burning metal and phosphorous mixed with the stench of blood. To this day, whenever I smell smoke, that is what I'm reminded of. It smells like death to me.

The fire was coming from the radio and Electronic Counter Measures equipment. Momentarily I thought, good skills. These men had obviously had the presence of mind throughout this nightmare to deny this vital equipment to the enemy with a phosphorous grenade that burned through the metal of these devices.

Another man, again with multiple wounds all over his body, was lying on his back, motionless and unresponsive, on the steps to the doorway.

To the right of the door, propped up with his back against the wall, another soldier was sitting quiet and still, unable to stand, having suffered at least one abdominal gunshot wound. When he saw me, his eyes locked with mine in an unspoken plea for help.

I stood there in absolute horror, trying to take in what I was seeing. Manny ran round the corner to join me. I don't know how long I had been standing there, but it couldn't have been more than a few seconds. I looked at my medic and could see the utter shock on his face. I knew we had to act quickly now or else any momentum we had would be lost and the two blokes we needed to help would die.

I grabbed Manny firmly by the shoulder.

'They're all gone,' I said, pointing at each of the bodies in turn. Then, to focus him on the job at hand, I bodily turned him away from the dead and directed him to the guy sitting there holding onto his belly.

'He's in a bad way.'

It worked; Manny shook off the shock and sprang into action, throwing his med-Bergan off his shoulder and tearing at the zip to get it open.

'Sir, I will tell you what I need, and you get it out, okay?'

His voice was rapid and high pitched. Not with panic – he was just fucking serious. He began to reel out a list of the kit he needed.

The previous week, on a slow day at PB Zoo, our medic had taken it upon himself to sit us down and give us a lesson on the names of the medical items he carried in his bag in preparation for exactly this sort of scenario where he would need a second pair of hands to deal with a casualty. However, if I was to get a handle on this situation I could not be here with my head in a bag. I told him he was on his own for the time being, and he cracked on while I got on the radio and told Zero what was happening. I told them how many dead and, importantly, how many wounded we needed to get out of there.

As I was talking into my radio, I looked round the corner to the first wounded soldier we had encountered. By that time Corporal Fiji was with him treating a femoral bleed. As Fiji stemmed the flow of blood with his knee in the man's groin, I rushed over and helped to prepare the life-saving tourniquet.

Coops was making his way towards me and nothing I could have said would have prepared him for what he was about to see. As he turned the corner I watched him physically recoil then check himself and look at me for direction.

I was satisfied that although I had only a handful of men, we had established all-round defence if the enemy that had perpetrated this atrocity decided to return. There were not enough of us to repel a coordinated assault, but we were not going to get snuck up on. I had men working on both the casualties, and a MERT had been requested. I told Coops to help Manny and as I did the medic called out.

'Sir?' He had only been with the team for two days and was not comfortable calling me Boss at that point. 'Sir, that one's not dead.' He pointed to the three bodies lying together.

I looked back at him incredulously, and he repeated himself.

God knows how Manny had seen that this poor soul was still alive. You could barely see him underneath the body of the man that lay across him, but he told me after that he had seen his arm moving.

I couldn't believe what we had to do next. I had never seen a dead body before that point, let alone touch one. I was scared, I was nauseas and I really, really didn't want to have to pull this young man out from under his fallen comrades.

As I stepped towards them, I kept telling myself that these were my friends and colleagues. I had been laughing and joking with them over the preceding week as we shared an overlapping area of operation. They were good men, not just dead bodies.

The medic started working on him and I held his hand and tried to tell him it was going to be okay. I knew it wasn't. Up close I could see the full extent of the man's multiple injuries all over his body.

I was shaken from my shock by the sound of shouting and commotion. A British soldier wandered round the corner. It was as if he couldn't see the horror all around him. He stepped casually over his dead comrade and put his arms around me like a pissed-up buddy.

'Thank God you're here. Thank God,' he cried.

He couldn't have been more than 20 years old. He was wearing desert trousers and an under-armour shirt. His eyes were wild and his fair hair was matted with sweat. He was confused and scared but obviously relieved we were there. He was suffering from a clear case of battle shock.

I grabbed him by the shoulders.

'It's okay, mate, it's okay. I'm David.' I needed to calm him down. Despite talking to a guardsman, I thought it best to use my first name rather than speak to him formally as Captain Wiseman.

A second soldier was behind him: the guy I had seen in the Mastiff. He was older, maybe in his early thirties, short and quite portly with the kind of moustache that soldiers love to grow when they are on tour.

He was standing meekly behind his buddy and clearly had a better handle on the situation but was also obviously distressed by the chaos that had unfolded around him.

There could be no disrespect for any of the men involved in what transpired in the police station that day, no matter what state they were in when I rolled in with my unit. What those men went through in the minutes before we arrived is unimaginable, and the things we all witnessed have left an indelible mark on each of us in different ways. The battle-shocked soldiers were no less valiant than any others. Battle shock is a medical condition; it is essentially where the brain has had enough. It has seen things that it cannot explain and decides to switch off temporarily, leaving the poor bastard dazed and confused.

I knew that a man with battle shock is a casualty and, if not treated properly, can cause problems for the other soldiers through erratic and dangerous behaviour. I did not have enough men to give these guys the attention they needed, so the best thing for them would be to keep them busy with small, easy tasks that their confused brains could deal with. But first, I needed to find out what the hell had happened.

One of the men started to explain.

'They've gone. I think there were two of them.'

The sketchy details he gave me turned my stomach. These poor guys had been betrayed by the very men they were there to help. They had been attacked from within the compound by one of the police officers they were mentoring. It was an inside job. The dead and wounded hadn't stood a chance. They had been caught completely unaware after returning from patrol. They'd got back to the assumed safety of the compound, thrown off their helmets and body armour and put down their weapons for a break as all of us had done hundreds of times before.

I could picture the scene. They were sitting relaxing and prone, leaning against the wall smoking fags, drinking water, reading *Nuts* and taking the piss out of each other. Then all hell broke loose. The guys on the roof and in the Mastiff heard the shooting and immediately looked to their arcs, thinking that the attack was coming from outside and the rounds being loosed in the compound were boys returning fire. It must have been exceedingly confusing, and it would not have crossed their minds that a murder scene was unfolding beneath them.

When they saw the policeman (or men) running away, they must have presumed it was a coward fleeing battle. Again, this would have made sense to them, as the ANP in Shin Kalay at the time were not a well-trained and well-drilled fighting force, but more a motley crew of locals given a uniform and a rifle.

Much later, when I met one of the survivors again, I learned the full details of what had happened from the viewpoint of the first wounded soldier we had come across. He explained that when the slaughter started and he realised he could not get to his weapon, his survival instincts kicked in and he ran across the courtyard away from the sound of gunfire. He was catapulted into the air when a volley of shots smashed into his legs and he lay on his back in the dirt. He could see his dead colleagues and heard shouting and more automatic gunfire from inside the building as he tried to crawl away from the chaos.

He had blacked out but was roused by a boot kicking his side. He opened his eyes and stared right into the barrel of an AKM assault rifle that was trained at his face. Instinctively he grabbed the red-hot barrel to shift the aim away from his head. The attacker let off a short burst at point blank range; one 7.62mm round passed through both of his forearms, another punched into his face and the rest slammed into the ground around him. He lay motionless as he was kicked again. He knew his only chance was to play possum. Finally, he heard shouting in Pashtun and the scrape of boots running away from his motionless body.

There was no mercy shown by the enemy that day.

After the details of what had happened sunk in, I set about tasking the men while we waited for the MERT to arrive. I got the older chap with the moustache up in the northern Sanger. He was still compos mentis and could handle a weapon. I was still aware how brutally thin we were on the ground and if the Taliban closed in we would have a fight on our hands.

I had the younger bloke cut around and fetch me things or send messages and water to my guys on the perimeter. Anything to keep him busy, to keep his mind focused and stop it wandering.

The first thing I got him to fetch me was the washing from the line. The Brits had hung up some string so they could dry their clothes. In order to give the dead men some dignity and to save my other soldiers from seeing them, I asked their faces to be covered with this clothing.

Just when it seemed things were under control, I heard a shout.

'CONTACT!'

I could hear rounds streaming overhead. At ground level they posed no threat, but for the two guys on the roof who I had yet to talk to it was a different story. I had to get up there and assess what was going on.

The attack only lasted a couple of minutes. The enemy were probing to see what condition our defences were in. The Taliban knew something was going on, and they were here, but not in force. It was probably the nearest couple of bad guys on a motorbike.

'Sir!'

Manny was yelling at me as he continued to work on the two guys by the doorway. He pointed into the building.

I looked down the corridor. A guy stood at the far end of the corridor. He was the first soldier I'd seen fully kitted out and therefore had obviously been on stag when all this had kicked off.

'We need a medic up here, NOW!'

My head did a back flip. I already had three dead, three very seriously injured and one battle shock and with only six men in my team and the Taliban warming up around the compound.

'How many injured have you got?' I called to him.

'Two bad, one not so bad!' he yelled back.

He proceeded to give me a concise battle picture. He was the only chap on the roof who was completely uninjured, yet he and another young soldier had maintained discipline, aided wounded comrades and helped to fight off the first probing attack. I was so impressed by his cool head and the leadership he showed that I later reported up my chain of command that he be formally recognised, I do not know if he was.

My shouting down the hallway obviously stirred things up in the building. Due to the fact that I had not yet had the chance to clear the rooms on the bottom floor, I did not know that they were occupied. The first guys to come out were three ANP.

Three of them came from one of the doors on the right hand side. One had been shot in the thigh and blood was pouring down his leg, he had his arms around the shoulders of his police comrades, one on each side supporting him as he made his painful walk down the dark corridor. Knowing what had happened to the dead and wounded in the past ten minutes at the hands of an ANP officer, I wasn't taking any chances.

Every expletive under the sun ejected from my mouth as I levelled my rifle towards the small group of men. They had about a second to comply and thankfully they understood, putting their hands in the air to show they were unarmed. They had no idea how close to death they had come.

In cover behind the doorway with only my head and one shoulder exposed and my rifle firmly lodged against the frame pointing directly at them, I beckoned them forward, and they edged the 10 metres or so down the hall, dragging their comrade with them, who I recognised as one of the commanders at the station. I had drunk chai with him only a couple of weeks before. I recognised one of the other policemen but not the third. My spider sense was definitely twitching.

I kept my weapon trained on them until they were outside and up against the wall that formed the boundary of the compound. As I covered them, Coops searched all three for weapons or comms equipment. Once he was happy, I was happy, and was about to head down the corridor and up to the roof when three more men strolled out into the hallway.

They were our boys; all scared, two in obvious shock. The first was an NCO with a cool head. The second had been shot through the hand but was otherwise fine. The third guy had also been shot through the hand. He strolled out in just a pair of boxer shorts and bumped into the doorframe. His eyes were completely spaced-out and he asked for the way to the exit. He had a serious case of battle shock and repeatedly tried to walk out the front gate.

I sat the two wounded guys down on the wide step that ran around the front of the building. I didn't want them round the side where they could see their dead and badly wounded mates. Even though the first guy had been shot in the hand, he was completely fine. I've seen guys on the rugby pitch with dislocated fingers make more fuss. I told him he needed to get a grip of his mate and not to let him wander around.

Just then a police pick-up truck raced up to the entrance. Three guys jumped out the back, picked up their injured commander and pulled him onto the back of the vehicle. The two guys who had helped him out the building moved as if to get the hell out of dodge as well. I grabbed my terp:

'Tell them they are staying here. I haven't finished with them yet.'

They didn't protest, and retook their positions against the wall as the injured commander was transported away for treatment on his wounded leg.

I figured I'd best get down that corridor to make sure no other injured blokes were going to come out of the woodwork. I have no idea how long I had been at the police station, but so much had happened that it felt like an hour.

I crossed the doorway into the building. It was like a scene from a nightmare. There were no electric lights. Immediately on the right, just inside the doorway, the burning electrical equipment crackled away, giving off a small amount of light with its withering flames. The shadows on the walls danced in time to the flickering. The only other light source was the main door further down on the left hand side.

Along the corridor there was one door on the left and three on the right at even spaces. There was blood all over the floor, and I couldn't believe how much there was.

The smell was horrific, and I gagged. The metallic reek of blood mixed with the phosphorous smoke that hung in the air like a special effect in a bad horror movie.

Alone, I cleared each room as I went passed, rifle in first followed by my head. The hallway ended with a concrete staircase to the front and the main entrance on the left, through which I could see Fiji still with the first injured bloke. Halfway up the staircase, there was evidence that someone had been shot there before they had managed to get up onto the roof away from their assailant.

I followed the trail of blood out of the cloying darkness and into the hot sunshine, I ached for the light after walking through that scene. At my feet in the Sanger was a large bloke with blood covering his abdomen. The guy who had given me the situation report five minutes before was standing watching his arcs out to the south. Another bloke with a patch of blood on his back was kneeling by the wounded soldier on the floor.

'He's been shot in the stomach, and we've got another over there, shot in the arse and legs.' He pointed to the next Sanger. 'He's okay, but bleeding quite a bit.'

'What about you?' I asked the soldier pointing to his back.

'Nothing, just caught a bit of frag,' he sniffed.

'Good, you can still work for me then.'

I knew we were desperately short of stretchers. We carried two light stretchers (nothing more than a square of material with handles round the edge) and we had one fixed stretcher on the vehicle. So I tasked the soldier who was bleeding from his back to start cutting down a couple of sheets of fabric that they had placed around the Sanger as a form of obscuration to use as makeshift bearers.

I later found out that that the 'bit of frag' the soldier mentioned was actually a ricochet round. It had bounced off a couple of walls losing a bit of energy before smashing into this back. He was a very tough young man, who, despite his painful wound, was a great help to his comrades.

The radio crackled in my ear.

'Amber 13, Zero. MERT ETA in figures 5. Pop smoke at HLS, confirm what colour.'

After a hurried reply, I legged it to the edge of the roof and yelled down for Coops.

'COOPS! Start getting these lads on stretchers and assemble them at the gateway ready to be shipped onto the chopper.'

I passed Manny on the stairs. He was on his way up to have a look at the two guys on the roof. I told him he was doing a great job and gave him a quick report on the injured I'd just spoken to.

By the time I had got to the bottom, Coops had already got the guy with the abdominal injury on a fixed stretcher over by the gate. The lad we had pulled from under the bodies was there on his own. I was pissed off that he had just been left and knelt down beside him to tell him the chopper was on its way. I put my face near his to check for breathing, I felt a day's worth of stubble rough on my cheek but felt and heard no breath. My own breath quickened and I thought I was going to lose it. I realised he was dead. I put my hand on his cheek and looked at his face, just an inch away from my own. I closed my eyes and felt a huge wave of sorrow. I held his hand and said a quick prayer for the poor boy and then I too left him.

I could hear the Chinook coming in but couldn't see it. I knew where I wanted it to land. The field near the bridge outside where we made our final stop before entering the compound was a pre-arranged HLS that had already been cleared for IEDs. I ran out of the police station and back over the bridge, knelt at the corner of the field and dug out the smoke grenade from my webbing. I threw it as far as I could into the scrubby grass.

I wanted to get four guys on the back of the MERT: the two men from the roof, the young man with the femoral bleed and the guy with the abdominal injury at the doorway. It would have to be all hands to the pump. I didn't care if you had battle shock or had been shot in the hand; you were getting a stretcher and shifting these guys to the chopper. I wasn't going to bring my guys in off the perimeter because it was a critical point when a helicopter came in. At a previous CASEVAC my callsign were providing the flank protection and the Taliban had waited until just prior to the MERT landing to open fire. It would be a great prize to bring down a Chinook with all the doctors and equipment on the back.

The first stretcher-bearers were mostly wounded. Led by Coops, Fiji and Manny, I saw the two lads who had been shot in the hand and the lad with the ricochet in his back primed at the gate 100 metres to my right.

The MERT saw my smoke, circled and then decided not to land where I had requested but to put down a further 200 metres away, which does not sound much, but is a bloody killer when you are carrying a bloke over a ploughed field, wearing full kit, with the knowledge that every Taliban in the local area would love to take a shot at you and your chums.

Just as the stretcher party left the compound and the chopper circled overhead, our reinforcements arrived: Amber 12 from PB Chilli. I met their commander, Manfat, by the bridge and got them to leg it into the compound and grab a stretcher. Anyone not on a stretcher was to fill in the gaps around my perimeter.

I ran back into the police station to see what else needed to happen. The blokes were struggling to get one of the injured from the roof down – he was a big lad! I grabbed onto the stretcher and we man-handled him down the stairs. It was hard work and I was conscious about how long the MERT, which had touched down by then, was spending on the ground. I was straight on the net, demanding that the pilot did not lift off until we got our man on board. He would not last long if we didn't get him on the flight.

A lot of stick gets given to the RAF; however, that day the pilot pulled a blinder. Despite the fact that the bugger had not landed where I wanted him to, he stayed on the ground until he got the thumbs up from me that all our wounded were on board. It was dangerous for him, and it took nerve to sit there in something as big as a Chinook.

As we carried the stretcher over that uneven ground, I could see some of the lads on the stretcher starting to fail.

'Last push guys!' I shouted, trying to make myself heard above the gale force wind that was whipping up from the helicopter.

A lad stumbled. He was knackered and did not have the strength to right himself. The stretcher tipped, the injured soldier half-spilled out onto the ground. He had been holding onto my wrist and I felt his grip tighten. He must have been in agony.

I looked up to see some RAF guys in the rear of the Chinook waving at us to hurry up. I could have very easily butt-stroked them right then. Could they not see how shattered some of these guys were? Did it not cross their minds to run the 50 metres to us and use their fresh arms to help carry him the rest of the way?

We finally got our man back onto the stretcher and got him on the back of the helo. I signalled for them to take off and jogged off the back of the ramp. The heat from the exhaust of the huge vehicle hit me like a wall, and I crouched down and looked away as the engines change pitch. I was caught in the brown out: the part of a take-off and landing when the world around the chopper descends into darkness as a huge cloud of dust envelopes everything for hundreds of metres.

As the dust settled, I looked up to see the Chinook speed into the sky. For such a big object, it can shift.

I stopped for a few seconds, breathing heavily; my nose and throat were clogged with dust. I was physically and mentally exhausted. I was kneeling down in the middle of the field but knew that any Taliban weapons would be trained on the chopper.

After a few deep breaths I picked myself up and jogged back to the compound, already thinking about the next task of respectfully dealing with the fallen soldiers.

CHAPTER 9
AFTERMATH

Back in the compound I arranged for Barney to drive the walking wounded back to Shawqat in the Vector. I tried not to focus on the blood splashes that had dried to black stains on the compound walls.

The injured men were still in a fair amount of pain. The immediate threat had subsided and with it so had the adrenaline rush that masked their injuries. As I explained to them what was going to happen I realised that none of them had been given any painkilling morphine. We carried doses of it around in our kit in easy to administer jabs, much like the stabs that peanut allergy sufferers have. I decided to administer the painkiller myself and pulled one of the syringes out of my bag. I looked at it. One end was purple; one was end red. I naturally assumed the needle would pop out of the red end – red for danger, right? Wrong! I hadn't conducted the full pre-deployment training so I hadn't memorised the phrase 'purple pointy', and as I smashed what I thought was the sharp end of the self-administering device into one of the men's thighs, a large needle sprung from the end I was holding and shot straight into my thumb.

'Damn it!' I yelped, shaking my hand.

I'm not sure how much opiate went into my system as I obviously pulled it out straight away, so I assume I didn't cop the full dose. However, Coops and Manfat, the commander of one of the reinforcing platoons from Amber 12, made a big fuss of me and got me to sit on the steps and not move, which really pissed me off.

'If I feel shit, I'll let you know,' I told them. 'In the meantime, I'm still in command.' They were only following protocol, and it may have been pride over common sense, but I didn't care. I'd managed to command ops there up to that point and I wasn't going to let go of the reigns because of this silly mistake.

I busied myself with securing the compound. I tasked the remaining personnel to find the nominal roll of the callsign that had been attacked and bring it back to me marked with who was dead, who had gone on the chopper, who was wounded and about to be taken back to Shawqat by Barney. I relayed all this back to Zero.

Next, since I did not know what higher command intended to do with the compound, I got one of the men to retrieve all the equipment in the place and lay it out in front of the steps to carry out an inventory. The callsign that had been stationed there carried some sensitive communications and weapons systems that couldn't fall into enemy hands. We needed to know what, if anything, was missing.

Then I went to chat to the two ANP officers who were left. They were understandably sheepish. I gave them water, and they gave me cigarettes and told me what they knew, pointing out which weapons they thought had been used by the 'rogue policeman' (as the attacker or attackers were later described) from the arms that had been left in the courtyard. They were both AKM assault rifles. One had a UGL. Corporal Fiji put them to one side, ensuring he used gloves to avoid contaminating them with his prints.

Everyone knew what they were doing, and once I was happy that all was under control, I released Barney to drive the wounded guys to Shawqat. It was a short round trip, and when he returned he brought body bags for the poor souls still here.

George, a major and the OC of the Duke of Lancaster Company back at Shawqat, then called over the radio. Helmand was split into districts, such as Nad-e Ali and Sangin. Shawqat was the centre of Nad-e Ali, and the base there consisted of a battalion of Grenadier Guards who were under the command of Colonel Roly Walker. They were reinforced by George's company and four OMLT teams from The Yorkshire Regiment. Major George was en route and wanted to see what he and his callsign could do to help. As a superior officer he could have rocked up and seized command. Instead, he came and saw that everything was under control, offered assistance and took a lot of pressure off me by being a reassuring presence and taking care of a lot of the comms traffic over the net.

With the compound secure, the priority was to take our wounded, then our fallen, back to Shawqat and await further direction which we did. There were four dead, and I learned later that another casualty sadly died in the chopper.

As the sun started to set, we noticed the dust trails of vehicles approaching. Given the day's events, everyone was jumpy, so when three vehicles filled with ANP arrived and started debussing at the gate, I acted quickly and defiantly. As far as I knew, the murderers or further Taliban infiltrators were among them.

'DROP YOUR FUCKING WEAPONS AND GET AGAINST THAT WALL!' I yelled, drawing my rifle. Thankfully they complied and didn't open up on me. I didn't care about my safety. I wanted them out of there and got on the net to explain that I was seizing their weapons and sending them on their way.

The bosses at head shed (HQ) started negotiating and soon came back to me.

'You can get rid of them but they take their weapons,' I was told.

I wasn't too happy about re-arming potential enemies, especially ones that I had just lined up against a wall at gun point. But, I could understand the politics of the situation and told the ragtag gaggle to clear off, which they did gladly. I'm pretty sure they didn't want to share a compound with a crazy commander after that episode anyway.

Relations between the ANA and the ANP were historically tense. The warriors hated the police. In the weeks leading up to this shooting, firefights had broken out between the ANA and the ANP in other parts of the country. Blood had been spilt. The ANP were mainly Pashtun's recruited from the local area, and the ANA, who were recruited from the north where the Taliban had less influence, largely believed that the police were Taliban spies and sympathisers. The ANP also had a reputation for corruption, abuse of power and taking young boys.

The compound was becoming a hive of activity. Word had obviously got out about events, and soon after the ANP scuttled off in their flatbed vans another bunch of Afghans rocked up. This time I was happy to see them. It was the ANA company sergeant major from Shawqat, bringing around 20 of his men.

In the back of my mind I was aware that since the shootings our defensive position had been desperately undermanned, which would be disastrous if the Taliban decided to launch an coordinated assault rather than the sporadic probing attacks we had experienced up until now. The arrival of a large ANA platoon gave us numbers in the event of an enemy action. The warriors didn't even have time to get in the compound before their assistance was required. Their presence must have attracted attention because as they started getting out of the vehicles rounds began to ricochet off the walls and the dusty ground. And it was no probing attack. The enemy, who must have been watching what was unfolding and who viewed their ANA countrymen as traitors, were trying to pick them off before they reached the cover of the compound walls.

'Contact!'

The shout went up, and the Afghans launched into action. They raced inside unscathed and went up the stairs to the rooftop Sangers where they started unleashing a hail of rounds in the direction of the enemy. What the warriors lacked in accuracy, they made up for in enthusiasm.

The contact was protracted and lasted on and off for several hours. When we'd first gone into the police station, the situation was unsure. I had a few men and everyone left inside was dead or wounded. As the day's shadows began to lengthen, I had reinforcements in the shape of Manfat's callsign, 20 ANA warriors and Major George. We were in a fortress by that point, and the Taliban were pissing into the wind with an attack launched far too late in the day to have an effect. The attacks were repulsed time and again as darkness fell and Shin Kalay went quiet. But I wasn't confident that we had seen the last of the enemy.

Coops and Manny had worked tirelessly under extreme circumstances all afternoon. Between them they had saved lives as they had been the principle guys administering first aid and coordinating the CASEVAC. They were physically and mentally exhausted. They had witnessed every horrifying scene, every injury, every dead man's stare. They were both completely drained, and with no more tasks to keep them occupied, they started to come to terms with what had happened. Exhausted, they sat with their heads in their hands and broke down.

I walked over to where they were sitting. With their helmets off, hair matted with sweat and faces smeared with grime, they looked dreadful. They were both overcome with emotion. The wounded had gone and Manny's work was done for the time being, and the reinforcements, especially the arrival of his fellow sergeant, Manfat, had taken the pressure off Coops. In the lull, both of them had started to compute the enormity of what they'd seen and experienced. Momentarily, I remembered the look on the face of the officer I met in the canteen at Bastion, it was the same look I could see before me now. Grizz, I thought. That had only been a few weeks ago, but it felt like a lifetime. I knelt in front of Coops and put my hand on his shoulder.

'Mate, you've done a blinder. CASEVAC is your bag and we got all those men away. You did that. Take five minutes now. I don't need you right now but I probably will soon. We're not done yet.'

I was just about to move on to Manny and tell him much the same when again the sky once again erupted with the crack and clatter of a fresh contact.

I looked across at Coops, wondering how he was going to react. I needn't have worried. He was British infantry; he was nails. He wiped a dirty, blood-stained hand across his massive nose, stood up and charged to the stairs. On the way he bowled into one of the other troops and wrestled a Gympy and a box of rounds from him.

'That's my gun,' he growled.

I followed in his wake and we stood shoulder-to-shoulder in the Sanger. Coops hung off the back of the gun as it spewed out a relentless hail of ammo. He was raging. I launched grenade after grenade from my UGL towards the enemy just a short distance to our south. In the dusky half-light we could see the muzzle flashes as the enemy sent burst after burst of 7.62mm our way. We aimed for those flashes and arc after glorious arc of trace spewed out from our weapons. I glanced to my right and further along the roof I saw Manfat and a handful of other British soldiers, side by side with our ANA allies joining in the fray.

The Taliban kept coming at us on and off for around two hours. They never stood a chance and never got within 200 metres of the compound.

The firefight was loud as hell. The sonic cracks of bullets filled the air. It was intense but there were lulls in the battle, which were eerie. Everyone was waiting and on edge. There was forced laughter and nervous jokes, and people ducked behind walls to smoke to avoid their lit cigarettes becoming aiming markers for marksmen watching in the night. The flat roof of the compound was awash with empty brass cases that were kicked around with clinking sounds whenever people moved.

In the final contact of the night, the enemy were attacking us from in and around the compound that my men had originally taken over when we first deployed to Shin Kalay three weeks previously. They spread themselves along the ditch that ran between the compound and the edge of town and gave us a perfect line of enemy troops at which to aim. Their commander must have been supremely confident or unbelievably stupid. It appeared he wanted to challenge our firepower directly with his own. There was no match. We rained all kinds of hell down on his position, and to make matters worse for him, two Apaches joined in. They had seen another group of enemy approaching from the south and the sky erupted with the sound of 30mm shells as they opened up, lighting up the sky with streaks of trace.

Another ANA callsign, accompanied by my OC, arrived as the contact finished. It was dark, and my blokes had been in the thick of it all day. We hadn't eaten, and all we had in the way of warm kit was a softie jacket each. After all the shit we'd been through, when my OC told us that we were being relieved and pulled back to Shawqat and that Amber 12 and the ANA were being left to secure the police station overnight, I almost shook his hand.

I gathered up the boys and we headed back to base in a convoy with the OC and Major George's Mastiffs. It was a cold and windy drive back to Shawqat in the WMIK, and everyone was quiet.

I held down the pressel of my PRR:

'Boys, extremely proud of you lot today. No one goes into the communal tent when we get back. Straight into our tent. Coops acknowledge?'

'Roger, Boss.'

I looked around at the boys in front of me back in our tent. Most of us were covered in other men's blood. Each one of them had contributed to saving lives that day. They'd stopped the Taliban from overrunning the place, killing everyone and securing the nearest crossing point into Shin Kalay. We later found out that we'd killed six enemy, including the local commander, and injured an unknown amount. I have never been so proud of a group of men in my life.

After telling my men how proud I was, I moved directly to the Ops room and checked on the two men who had been left at PB Zoo in a compound full of ANA Warriors. They had also had a busy evening, with probing attacks being made on their compound and some wounded locals at their door looking for help – they had been forced by the Taliban to run ahead as human shields against our fire. Humph had patched them up, and both men had kept their heads in what must have been a tumultuous period for them on the other side on the town.

I passed the company sergeant major of the Lancs Company, Major George's right hand man.

'Sergeant Major, I have no idea what TrIM entails or how we go about it, but I know my guys may need to get some of that. Is there anything we need to do tonight?'

TrIM is Trauma Incident Management, a mechanism by which psychological dramas can be identified and nipped in the bud or followed up later. After every punchy episode, those involved would go through this process, and every company should have some TrIM trained personnel, usually senior NCOs.

At that point I knew what we'd experienced had the potential to have an impact on each of us.

He started to explain, but I wasn't listening. My legs went weak and my eyes blurred. I thought I was going to be sick. Like Coops and Manny earlier in the day, the full impact of what had happened suddenly hit me, as my responsibilities reached their culmination point and I had no reason to remain strong.

I quickly excused myself and hurried out into the cool Helmand night. In a quiet corner of the base I dropped into the shadows and went into meltdown. I crouched in a ball, my back against the rough Hesco, and I cried. As I gripped my shins and buried my face in my knees, I shook with silent sobs. I didn't want anyone to see me like that. The wave of emotion came from nowhere. The enormity of what we had just done overwhelmed me, and I could do nothing to hold back the feelings.

Eventually I managed to get a grip of myself. I took a water bottle and splashed the cool liquid over my face before striding back to our tent behind a crumbling façade of control.

The lads were still there where I had left them.

'They've put on a late scoff for us, so make your way over to the cook house,' I told them, trying hard not to let them hear the crack in my voice.

The lads went to eat but Coops and Barndog remained behind, and I pottered around my bed space, avoiding them.

'You not coming, Boss?'

'I'll be there in a minute,' I answered, avoiding eye contact. Every sinew was straining to stop my emotions bubbling to the surface again.

'Boss … you alright?'

I looked up to see concern written across their faces.

'Yeah, I'll be fine.'

But I wasn't. Everything came to the surface again, and I felt Barndog's arms wrap around me as I broke down in front of them. I had managed to hold everything back for the whole action but now the floodgates were open and I couldn't hold it back.

'Don't let them see me. The boys can't see me like this,' I said.

They led me to the back of the tent into our small briefing area. My face was wet with tears and snot, and for a minute we held each other, all three of us. As the emotions quelled we talked quietly and chain-smoked filthy Pines. We reassured each other that we could have done nothing for the boys who had died and we could not have given more.

Composed, we headed to the cook house for food. Eating was merely a mechanical process of shovelling fuel into my body, chewing and forcing it down my throat. As I ate, I looked down at boots lined up under the table. They were splashed with dark red blood, crusting to black in places. I felt numb.

First thing in the morning we burnt our clothes and were issued fresh combats. There was no point trying to wash out the blood by hand.

After breakfast we loaded up the wagons and headed out to Clarky and Humph, who had done an amazing job back at PB Zoo. We turned right along the dusty track by the petrol station and continued for a few hundred metres until the police station came into view. We pulled in and surveyed the busy scene.

Manfat came out to meet us and we shot the shit with him for a while as the clean-up went on around us. A Royal Military Police incident investigation team were packing up to make way for a group of Royal Logistics Corps blokes with specialist cleaning equipment whose unenviable job it was to remove the gory evidence of what had happened there the previous day.

I took a walk around to take it all in and revisit the jumbled memories I had. I walked the same ground where I had found the dead. I kicked the empty cases of rounds I had fired from the rooftop towards the advancing foe and I passed the spot at the top of the stairs where I had stolen a minute in a lull to sit and draw on a much needed cigarette.

It was surreal. It seemed like something that had happened to someone else in another time, or maybe a bad dream or movie I'd seen.

I made my way back down to where Coops and Manfat were still talking.

'I certainly wouldn't have wanted to stay here last night. It would've properly shat me up.'

'Aye,' Manfat nodded, gesturing to a room at the front of the building, where, just inside the corridor, a soldier was scrubbing a blood splatter from the wall.

'I set up the radio stag in that room, but the guys were proper spooked and didn't want to be in there on their own in the dark. Don't blame 'em. I was fucking shat up myself,' admitted Manfat.

CHAPTER 10
GRIZZ

In Nad-e Ali death and danger had become almost normal; people were being hurt every day. In the blood and guts of combat it was easy to get blasé about the destruction that was unfolded around us, but in the quiet, when the adrenaline subsided, there came a time when we each had to face our demons. To stave off those times we immersed ourselves in day-to-day tasks such as washing clothes by hand, writing to loved ones or routine weapon and kit maintenance.

A few days after the police station shooting a few of us were outside doing just that – cleaning weapons in the never-ending effort to scrub dust from the working parts – when Coops came running over from the direction of the Ops room.

'Where's Manny?' he asked.

'What's up, Coops?'

I leant forward, halfway out of my crappy fold-away chair, concerned over what was unfolding, as Manny emerged from the folds of the tent behind me.

'ANA vehicle inbound. It'll be here in a couple of minutes. One of their lads trod on an IED. Manny, the sergeant major wants you there at the gate to meet him and work on him as soon as they come through.'

Manny dashed back into the tent to grab his medical kit.

I went too to see if I could help.

At the gate the green pick-up we'd watch race in slowed down. Even though it was an emergency, the driver knew better than to rush the guards who were veterans of this godforsaken country and all too wary of suicide bombers.

ID quickly verified, Manny and I ran up to the passenger window. The casualty was in his early twenties, clean-shaven with straight black hair in a long fringe to his eyebrows. His head lolled on his shoulders. He was still conscious but his eyes were glazing over with pain and shock. Dust covered his whole body and in places it congealed with blood in a horrible dark paste that smeared across his clothing.

Manny opened the door, and as it flew open I got a full look at the damage to the young man's body. His leg was a complete mess. I didn't need to be a doctor to know that the surgeon at Bastion would be reaching for his saw within the next 30 minutes, if the poor bastard made it that far. His twisted and shredded limb must have held just fragments of the bones that once supported them and gave them form. Without the rigid bone the leg was just a broken slab of meat. It was impossible to assess where the bleeding was coming from: the whole area was a slick of bright red blood. Patches and trails of clothing hung about the limb, either blown off by the blast or plastered flat to the skin with gore.

The upholstery of the new pick-up was soaked through, and the footwell on the passenger side was filling with blood. He sat there motionless, aside from his rolling eyes. His whole face was sagging, as if the effort of keeping his eyes open was using up all his energy and he had nothing left in the tank to hold up the rest of his features.

Manny only took a second to make his decision.

'This is pointless. I can do nothing for him here; just drive straight to the med centre,' he ordered the driver.

The precious seconds it would take administering first aid would be better spent driving the few hundred metres to where the doctor was waiting with a medical team and an array of equipment to give this guy a chance of survival.

We waited around to help carry the stretcher to the MERT when it arrived, and a quarter of an hour later the rhythmic beat of rotor blades could be heard approaching in the distance. The huge frame of a Chinook landed 30 metres from the entrance to the med centre, and the injured Afghan was carried out into the dust storm the aircraft had created.

We weren't needed, and watched as four medics, one of them holding a bag of fluid, disappeared into the back of the helicopter with the casualty. With the man on board they disembarked, and the pitch of the rotors got higher and higher as the chopper lifted with urgency to get out of small arms range. As the sound died away we ambled back to our weapons, still in pieces but now covered in a thick layer of dust.

We were back on the ground and we had been tasked with new orders which meant it was time to say goodbye to PB Zoo. We were sad to leave the little compound as it had been our home for such a long time, but we had received orders to push south in order to provide a screen for the Royal Engineers who were moving in to build up a more permanent and defendable PB to replace PB Zoo at the south-western corner of Shin Kalay. Along with our ANA colleagues, we took over an unused compound to the south of the build in order to protect their work at the edge of the town. To our right and left, two other callsigns occupied neighbouring compounds. There was a road running left to right in front of us and beyond that were fields and ditches. As ever, vigilance was imperative. The area was a nest of snipers, IEDs and potential suicide bombers.

The idea was to have a tactically sound base to house around 30 people with proper Sangers that could withstand repeated enemy assaults. The position in the south-west of town was chosen to extend our sphere of influence and allow us to increase the effectiveness of the disruption of enemy activity within Shin Kalay. Unlike traditional wars, there was no clear 'front line' and the insurgent was able to move amongst the population. Building permanent defensive positions enabled us to launch effective patrols to deny the enemy freedom of action, disrupt enemy activity and to reassure the local population of our security. The intention was for these positions to act like ink drops on a blotting paper, with the influence of different sites spreading and eventually joining up over a large area.

The engineers toiled day and night about 300 metres to our rear to make sure the job was completed quickly so we wouldn't be left out longer than necessary.

A few days in and I was on the roof on stag, casually surveying the intersection up the road from of the compound, when an enormous brown sphere rose up from the ground. It was as if a giant was blowing a huge bubble from below the earth. It was an almost perfect sphere of dirt, dust and debris that plumed into the air. I managed to mutter 'What the f...' before the sound wave hit. A ground shaking boom resonated in my ears as I turned to Cowhead for assurance that what I was seeing was real. The look on his face confirmed that I wasn't dreaming.

I got on the net to call in the detonation.

'Hello ZERO, this is Amber 13A. Large explosion 300 metres to our south. Suspect the device was detonated by a civilian. Confirm no friendly callsigns in that location. Do you want us to push forward to aid with any casualties? Over.'

I was told to stand to, and relayed down to the men that it was likely we would need to send a patrol out to help with any casualties. They knew there weren't any friendlies to our front, so, like me, they suspected a civilian casualty. I only hoped that it was a stupid dog like the week before and not some poor kids.

As I climbed down from the Sanger, the Afghans started cheering and dancing about the compound with their weapons in the air. It looked like a scene from a National Geographic documentary. Bemused, I shouted down to Rayes, who was also grinning like a Cheshire cat.

'What is all this about then, mate?'

'Over the Icom, David. The explosion was the Taliban blowing themselves up by accident,' he chuckled, as he explained that the enemy were now calling in for assistance.

My face broke into a grin. It was exactly the injection of morale we needed after the previous days. I relayed the good news.

'Hello ZERO, Amber 13A. Reference that last explosion. We've got it over the Icom that it was an own goal. They are calling in for some assistance and a vehicle is en route to pick up the casualties. Over.'

'Zero, Roger. DH3 en route now. Will get eyes on the recovery vehicle. Out.' A DH3 (Desert Hawk) was an unmanned aerial vehicle with a camera on it and was used as an effective reconnaissance tool at a tactical level.

By standing back and watching the Taliban CASEVAC unfold, we would be able to gather valuable intelligence about enemy logistics and command elements. Finding out where they took their dead and wounded would be immensely beneficial.

The Icom was going mad, and Rayes was struggling to keep up with the near constant traffic and to keep me abreast of what was going on.

'The vehicle is coming now, David.' I felt like a spectator listening to a radio report of a football match.

I scanned the road with my binos, and sure enough, a small mini-bus appeared on the road. It looked like a VW camper van. It kicked up a small dust cloud as it bounced down the road.

'Zero, Amber 13A. I think we have eyes on the CASEVAC vehicle now. 400 metres to the east of the contact point and travelling west. Over.'

'Zero, Roger. DH3 has eyes on. Out.'

The van passed in front of our allies sitting across to our left. As it did so it dropped out of view behind a lone compound. It did not reappear.

I could not believe what I was seeing as another explosion, smaller than the first, ripped the earth apart less than half a kilometre away on my left. The noise of the explosion that followed stunned me.

This cannot be happening, I thought to myself.

The dumb fuckers had only gone and driven over another IED. I could only surmise that the party that had so gloriously spread themselves over the road not ten minutes before had been laying a belt of IEDs all along the road in anticipation of us pushing further south, and the CASEVAC vehicle had not been told and had obligingly removed another one for us. The irony was that it was never my intention to push onto the road.

The boys were ecstatic when I relayed details of what I'd just seen from my vantage point down to the compound floor. The ANA carried on with their funny dancing, hugging each other and wallowing in the misfortune of our enemy with no thought of mercy or sympathy. I harboured none either.

The spectacular own goal, while a blessing for us, also focussed my mind on the inherent dangers of our situation. The tension was palpable. Every day there was contact, and from the locals who lived and worked in the town it was hard to tell who was an innocent and who was in cahoots with the Taliban.

The author after completing his 11 month training course at the Royal Military Academy Sandhurst, with his future wife, Lucy.

The author poses with 1 Platoon, A Company beneath the famous Crossed Swords in Baghdad.

A trader tries to take his camels through an IED clearance. The dog (right) was shot by the author after attacking Rayes days later.

Callsign Amber 13 at FOB Shawqat about to leave for its first patrol in Afghanistan.

Amber 13 pauses during a patrol north of Shin Kalay.

Patrolling in Nad-e Ali, a district right at the heart of Helmand Province.

PB Zoo, so named due to the number of creatures stationed there, was Amber 13's home for a little while during their operations in Shin Kalay.

Amber 13, fatigued after holding a compound from repeated contacts with the Taliban, north of Shin Kalay.

The author enjoys lunch with Rayes (ID protected) and his ANA comrades. Captain Imam sits laughing to the rear and right of the picture.

The author poses for a photo during a break in a patrol in the safety of a disused compound, Nad-e Ali, Helmand Province.

Barney and the author pose with the bomb that nearly killed them both but for a poorly placed detonator.

Central Shin Kalay; life still goes on for the civilians despite the military presence.

The author with a 25kg IED about to blow.

An IED in Shin Kalay. The main charge (yellow) and the black and red wires are clearly visible.

One of the 'pets' from PB Zoo. This dog belonged to Faraz and was later shot by an American.

The Police Station, Shin Kalay.

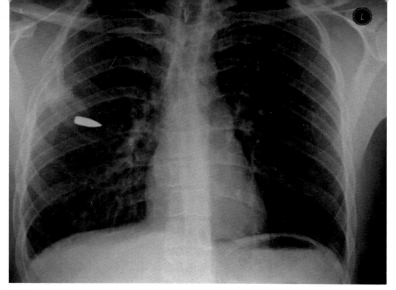

This X-ray shows the bullet still lodged in the author's chest.

The author training in the Alps before his Everest attempt.

MAIN IMAGE • Camp 2 on Mount Manaslu, further training for the attempt on Everest.

LEFT • The author and Jaco utterly exhausted after descending from the summit of Manaslu.

FAR LEFT • The Puja prior to climbing Everest; monks ask the mountains for safe passage, blessing the climbers and equipment.

Night falls just below the summit of Lobuche. Everest base camp is just to the left of the picture. (Courtesy of Petter Nyquist)

Descending from the summit of Lobuche, the author takes in the view. (Courtesy of Petter Nyquist)

Crevasse crossing above camp 1 on Everest.

The author trains below the ice fall on Everest. (David Cheskin/PA Images)

LEFT • As part of the Everest expedition, the author trains below the ice fall. (David Cheskin/PA Images)

RIGHT TOP • The Lhotse ice wall. The third highest mountain in the world towers above us.

RIGHT MIDDLE • The author descends through the Khumbu ice fall after six days at camp 2, Everest.

RIGHT BOTTOM • The author below the ice fall, the most dangerous section on the south side of Everest.

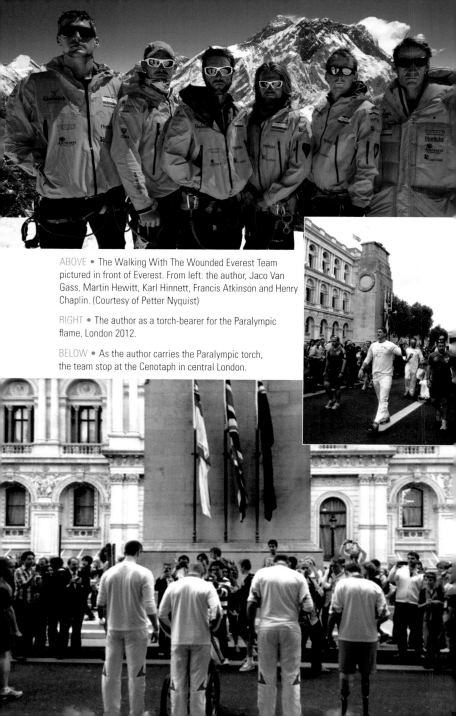

ABOVE • The Walking With The Wounded Everest Team pictured in front of Everest. From left: the author, Jaco Van Gass, Martin Hewitt, Karl Hinnett, Francis Atkinson and Henry Chaplin. (Courtesy of Petter Nyquist)

RIGHT • The author as a torch-bearer for the Paralympic flame, London 2012.

BELOW • As the author carries the Paralympic torch, the team stop at the Cenotaph in central London.

I was tetchy and beginning to harbour a deep-seated unease about the whole situation. The day after we had watched the enemy blow themselves apart, a motorcycle spluttered towards the compound.

The motorbike is the preferred mode of transport for the Taliban over the rough, uneven tracks of Helmand Province. Most of the tracks are too narrow for a car and the bike allows the enemy to move rapidly from one area to the next, carrying all they need for their ultra-light style of combat. They often have weapons cached so they just pick up and drop off munitions as needed without holding on to the incriminating weaponry. They pose as ordinary farmers going about their business. They blend in with all the other locals, which allows them to perform the closest possible reconnaissance missions, simply riding from one area to the next before dismounting and walking past an intended target without raising too much suspicion.

The motorbike is also a great tool in which to hide a suicide bomb, so when I watched the ANA troops at the checkpoint to the north of our position casually question the rider of the bike and let him continue towards the base without searching him, I cursed.

'Lazy bastards!'

There was no way that the potential bomber was getting anywhere near my men. I grabbed my weapon, yelled for Rayes and legged it out of the compound. The motorbike had not got far and was now only 25 metres away; I held up my hands and shouted.

The rider was a thick set man wearing dark clothing. He had a huge black bush of a beard and peered out from below a traditional round hat that fitted snugly on his head. I shouted at him to stop. He carried on. I was awash with rage to think that this bastard was defying me and that the stupid wankers at my checkpoint were merrily sending him forward without a proper search.

'Fucking stop the fucking bike now!'

I was screaming blue murder at the bloke. It was as if he hadn't noticed me until I was just 15 metres away, standing my ground with a weapon pointing at his face. He didn't know what to do. One set of soldiers had waved him forward and another was now standing in front of him yelling and threatening to kill him if he moved.

By now, several soldiers were on my shoulder. Coops was right next to me with his own weapon in his shoulder.

'What is it, Boss?'

'This guy hasn't been searched at all. Look at the pile of blankets on his saddle. Could be anything under those.' I gestured to the pile of rags he was sitting on.

He was nervously looking back over his shoulder at the Afghans. We are trained to look for nervousness in potential suicide bombers, and this bloke was most certainly twitching – however, this might have had something to do with the line-up of armed foreigners standing in his path.

Rayes translated for me as I shouted, calmer now, over to the rider.

'Get off the bike and lift up your shirt!'

He didn't move.

'Get off the bike and lift up your shirt,' I repeated.

He looked around again at the soldiers behind him.

'Get off the fucking bike and lift up your fucking shirt!'

Someone was going to die. I could feel the electricity in the air. I took the safety catch off my weapon and shifted its weight in my shoulder. I was going to use it. The rider's frightened eyes widened as he saw my intent but still he didn't move. Our eyes met for a fraction of a second.

'Is this right?' The question went through my mind.

I took the slack off the trigger, and his life was mine to give or take.

He was so close; I would see everything. I would see his throat explode as hot metal tore through his neck.

I squeezed the trigger. The rifle recoiled. The round hit the ground next to the man. At the last second I decided against ending his life. He should have died. He should have bled to death on the dusty floor with a hole the size of squash ball in the back of his neck. He was posing a threat to my men and was not cooperating in a search. That should have been his death sentence.

He cringed against the sound of my rifle and his mouth gaped open with fear as he realised how close he had come.

The shock pulled him out of his petrified stance, and his shaking hands reached down to his clothing, which he pulled up, exposing his belly and showing me that he was not strapped with explosives. Once I was happy, two guys went forward and checked under the blankets, which turned out just to be there for his comfort on the bumpy tracks. I waved him away. He didn't continue on his journey but instead turned around and headed back from wherever he had come from.

I am not convinced that he was not Taliban and that he was not on a recce. However, I am glad that I didn't kill him. To have searched a dead body and a dead man's bike to find nothing worthy of taking his life would have weighed very heavily indeed.

I was angry and on edge.

'He was just shit-scared, Boss.' Coops patted me on the shoulder as we walked back into the compound.

Over the following days I couldn't shake the feeling that something bad was going to happen, something worse than the threat, death, danger and injury we were exposed to every day.

A sniper had been bothering us for days, opening up whenever we left the compound. One afternoon I looked out and saw him on a compound roof about 300 metres away. Under the rules of engagement for the conflict, we could engage any positively identified Taliban. I was sure I was looking at one such bastard along the length of my rifle when I spied a man with a long barrelled weapon moving along a compound roof in the general vicinity from which we had been repeatedly engaged by sporadic single round rifle fire for days.

It was a seriously long shot with this weapon and at a moving target. I levelled my rifle, using the low compound wall to support the weight. I would only have a few precious seconds before he moved into cover but I needed those seconds to steady my aim. I would only get one shot and I wanted it to count. I levelled my target off in the sighting system and took up the slack on the trigger. I gently applied more and more pressure until the rifle jolted in my arms and let fly a tiny piece of metal that I hoped would smash into my adversary's back nearly a third of a kilometre away.

I never knew for sure if I'd hit him. By the time my sight picture had realigned following the recoil, the enemy was nowhere to be seen. I hoped this meant that I had sent his body flying off the roof with my round in him, but he could just have easily have jumped off or ducked as the bullet was flying towards him, or, simply, I could have missed my target. Like I say, it was a long shot but coincidently that sniper didn't bother us again.

I was finding the nights hard. I hadn't slept for days and the strain was starting to show. The silence echoed around my head as I lay in my bunk in the dark, but sleep never came. Exhausted, I was losing my temper and I was losing my cool. Without the tonic of sleep, I couldn't think clearly and my temper was quick.

Sleep would solve all my problems. It would take me away from Helmand and my thoughts for a few blissful hours and help me regain the balance in my head. The rage I felt at intervals would be cooled and my confusion cleared. Fatigue was what was causing my mind to wander from the task in hand, to wander to places in the past that I didn't want to be.

My head was filled with intrusive thoughts, pictures that I couldn't shift. If I shut my eyes for longer than a blink, I would feel, smell and hear the sights I witnessed at the police station. I would relive them. One sight in particular lived on behind my eyelids; the poor soldier whom Coops and I had tried desperately to help by pulling him out from under his fallen comrades. It was the only place he lived now.

I felt him too. I felt his cold rough skin on my face as I pressed my ear to him, listening for a breath that never came. I could smell him. I couldn't block it out, so instead I didn't shut my eyes.

It was worst in the dark silence. There was no conversation to listen to, no music to distract me. The daytime was full of its own distractions: people to watch, checks to undertake, books to read. But the dark was a perfect canvass upon which my mind projected a jerky movie played over and over, where one scene would cut inexplicably to the next without warning or chronological continuity. The frustrating sequence of clips and stills made no sense. It replayed the horror of the police station over and again, pausing, rewinding and replaying over and over and over again.

Memories forged in traumatic situations are not the same as normal memories. This is why victims of violent crime struggle to remember important details and the correct sequences of events. Defence lawyers know this and use it to their advantage to pick holes in witness statements and attain 'not guilty' verdicts by creating doubt in the minds of jurors.

In a traumatic situation the brain becomes overloaded with information, much of it difficult to manage. In extreme, stressful life or death situations, the brain does not have time to process the facts. So instead it leaves bits out or mixes them up in a different order.

Later, when the brain goes back to review the events, it is unable to grasp exactly what happened and cannot fully process it. Think of it as an airing cupboard full of washing. Normally the washing – your memories – are folded neatly and placed in piles so you know where to get the towels or the sheets you need. In a traumatic situation that washing is thrown in haphazardly as there is no time to fold it and put it away in order. When you return later and open the door, all the washing spills out on the floor. If there are important items missing, the person becomes distressed and may have to pull everything out again to look for it. So the process starts all over again.

That was what my brain was doing and was why I couldn't stop revisiting the events. Every time a memory was accessed by my brain, the whole overwhelming experience would spill out and therefore it could not be processed or coped with.

I lay in the dark, my head full of confusion and haunted imagery. The ground was still radiating the heat of the day so I was not in my sleeping bag. I lay on my roll mat. I couldn't bear the movie that kept playing in my mind, and was getting more and more frustrated by the lack of sleep. I felt like I was going crazy.

There was no point trying to sleep. I didn't recognise myself. Would anyone back home know me anymore? Would Lucy know who I was? I was hit by a wave of sadness. Something in me had changed, and I didn't know what. I wasn't the same person. I missed home. I missed my wife and yearned to see her and feel the soft muffled kicks of my unborn son through her bulging stomach. I'd have sold my soul to have crept into bed beside her. Instead I crept to the foot of our ladder and started to climb up to the roof where Barndog was sitting on stag behind a small sand bag wall. I whispered into the darkness.

'Ey up, Barndog.'

'Y'alright, Boss?'

'Not really, mate. How long you got left?' I asked.

'Not long. You can go give Cowhead a nudge for me if you like, then I'll have a fag with you.'

I felt like a kid scared of the dark needing someone to talk to and for them not to go to sleep. We smoked tabs and talked for ages. I told him I couldn't sleep and what I saw when I shut my eyes. He told me things that had hit him hard from his previous tour and then he pulled out a thermos.

'Do you want a coffee, Boss?'

'Nah, I don't drink coffee, and anyway, I don't think I need caffeine right now.'

'Try it,' he urged. 'It's good stuff that I've had sent from home. None of that rat pack crap.'

'No, I'm okay,' I said.

But he was insistent, and, as he poured, I could smell that this was going to be a particularly good brew.

It was not just the temperature of the coffee that sent a delightful warming sensation right down to my toes, and I relaxed slightly more with every sip. It was good medicine for my tattered mind.

The next morning, I realised that key members of the team, myself included, were seriously fraying at the edges. We needed to get off the ground before this lack of sleep started to affect decision making, if it wasn't already, and before bruised minds were compounded with irreversible damage.

My boss, the OC, was visiting the site where the new PB was being built, and I walked over to explain the situation to him and ask that my team be lifted off the ground for a few days. I ended up in a right state, knowing that this was the right thing to do, the right decision, but at the same time feeling like a failure, believing that I'd failed in my leadership and the command that had been invested in me. I felt as if I was letting the OC down and letting my men down by not being able to shake this off, not being able to pull myself together and get on with the job in hand.

However, the OC agreed, and the next day we were pulled back to Shawqat for a few days of rest. Still not sleeping, Coops and I were seen by specialist medics and we took a course of sleeping pills for several nights, just to get us back on track.

It didn't work for Coops, and it was decided that he should head back to

Bastion for a few days to get some proper rest, to be right out of it and give him chance to get himself together.

A couple of days into our rest period, Major George came to see me. He was due to fly home to following day. I have nothing but the highest regard for George; for the brief period I worked with him he always struck me as measured and a realist.

We stood outside the tent shooting the shit. It was getting freezing at night, but I needed a smoke. I was up to and beyond 20 a day at that point and I needed the harsh Afghan cigarettes with 'American Taste' just to keep my head in check.

George had something he wanted to say, but we both remained silent as I took the first couple of drags. We exchanged small talk about how it was getting 'a bit crazy out there'. Then he looked me in the eye and the conversation turned serious. We began to talk about the police station and about what a mess it had been. I looked him dead in the eye and thanked him for his help that day.

He told me I had done a good job. Other people had echoed the sentiment but it meant more coming from him, and hopefully we shared mutual respect for each other at that moment.

The mood remained sombre as I lit another cigarette from the stub of my first.

'You know, mate, I think I've reached a point where I honestly have come to terms with the idea that I will either be killed or very badly injured over here,' I told him. It was the first time I had articulated what I had been feeling to anyone.

I had been feeling it for a while. Christ, what a terrible thing to feel, but I truly had come to a sense of acceptance. I felt sad for Lucy and my unborn son but no fear or sorrow for myself.

George looked at me.

'I know what you mean.'

It was not what I expected to hear from him. I thought he'd put a hand on my shoulder and say something bone like 'You'll be okay, mate,' but he didn't. The lucky bastard was on the first flight out of there the next morning but he also had had that nagging feeling of impending doom. It was a crazy mindset to be in.

CHAPTER 11
MAN DOWN

15 November 2009, 12 days after the police station. Coops was back in Bastion. He still wasn't himself and he needed to get away from it for a while. He was having trust issues working so closely with the Afghans because of what he had seen 'one of them' do to 'us'. I couldn't shake the foreboding sense of unease I felt each time we went outside the compound on patrol.

With Coops away, Barney took over as my right hand man. He was a character, a good guy in a tight spot and had a great sense of humour. He was more than capable of filling the role as he was a real grafter with years of valuable experience. He'd been in Afghanistan on previous tours and had picked up plenty of choice Pashto phrases he could banter back and forth with the warriors, which meant they loved him.

I'd been in theatre for two months but it felt longer. The one link to home was E-blueys: our letters. They were vital for everyone. It was important to have something physical from home, something that could be touched and reread and looked at. Lucy was five months pregnant. I'd missed scans, but she had sent me the pictures which were dotted around my pit back at Shawqat. When I showed them to my Afghans and told them I was having a son they were ecstatic for me. They sang and danced and waved their weapons in the air, sharing the joy that my first born was to be a boy.

We also had a satellite phone and I spoke to Lucy once a week. We couldn't talk about details, but I didn't want her to worry, so probably would have glossed over things anyway. However, there's no avoiding some high profile incidents, so I called her after the police station; she knew I was in Nad-e Ali, and I knew she would have heard about it on the news. I got the answer machine and explained that I was okay, I had been there and that she would have been proud of what I did, leaving it at that.

Hearing about stuff going on back home felt strange. I knew things like going to the supermarket and getting the car MOT'd were normal, but to me they also sounded alien and very far away.

We were in Shawqat, kitting up for a patrol with another company of warriors. They were the Heavy Weapons Company, even though they didn't have any heavy weapons. They were stationed in a PB called Blue 17 further north with a small team from The Duke of Lancaster's Regiment. These Brits weren't OMLT and therefore felt they needed some support from guys that were used to working alongside our ANA allies.

This was a raw area, recently won during the extensive fighting that had pushed the FLET north to its current position just a small number of weeks before, the same action in which my callsign extracted the casualty who had been shot in the helmet. A question mark still hung over this new ground; the Taliban obviously still thought it belonged to them and were hitting the tiny PB at Blue 17 hard on a regular basis.

As we prepped the vehicles that day I really didn't feel great. I hadn't felt right for a while, but something about the conversation I'd had with George was nagging in the back of my mind. At the start of the tour I had felt invulnerable. I had felt that way all my life: that nothing really bad would happen to me. But not that day. For some reason I felt something very bad was going to happen. I am not claiming to be psychic but I definitely had a bad feeling. Bad enough to mention it to Barney.

'I've got a bad feeling about this one,' I told him. In hindsight, not the most inspiring thing you'd want to hear from your leader.

'Don't say that, Boss,' he replied, as he cracked on loading up the vehicle. I supposed he was right so I thought nothing more of it as I pulled the heavy body armour over my head and let it drop into position, feeling the reassuring weight on my shoulders.

It was only the second time we had gone out in our new body armour and helmets. The familiar desert pattern had been replaced by a light sandy colour, and the new protective wear fastened more securely around the middle, so the weight sat on the hips rather than on the shoulders like a backpack. I liked it; it felt more secure and didn't wobble about as much as old version. The downside was that it was more restrictive. The extra straps around the midriff meant it was harder to turn and bend and it made you move a little like a robot.

The new helmets were lighter and looked similar to the distinctive Second World War German ones, with a ridge high over the eyes which curved down over the ears and back of the head. The new kit wasn't perfect. The armour came with no plates so we had to ram our old ones into place despite the fact that the new outer was designed to carry a thinner plate.

The helmets did not come with covers so were just stupid looking shiny domes. I was not having any of that. Every army officer has his tour photo up in his downstairs toilet – don't ask why, but we all tend to put tour photos in there – and it wouldn't do to look silly in the photo, so I'd given my helmet a military makeover. I had taken an old dhobi-sack (netted wash bag) and cut away a square large enough to cover the whole piece. I then took my cam cream and an old toothbrush and completely covered the material in a nice mixture of brown, black and green before stretching it over the helmet and holding it in place with my favourite sniper tape, which made the most mundane objects look ally. Even though people called the plain green, cloth-like tape 'sniper tape', it was actually canvas repair tape for fixing leaky tents.

I booked out of the Ops room and checked comms with them before switching on PRR and checking comms with all the boys. I pulled on my pimped-up helmet and climbed into the front seat of the WMIK before pulling my grab sack off the bonnet and onto my lap. My SA80 A2 with UGL was down my right side lodged between my leg and the central column, and I pulled the GMPG towards me on its cradle.

With all the heavy equipment, this was the most comfortable I could be. However, it was not a long journey, and I always enjoyed rocking around in the WMIK with the Gympy pulled in close and the warm breeze finding gaps through my kit and refreshing my skin. Every now and again I would jump suddenly as the gunner standing in the back with another Gympy on a cradle would fire off a mini flare at someone getting too close to our patrol.

MAN DOWN

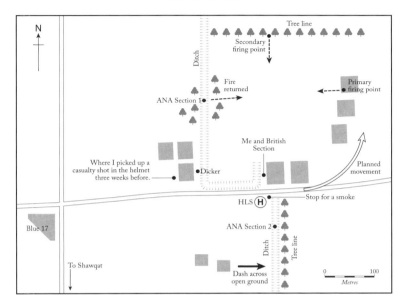

This sudden loud crack in my ear was never welcome as it really is not dissimilar to a gunshot when it takes you by surprise.

We bumped along the dusty road, kicking up clouds of choking filth to our rear. I waved at the locals we passed, most of them digging sections of ditch or carrying sacks of produce on tiny motorbikes. Any one of those sacks could have contained weapons, drugs or IED parts. I didn't trust anyone and watched closely, tightening my grip on the gun when someone I deemed suspicious passed by. They all stared with wide eyes that gave nothing away.

We pulled into the compound. The ANA company was ready to go, and even as I was sorting out the last details with the company commander (who was not joining us), the first of his men were out the gate. I would've liked to have found out the last time this gentleman had been out with his company. Judging by his demeanour and the size of his belly, I would've reckoned it had not been in the near past!

We stepped off on what would be our first patrol since our rest at Shawqat. The Icom was going nuts all through the patrol.

'Bring up the big stuff. We'll hit them in the next field. The next field.'

Something was going on. An ambush was being planned. We knew there were quite a few guys in the area just by hearing different voices over the net.

We patrolled on foot, and when we came to a small collection of compounds I pushed forward to speak to the point ANA section commander. We had to cross a section of open ground to get to the next piece of cover: a ditch line with relatively tall trees offering fairly good cover from view and fire. We would cross the open ground in stages, never having more than a couple of guys moving in the open at any one time, with soldiers static, primed and ready to engage any enemy that opened fire on the poor bugger out in the field.

One at a time the men sprinted as fast as a fully-laden bloke could across a ploughed field. I was expecting the rounds to come flying in at any point as we made our way through this vulnerable position. It was then my turn.

I waited for a decent gap in front of me, as I knew I could move pretty fast with weight due to my size and I didn't want to catch up with the mucker in front to make us an even juicier target. I ran, making a half-hearted attempt to 'hard target' or zigzag my way across the field before deciding 'sod this' and sprinted hard and straight for 100 metres until I reached the apparent safety of the tree line and shallow ditch.

It took a while but we all got across and not a shot had been fired, despite the excited voices over the Icom. They were either bluffing us or were waiting for us to cross into their killing area.

We pushed up the tree line in a long line, keeping well-spaced apart as the terp reported back that he thought an RPG attack was imminent, due to him recognising a frequently-used code word on the net.

We were following the tree line north. The best cover was the ditch, but recent intelligence reports informed us that likely points of cover were being bobby-trapped with IEDs, and there had been numerous stories of callsigns being bumped by small arms fire then jumping into the nearest ditch and not coming out of it.

I looked over my shoulder at the cluster of compounds we'd just passed. A group of locals were standing on the edge watching us. I took it as a good sign that there were still civvies hanging around.

The treeline ended when it hit the road after 300 metres. My front ANA section had gone firm at the tree line and I moved forward to speak with the section commander.

'OK, we'll clear a safe lane across this road then we'll just continue the advance.'

I could see the doubt in the eyes of the Afghan warrior. He looked at his PB just 400 metres to the west. This was the longest patrol that he had conducted from his small base, and he was obviously very keen to return to it sooner rather than later.

The same doubts were going through my own mind. We knew the Taliban were out there waiting for us and that an attack was imminent. My spider sense was going nuts, and the constant updates from the terp about the threats coming across the Icom were drip feeding tension into this patrol. If we turned and headed home the bastards would have hit us in the tail, forcing us to fight a difficult rear action. Moving forward gave us an element of unpredictability. If every patrol in the British Army turned back when it got a bit scary, where the hell would that leave us?

So I decided to push on as planned.

The enemy had control of the area we were in. They dominated the ground. Without consistent and extensive patrols, a fighting unit is unable to enforce its will on the local area. If it cannot enforce its will then it is unable to fulfil the political objectives that put it there in the first place. By advancing to contact we were challenging the enemy's control and attempting to eventually become the dominant force. It was not a process that occurred overnight, but I wanted to take the first steps.

I explained the plan.

'Over the road, push left and advance to the next field and up to the small copse of trees at the far side. We will cover your advance from that compound.'

I pointed over the road to the building directly in front of us as Rayes interpreted what I had just said.

'Once you get to the copse, go firm and cover our movement to the trees. Okay?' The warrior nodded and set off, his front man sweeping the road with his metal detector, thus clearing a relatively safe path for the rest of us.

I took the opportunity to have a drink of water, and Barney came up to get a heads-up on the plan. We exchanged a few words and a bit of banter and I briefed the lads over the PRR.

Humph pushed on over the road with the metal detector. We crossed a steep-banked thigh-depth ditch. Cowhead was carrying the GPMG and I wanted him to take up a position at the far corner of the compound so he could cover the movement of my front section with our most formidable weapon.

The baked mud compound wall was around 20 metres long. A narrow path, only a couple of feet across, ran alongside it, and to the left was another ditch. Between the ditch and the narrow path was a tangled line of small trees.

'Boss, I've got a reading.' Humphries, who was 5 metres in front of me, called out. His detector was squealing away as it picked up metal below his feet. This was not ideal. I needed to get Cowhead with the gun up into that corner fairly sharpish to cover my forward section of warriors, and it would be hard to call them back with unreliable radio communications between us and our Afghan friends.

I looked back. Only half my team had got over the ditch. The rest were on the other side of the road waiting patiently with the rear ANA section. It only took a few minutes before Humph gave the all clear and we continued to the corner of the compound to support the front section.

Humph and Cowhead got in position. I looked through the trees to my left and could see another group of compounds about 150 metres away.

Crack! Crack! Crack!

It was a stuttering start: a single MMG, a PK no doubt. But the contact built after a couple of seconds into a cacophonous crescendo of sharp cracks with what sounded like a section of men firing – a couple of MMGs and maybe half a dozen assault rifles (AK47s or the like). The rounds were not landing near us, nor were they passing over our heads; they were aimed at my forward section. I reached for my pressel switch on my radio whilst simultaneously scanning the ground around me for the enemy.

'Amber 13A, contact. Wait. Out.'

I called forward to Humph and Cowhead, but they couldn't see anything. The Afghans had all gone to ground so I could not see what they were firing back at.

I stopped where I was and had a think. It sounded like the enemy were firing from a position to our front and right. I had a quick look at my map, and, sure enough, there were a couple of compounds in the area. I had a rough plan: loop back on the other side of the road with my two remaining sections, use the tree line as cover and push east to positively identify the enemy position. Then destroy them.

Before doing this, however, I wanted to push forward to the corner of the compound to see if I could get eyes on the enemy and to ascertain the nature of the ground which we were about to cross.

Before standing up I reached up to my helmet mounted camera and switched it on. I was back on my feet but crouched as low as I possibly could, bent over at the waist. There were no rounds coming our way, but that didn't mean I wanted to wander around as if I was taking a walk in the park.

As I pushed forward through some thin cover I saw a bloke 150 metres away at the edge of the compounds. He was just standing there on his own, watching the firefight.

Bastard, I thought to myself.

'Guys, we've got a dicker. Left, 150, reference entrance to compounds. I'll fire a couple of warning shots.'

This guy was reporting our progress to the enemy. If I was about to perform a sneaky right flanking assault on these insurgents I didn't want the dicker calling them up and telling them from where and when we were approaching.

'Tza! Tza!' Move on!

I shouted over to the guy in Pashto. He couldn't hear me over the noise of the fight, so I took aim and sent two 5.56mm rounds in his general direction. I aimed at the soft ground to the right-hand side of him. This did the trick. He experienced the sickening sensation of the sharp whip-crack that explodes in your head when rounds unexpectedly pass very close. It's not like in the movies where people stand around unflinching when the rounds begin to fly. You have an involuntary primeval reaction: you either hit the deck or run for cover, and this guy ran like the wind.

As soon as he was gone, I had the same thing happen to me. A round whistled passed my head and a loud sonic crack filled the air around me. I jumped, but I did not have time to react before the second round found its mark and slammed into my shoulder.

The whole fucking world exploded in my body. Someone had just smashed me in the chest with a bastard sledgehammer. Everything cartwheeled and span in front of my eyes. I wasn't there – my conscious self was knocked into next week – but I must have been picked up off my feet and dumped unceremoniously on the ground as the bullet hit with several tonnes per square inch of pressure. A tsunami of adrenaline-soaked pain bought me back to the present. I knew immediately I had been shot and tried to get into the cover of the ditch to my left. My hands slipped underneath me in the mixture of mud and blood that was all around me as I crawled across the cold ground. It really is amazing to see how much a body can bleed. The stuff was pumping out of me. Slipping and sliding through the filth, I called out, 'Boys, boys! I've been hit. I've been shot.'

As I entered the water, I heard the call being passed down the line.

'Man down!'

'Manny, get up there: it's the Boss!' someone yelled.

The filthy water was deeper than I expected and I couldn't find the strength to stay above the surface with all my kit on. I began to sink under the putrid, dark water. As I slipped below the surface I started to slip out of consciousness. I was tired, so very tired. And all I wanted was to close my eyes and give in to my body's desire to shut down. I was dying; I accepted it and I was calm.

Someone plunged into the ditch next to me, grabbed me and pulled me up by my webbing straps. The pain shot through my upper body like acid. I was burning from the inside. This broke the spell of calmness. I looked up; it was Fiji.

'Boss, Boss, where are you hit?' I couldn't understand his urgent, Fijian accent. My brain wasn't working. 'Where are you hit?'

I tried to reply but couldn't take in enough air to form a word.

'Armpi…' is all I managed to slur.

My lips were painfully numb.

I hadn't actually been shot in the armpit but that was where I felt most of the pain. I learnt later that the bullet had grazed the tangle of nerves called the brachial plexus which sits in the armpit, hence why I thought that's where I had been hit.

Fiji held me up with his arms before slipping his knees under my back to stop me sinking. With his hands free he started stripping the kit off me. This was all slung onto the narrow path. Each movement sent bolts of agony through my body. As he manhandled me, I noticed it was not just my lips but everything from my mouth down to my hips on my right side that was painfully tingling, as if electricity was running through it. It was also completely paralysed. I wanted to help as Fiji took off my day sack by pulling my own arm through the hole, but it just was not happening. Nothing would move. Nothing was working in the way it should have been and the tingling pain was building up, as if a thousand bees were stinging me. This excruciating feeling was backed up by the agony from the pulverised bones and flesh that the bullet had created.

Another man dived in the ditch, and I saw Manny's face, inches from my own.

'Boss, you're going to be okay. You're okay. Don't worry.' We both knew I wasn't, but I admired his optimism.

His voice was high-pitched and his speech was quick. As he worked he kept up the reassurance. I couldn't reply but I tried to keep eye contact so that he knew I could hear and understand him. Why couldn't I breathe?

Manny barked orders to Fiji as he started to cut away my shirt to expose the wound. Blood spurted from it rhythmically in time with my pulse and with enough pressure to form arcs which splashed on my face. It was so small: a tiny little hole just below my collarbone. It didn't look like my shoulder; it didn't feel like it was attached to me somehow. All around it was so pale, seemingly more so with the contrast of bright red blood at the entry wound. I looked away.

I was lucid enough to realise that I was in danger of bleeding out, but what really worried me was the increasing struggle for breath I was having; the round had obviously pierced my lung. The layers of clothing and body armour had formed a partially air tight seal over the wound. Now it was exposed to the open air (and the shitty ditch water), there was nothing keeping the air that I was breathing inside my lung. It was like a burst balloon flapping helplessly in my chest.

Each time I tried to breathe in I was pulling air into my chest through the wound itself, which made a sickening sucking noise on the in-breath and bubbled disgustingly when I exhaled.

Manny understood what was going on.

'We need to get a chest seal on him: he can't breathe.'

A chest seal is a square patch that is placed over the wound and stuck down on three sides. When you breathe in, the suction closes the patch onto the wound, making it air tight and giving the lung a chance to fill. When you breathe out, the air blows the patch away from the wound, allowing air to escape through the side that is not stuck down.

But my chest was slimy with blood and ditch water. Manny went through several patches but couldn't get one to fix.

Manny and Fiji had twisted me to try and find the exit wound. This would be much bigger than the entry wound and normally much more serious. I moaned and groaned as they pulled my big frame in all directions and I thought I was going to vomit with the pain. But there was nothing. The round was lodged inside me.

With me incapacitated Barney was in command and scampered over to assess the situation before he headed back to control the CASEVAC. Up front Cowhead and Humph were with the Gympy that was singing away, sending a deadly cone of fire towards the insurgents who had just hit me.

'Boss, we need to move you,' Manny said.

Barney was back after a few minutes. I could see a few guys with the lightweight stretcher ready to carry me out huddled in the ditch further down the path. If I was a sniper that had just whacked someone, I would be waiting for the moment the stretcher bearers arrived, as a group of slow moving guys makes a very juicy target.

'I'll walk,' I managed to slur.

'What?'

'I'll walk,' I mumbled again.

With a great deal of grunting and moaning, I was dragged out of the ditch and onto my knees before being hauled up onto my feet. The path by the ditch was too narrow to have guys either side of me to keep me up.

Manny was in front of me and momentarily I grasped hold of his shoulder for balance. Fiji was behind carrying my kit. I bounced off the wall as I staggered step after painful step. I locked eyes with one of the ANA boys. He had a black, well-trimmed beard and his eyes were like dinner plates as I stumbled passed him. He sat in the ditch staring up at me; I must have looked a right ragged state with my shirt all cut open, covered in blood and being half dragged off the battlefield.

I was pushed and pulled through the bigger ditch and by the time I was up and over I was completely spent. I could not move another muscle and collapsed on the hard dusty road.

I lay there looking up at the sky, struggling to breathe. The pain in my chest was becoming unbearable and I was dizzy as hell. I listened to the ongoing battle with rounds whistling high over my head and the crash of an RPG landing. I felt useless and helpless.

Manny should have stayed in the ditch where it was safe. He should have stayed in cover so that if the enemy surged round the flank he would have at least stood a chance. But he didn't. He got out of the ditch and lay across my body, using his own armour as a shield for my unprotected body should any of those RPGs land close enough to pepper me with shrapnel. He lay across me and started to pray. He recited the psalms:

'… and ye though I walk through the shadow of death I shall fear no evil…'

He repeated the Lord's Prayer over and over. There was not much else he could do for me medically, but I drew from his great strength and I moved my lips in time with his own, though I did not have the breath to keep up with the words. I reached under him and weakly held the gold crucifix my Aunty Jane had given me before I deployed to Iraq. I held the icon in my bloody fingers.

We remained there for several minutes before the pain in my chest suddenly increased. I tried to roll onto my side, but Manny held me in place. I was beginning to panic as my breathing had now completely stopped. I tried to force air into my lungs, but nothing was going into my throat. I frantically pointed at my mouth and tears formed at my eyes. This is it, I thought. This is absolutely it. Everything sounded distant and far away. I was dying.

Then, as I edged towards a darkness and a peace, Manny saw what was happening, grabbed me by my ragged shirt and began to rock me fiercely back and forth. My head lolled around, the world spun back on its axis and the sound of Manny' frantic prayer filled my ears again.

'… have I not commanded you to be courageous? You shall not be terrified for the Lord our God is with thee.'

A fraction of sweet air crept into my left lung and then a fraction more as Manny continued to throw me around the floor. Eventually I was back to the same level of laboured breathing that I had been before. Painful and shallow, but enough to keep me alive.

'Boss, your chest cavity is filling with blood. The sheer amount of blood is stopping the other lung from filling with air. There is nothing I can do. As soon as the chopper gets here they will put a drain in your chest and that should help.'

Manny was a genius. By violently tossing me around he'd managed to shift enough fluid around in my chest cavity to literally give me a bit of breathing space.

I nodded weakly and tried to move to ease the discomfort. Manny had placed me on my injured side to ensure gravity pulled the blood around my useless collapsed lung and gave my good lung room to work. But the pain of lying on that side was unbearable and I had to lie on my back. I couldn't explain this to Manny, and he kept pulling me over onto the side that had been shot, with a collapsed lung and a back full of broken ribs. I gave up trying to lie on my back and instead sat up. It was the only way to take the pressure off my injuries.

'Boss, get down! Do you want to get shot again?' the medic urged.

I was more scared of stopping breathing again, and there was no way I could lay on my right hand side, so I remained in a half-sitting position which made breathing a great deal easier.

I know it was cheesy, but I just had to ask the question, and thought I might as well ask it while my breathing was okay.

'Manny, am I going to die?'

He looked me square in the eyes.

'Sir, you know I'm a good medic. You are all I care about at the moment. We're getting you out of here now.'

It wasn't a straight 'no' but it was good enough. When Barney ran over seconds later, Manny's demeanour was less reassuring.

'We NEED to get him out NOW! Where is that FUCKING helicopter?'

He was screaming at Barney. I had never seen him get aggressive before and I had never heard him swear. Shit.

The news from Barney was not good.

'They're arguing over the net about bringing the helicopter in while the firefight is going on. They're going to bring up the vehicles from Blue 17 and take him back to Shawqat where the chopper will pick him up and take him to Bastion.'

Barney looked stressed. We all knew that wouldn't work.

If I didn't get to Bastion very soon I would die. I wouldn't make the bumpy journey back to Shawqat in the back of a WMIK. At that moment I couldn't comprehend the danger that a helicopter would face trying to land. All I wanted to do was get out of there. Selfish self-preservation.

'Barney, please get me a chopper,' I begged.

'I'm trying, Boss. I'm fucking trying. Dig deep man.'

He was off again and talking on the net.

I lost the strength to sit and lay down again. The pain was all encompassing and it didn't seem to matter if it hurt more to lie on my bad side anymore. Manny couldn't give me any drugs. All he had was morphine which was no good for respiratory injury because it slows the body's systems, including breathing. A big hit of morphine might be all it took to stop my meagre breathing altogether.

Manny held my hand as he shielded my body with his own and prayed. His face was just inches from mine. He put his own life in danger to protect me, gave me strength and hardened my spirituality through his own strong faith. Some actions are too great to ever possibly be sufficiently thanked for.

Despite his attention, I could feel myself slipping away. A cool relaxed feeling washed over me and I began to feel very tired. I was no longer praying with Manny but concentrating on his words and trying to move my lips in time with his own. Whispering and murmuring I could barely hear the noise of the battle, just his words which were slipping to the back of my consciousness. He kept shaking me to keep me with him but he was losing the fight. We both were.

Then Barney jogged over.

'Just a few minutes, Boss. Chopper's coming for you.'

It was incredible news. For some reason I knew that if I got on that helicopter I would be okay. If I could dig a little deeper and give one last surge I would make it. But I had nothing left in the tank.

'We need the stretcher, Barney. He can't walk again.'

When I heard those words from Manny it sounded like a challenge. He continued to recite passages from the Bible:

'… have I not commanded you to be courageous?…'

Something strange was happening. I felt something coursing through my body. It was a sudden and profound strength and a sense of clarity.

'… You shall not be terrified for the Lord our God is with thee…'

Many weeks later my Aunty Jane gave me the famous 'Footprints' passage. In the text a man describes a dream in which he is walking on a beach with God. They leave two sets of footprints and each indent represents a stage of the man's life. At some points the two trails dwindle to one, especially at the lowest and most hopeless moments of the character's life. When questioning God, believing that he must have abandoned his follower during those times, God gives the explanation: 'During your times of trial and suffering, when you see only one set of footprints, it was then that I carried you.' That strength I felt was me being carried.

I told Manny that I would not need the stretcher and instead I was pulled to my feet and walked.

I could hear the helicopter in the distance. With my new found hope, and more than a little help from Manny and Fiji, I was bundled to my feet. I could see an American Black Hawk preparing to land high above our heads. I heard a snap and a hiss as someone threw a smoke grenade into the field on the other side of the road. A thick red cloud filled the air around me as I half-walked and was half-dragged to the landing site with Manny on my left and Fiji on my right holding me up. I was trying to tell Fiji to let go of my arm, as the pain he was causing was excruciating, but he heard nothing over the deafening sound of the helicopter as it neared the ground.

The red smoke was blown away immediately and replaced by an even better screen of brown dust that shielded the entire area from view as the rotor blades picked up every grain of dirt in a 50 metre radius and threw it into the air. We staggered forwards, unable to see but following the thumping sound of the blades, the screeching of the engine and heat of the exhaust.

All of a sudden I could see the large open doorway with a guy hanging out, arms outstretched, ready to drag me in. I fell forward, spent and completely at his mercy. He manhandled me onto the aircraft and in what seemed like seconds the pitch of the screaming engines changed and I felt the airframe lift off the ground.

I started to lose consciousness again as we ascended rapidly in a race to gain height and get us out of RPG range. I could see a metal panel of the ceiling above my head with several dials. My senses were overwhelmed by the noise as we hurtled over the barren countryside of Helmand Province towards Bastion. Lying on my back again and unable to move, I felt my chest filling with blood once more. It got harder and harder to breathe.

The guy who dragged me on to the chopper and strapped me to a gurney was fishing around in his med pack. I wanted to attract his attention; I needed him to rock me about, to get the blood away from my good lung so I could breathe. He moved swiftly around the body of the aircraft, and when he looked over at me he could see terror in my eyes. I tried to motion to my mouth but my arms were strapped down tight. I opened and shut my mouth like a fish. I was panicking. I'd made it onto the chopper but right now I was going to suffocate. I was struggling, my oxygen was running out and I could do nothing about it.

The American lent across and pushed his face against mine. I don't know if I was hallucinating but he looked like a character out of *Apocalypse Now*. He was wearing aviator sunglasses that completely shielded his eyes. His skin was very tanned and his eyebrows had grown fair in the sun. Most striking of all was the enormous Mexican bandit moustache that he majestically sported and which hung down to his chin. I felt it scratch against my face as his pushed his own close to my ear.

'Don't worry, man. I'm about to give you the good shit!'

He waved a syringe in front of my face before plunging the needle into my body. I felt like I'd gate-crashed a Vietnam movie.

I was incredibly dizzy due to lack of oxygen and the dizziness started to increase. The medic had filled my veins with Ketamine.

After that it all got a bit intense. I could not understand what was happening. I could not see a thing. I felt the weight of a man on top of me. My face was buried in the medic's flight suit. I could smell him. It was the pungent smell of a man who had been working all day in the Afghan heat. My world was covered in the rough dark green of his clothing. The beating of the helicopter's blades blocked out all other sounds, and I had no breath to scream. But in my own head I was pleading, I was begging and I was screaming for him to stop whatever he was doing to me.

He was putting a scalpel into my right side. He was stabbing it through my ribs. Unbelievable pain wracked my chest as the blade was pulled out, and then he put his finger in the hole. He pushed it deeper and deeper into my chest. I could feel it wriggling against my shattered ribs as he worked his finger into the stab wound he'd just made. I was squirming and gasping for air like a landed carp. Then, suddenly, he stopped and the pain subsided to an ache.

The paramedic on the helicopter had just cut a hole in my side and through my ribs then stuck a length of tube around 1cm across through the hole. It was a drain to take the blood away that was filling my chest and it allowed my good lung to open. I did not understand this at the time, and it was only later that I was told what had happened. The drugs he had given me were beginning to addle my brain and I was starting to lose lucidity. Helmand melted away. Blood flowed out of the hole in my side. Somewhere inside me sat a Taliban bullet; a souvenir of Helmand. One war was over for me, but another was just beginning.

CHAPTER 12
CASEVAC

In his final act of heroic professionalism, Manny handed over a written brief to the medic on the Black Hawk highlighting my haemopneumothorax injury. Armed with the correct details, the guy had realised I was suffocating and had done the only thing he could in the circumstances. He manually and painfully placed a drain in my chest without anaesthesia. In hindsight, the pain was worth it. The moustachioed medic saved my life.

As the pain subsided, the full effects of the ketamine started to kick in. My head was spinning, creating sickening waves of nausea. It felt like I was horrifically pissed. I employed the same technique I'd used in the back of cabs or on trains on the way home from parties. I tried to focus on a single object. I stared at dials on the roof of the chopper. I had to focus on one dial in particular. In my addled brain it made sense that if I could just keep concentrating and keep my attention on that one dial on the ceiling of the helicopter then I would live.

I kept staring and staring. Everything else was irrelevant accept for the one dial, which continued to blur and fade in and out of focus. As I stared, the dial began to move and my vision became unsteady.

Then it all went black and quiet.

When I came too, a man was leaning over me. He was cleanly shaven and wore clean combats. I could smell soap on him. I was confused. I hadn't seen a clean person for two months and I couldn't understand who he was or where I was.

His hands were underneath me.

'Don't drop me. You're going to drop me,' I felt unsteady.

I was talking very quietly and I could hear my words slurring; there was no panic in my voice, but I was positive I was about to be dropped onto the concrete below. My head was fuzzy, and I thought it was funny. For some reason, I was sure this man was trying to lift me out of the helicopter on his own, using only his index fingers.

'I've been hurt and you're going to drop me.' I was matter-of-fact.

'Don't worry, I've got you. You're okay. I won't drop you,' the man reassured me.

It felt like I was floating. I was moving smoothly along the ground with no jolts or bumps. Suddenly it made sense. Wheels! I'm on a bed on wheels, I thought. And I smiled inwardly, proud that I'd been able to work it out.

The moustachioed face from the chopper came from nowhere and appeared close to mine. It said something. I had no idea what. I must have smiled or nodded, as the face smiled back and then vanished.

I felt like I was levitating and I glided through sets of doors. I was horizontal. Strip lights above me streaked along like space ships in *Star Wars* going into hyperspace. The long stripes of light merged into one continuous beam above my head. I loved it.

You're hallucinating, David. The thought popped into my head. Part of my brain was still acutely aware of what was going on and could reason with the world that seemed to be going crazy. The drugs he gave you, they're making you see things, I thought.

But my rational self was only a very quiet voice in the corner of mind. It was the tiny handle on realism that kept at least part of me grounded. It had no control over anything my body was doing. It was a spectator. My ketamine head was in control and it was having a whale of a trip.

Faces kept on appearing in front of me, uncomfortably close. They weren't normal. My vision was like looking through a fish eye lens: distorted and misshapen. Suddenly a lady's face loomed into my field of vision. It was the shape of a teardrop and her mouth was on her forehead. She was a living Picasso painting.

'You're talking out of your head,' I told her.

She was asking me questions but getting no sense out of me at all. I thought it was all very amusing.

I was wheeled down a long corridor and into a brightly lit room where a face appeared covered in a blue mask. I knew it was a doctor. He kept asking me questions. He wanted to know about my pain, about what had happened. As he talked I had the sensation of being completely naked. All my clothes seemed to have been removed in one movement. The nurses must have been cutting them away. And after that nothing of the real world exists in my memory. The 'good shit' finally smudged out the last little bit of lucidity I had.

I was told afterwards that ketamine is sometimes used as a medical sedative for children. It is effective as they have no real experience of terror and horror. They have wonderful hallucinations and out of body experiences involving teddy bears and gum-drop lands and are given the drug in a calm environment where everything is under control and relaxed.

Unfortunately for me, and for a number of my friends who had also been given the drug, administering it in the back of a helicopter during the pressure and panic of a CASEVAC created an unsettling and intense experience.

The drug-fuelled trip that I went on after I blacked out on the operating table felt as real as reality, and I remember it with the clarity and certainty of any past memory. It was tangible.

I honestly thought I had died and gone to hell.

I found myself moving very quickly down a flickering tube. I had no concept of how long I was travelling, as time had no meaning. There were no reference points. There was no wind and no resistance, but I knew I was travelling at great speed. It felt like static electricity was all around me, crackling across the surface as I raced along, before coming to an abrupt and jolting stop.

I couldn't move. I couldn't breathe. I couldn't blink. I was sitting bolt upright and encased in rock. Whilst I had been travelling down the tube I was too enthralled to think about the situation. I was distracted by the speed and the lights all around me. But as I sat in the prison of my immovable body my mind began to tick over.

Where am I? Why can't I move?

The frustration grew inside me as I willed my body to move, even if it was just a flicker of motion. I was conscious that I was not breathing, and the desire to draw breath was overwhelming. Frustration became panic.

I'm dead. This is it.

I stared blankly ahead and watched as a slideshow started in front of me. The picture in front of me began to change a segment at a time. Just like in a game of Tetris, one part of the picture drifted into my peripheral vision before lodging in its correct position. One brick at a time until the vision was complete.

The picture I was shown was a Sanger in Afghanistan. I was inside the Sanger, looking out over a dusty landscape. The colours were too vibrant and warm. It was hot, and I could taste and smell the dirt in the air.

As I sat there stock-still, I remembered how I had got there and I remembered my wife and family. I was not upset. I was numb. Just as I couldn't move, I also couldn't feel emotion. No warmth, only dread and panic. That was when I told myself I was in hell.

The scene began to change in front of me. Once again, one slow moving segment dropped into place at a time until the image changed completely. Another desert scene or another Afghan village passed before me. This process continued for what seemed like forever. The images were sometimes just landscapes and sometimes disturbing. At stages dead bodies filled my vision, along with images of the dying or bloody and burnt children. I came to accept the finality of my position. I accepted that I was there forever. It was my lot, and there was nothing I could do to change it.

What bothered me the most and what stayed with me for a long time afterwards was how quickly my mind accepted the new reality. I did not forget my past in a hazy, druggy blur. Instead I believed I was in a new phase of existence.

I don't remember waking up, but I was told afterwards that I was fighting and swinging wild, slow punches, ripping the wires and tubes from my body. The medical staff had to pin me down and take some of the equipment out of me so I wouldn't damage myself. Thankfully they had the good sense to remove my catheter during this process.

The next clear memory was of a middle-aged female nurse standing over me. She was smiling and talking to me very calmly. I tried to move but everything hurt.

My right hand side was immobile. My arm, face and side were buzzing with an electrical burning pain that would not ease. My arm would not move at all, and the unresponsive side of my face and neck made me look and talk as if I'd had a stroke. But I was unconcerned. It was probably a combination of good opiates, which don't always block the pain but make you feel indifferent to it, and the fact that I was alive and away from the hallucinogenic limbo that I had experienced.

I was barely aware that Coops and another guy were sitting by my bed.

'Alright, Boss.'

Coops was in Bastion following the police station massacre and his face was the picture of relief. He genuinely looked ecstatic to see me open my eyes. I found out months afterwards that he had been told by the doctors to expect the worst and that I was not likely to make it through surgery. When he told me this, months later, in a spit and sawdust bar in Blackpool, I was gob-smacked. I hadn't realised how close I had come.

I could barely keep my eyes open but I stayed awake for long enough to have a laugh with the man who had been by my side for the previous two months. Apparently the drugs had a strange effect on my levels of inhibition.

'Boss, at least you've got some fit nurses to perv at in here, like!' he joked.

With a great deal of effort and pain I shifted my weight so I could see who Coops was talking about.

'Hey! Pretty nurses!' I called.

A beautiful Danish lady with her equally pretty American colleague started to walk over. Coops and his mate were in fits of stifled laughter as they tried to look away. In my head I could see nothing wrong with my actions or what I was saying. Lack of constraint was obviously a common side effect, as neither of the extremely patient ladies seemed phased or surprised at my boldness.

'What are your names?' I asked, slurring like the worst drunk in a seedy nightclub.

They told me, but I lay there shaking my head.

'I'm never going to remember all that. So I'll just call you Pretty and you Gorgeous. Is that okay?' They laughed and, after checking I was alright, went back to their duties.

I slipped back into unconsciousness and when I opened my eyes again Coops had gone. I saw a tall man of around 50 striding through the double swing doors of the intensive care unit. He was in combats and had a shaggy mop of grey hair. He was carrying a long shepherd's crook that came to just above his shoulder. It struck the ground with each alternate step he took.

I watched him approach and he stood at the end of my bed. He introduced himself as the Padre and asked if I wanted to talk to him for a while. His voice was steady and calming. I told him what had happened to me, how I'd been shot and how Manny had lain over me in the open ground and I asked him to pray for my medic. I told him I had stopped breathing and that Manny had screamed the scriptures into my face and how then I was not only able to breathe again, but also stand and walk. He listened, took stock and leant on his crook (maybe the crook was something inserted by my drug filled brain but I remember it as clear as day!).

He prayed over me and offered me a blessing before reading from the bible. After a while he could see I was struggling to stay awake. He placed his hand on my shoulder and stood over me until I fell asleep.

My world was short bursts of consciousness. I fell asleep in the middle of situations, and each time my eyelids flickered open again everything had changed. It was very confusing, and I struggled to keep up with who was there and what was going on. The shift changed and Gorgeous and Pretty left; they both gave me a peck on the cheek and told the incoming nurses to 'watch out for that one!'

The new nurse came over. She had the phone and told me that a Major Hale wanted to speak to me. I was so full of drugs that I thought nothing of my mate Pete calling me up from Germany. I must have sounded flippant when I answered.

After a brief chat, Pete told me that he was going to call Lucy and tell her that she should expect a phone call from me in the following few minutes. I checked with the nurse to see if I could do that, and apparently it had been the plan all along.

Before we left Bastion, all the soldiers in my unit had been ordered to leave a CASEVAC bag should any be wounded. The bags contained a few personal items. We were also required to write down a list of phone numbers of people we would want to speak to and leave that in the bag. It was a wise plan, as there was no way I would have been able to remember the dialling code for Germany, let alone the subsequent 10 digits in the number. I held the phone to my left ear and heard it ring just half a tone before a worried and tearful voice answered.

'David?'

Lucy was not crying, but I could tell by her tone and the broken sound of her lovely voice that she had been recently.

'I'm okay, sweetheart. I'm okay.' I apologised for slurring my words but explained it was the drugs. I didn't tell her I was paralysed to my hip down my right hand side.

I found out later that Lucy had heard nothing about my condition between the fateful knock on her door first thing in the morning until the call in the early evening. Lieutenant Colonel Jonny Price, the CO of my parent unit, had delivered the news. He had received a phone call from the duty officer, who had himself heard from JCCC that I had been wounded. The only information he had was the bare facts, and it was those that he presented to Lucy.

'David has been shot in the chest. He is alive and has been taken into surgery, but we don't know any more.'

Lucy was devastated but held herself together with the greatest dignity that day and displayed amazing resolute inner strength as she sat by the phone and waited for it to ring. Her best friend on the street, Jane England, came over and sat with her for nearly the whole day, and for her support I will always be grateful.

Jane's husband, Captain Gary England, was assigned as the Visiting Officer to accompany Lucy to Birmingham the next day, as that was where I was being taken. He dropped everything, including his own young family and his busy job in Battalion HQ, to be on the first plane out early the following morning. He was a vital link and liaison through the army channels, speaking the foreign language that only those in the army can understand and in doing so helped my family and me. Gary and I were great friends before I was hurt, but I owe him a debt of gratitude for his help.

Lucy told me afterwards that I was so matter-of-fact when I called her, she was immediately worried there was something I wasn't telling her.

I phoned my mother after I spoke to Lucy. She sounded upbeat and matter-of-fact: it was her coping mechanism. In reality, she was in utter disarray. I commented on how well she sounded, but chatting for even a few minutes took all my energy and I was soon falling asleep.

The next time I awoke, someone was speaking to me.

'David, you are doing okay. We're going to get you back to Britain.'

The nurse was talking to me. I was being wheeled along a corridor.

'We're just moving you along to a different ward while you wait for your flight.'

In the new ward, a hulk of a man was waiting for me. Brad (obviously an American with a name like that) had upper arms as thick as my thighs and his head seemed to melt into his shoulders. His neck was nothing but a brief consideration. He was assigned to look after me until the C-17 Globemaster flew me home.

I bothered Brad regularly for cups of water. The general anaesthetic from the surgery had left me with a raging thirst I couldn't quench. Brad delicately held countless cups of water for me as I drunk through straws. He had the body of a boulder and the patience of a saint!

The intake of fluids had obvious side effects, however. My catheter had been removed during my violent return back to reality, and several hours and several pints of water later I found I was unable to urinate. The paralysis had most likely affected my bladder control.

When Brad's shift was over he handed over to a lovely blonde woman called Anna, who was the RAF nurse responsible for me during the flight back. Brad explained that I hadn't been for a pee for several hours.

'Well, we'll just catheterise him. Not a problem,' Anna said.

'Err, I have a problem with that!' I piped up. They thought I was asleep and were not expecting a response from me.

'There is no way on God's green earth that you are shoving anything up my penis. Absolutely no way!' I was insistent.

'But it's an eight-hour flight, and we won't be able to do anything about it once we get on board. It has to happen in the next hour or so,' explained Anna.

'No way.'

I was getting overexcited and pain was raging up and down my right side.

Anna obviously took a cue from Brad and made herself scarce so we could talk man to man.

'David, just look at yourself – that cannot be comfortable,' he tried to reason.

I was propped up on pillows and looked down at my stomach. My bladder proudly protruded from my midriff like a lady in her second trimester. Brad was right; it was bloody uncomfortable. I didn't feel like I needed to go; I felt incredibly full, as if I was going to burst.

'Maybe if you help tilt me, mate? Lying down flat is not the easiest position to piss from,' I said.

Brad tried to carefully push his shovel-like hands underneath my body and tilted me over onto my left side. It was agony, but I was willing to endure it if it meant avoiding a catheter.

I was lying completely naked, half-suspended in the air, while receiving an intimate bear hug from behind by an American body builder and nurse. I completely tensed up and was wracked with pain. My cock hung in the grey bottle and nothing came out. Maybe if I had been lighter then Brad wouldn't have huffed and puffed in my ear so loudly and I might have been able to distract myself from the situation enough to release my bladder. But it really capped it off when I saw the look on Anna's face as she pulled the curtain aside to see what all the commotion was about.

Shortly after, I was lying back down with a tube up my knob. It wasn't so bad, certainly not in comparison to the most uncomfortable spooning session I'd ever experienced 10 minutes previously! The relief was almost instant, as what must have been pints of fluid drained out of me. I passed out with exhaustion.

When I opened my bleary eyes again I was outside in the dusty night air. It was breezy and I could hear a roaring sound all around me. I was being wheeled up a metal ramp into a man-made cavern. I passed several other guys on beds, all wrapped up in various bandages with bags of fluid suspended above their beds. A couple of soldiers were sitting on the edge of the cavern; their arms were in slings and their eyes were as wide as saucers as gurney after gurney was pushed past them. Each contained comatose or semi-conscious figures lolling amongst the blankets. One of them nodded at me, but I felt so heavy that I couldn't move to return the gesture.

'We'll be taking off shortly, David. Do you mind me calling you David, or would you prefer Sir?' someone asked.

I was being wheeled aboard the flying hospital that ferried the war wounded back to the UK. Normally C-17s are used to carry troops and equipment in long haul missions. The four-engine transport jets are big enough to carry tanks and helicopters. But the ride I was being taken on had been converted into a flying hospital. Developed during the Afghan conflict, the plane was a fully functioning ward at 30,000 feet. It was on constant stand-by to take the worst of the battle-wounded from Afghanistan to the UK and could get injured troops home to medical facilities and to their families within 36 hours of injuries being sustained. Weeks before the plane had been used to fly several of the injured from the police station massacre back to hospitals in Britain.

The medics aboard were called CCAST (Critical Care Air Support Team) and all worked within the NHS but dedicated four months a year to help the military save its wounded. Because of the nature of the conflict they were trained to deal with traumatic blast injuries and amputations. Sadly they were kept very busy during 2009.

I must have drifted off again without realising, as the bed was static when I woke and Anna, her face, framed with blonde hair, was leaning over me; there are worse ways to wake up, trust me!

'David is just fine, thank you. Do you have any water?'

So it began; an eight hour cycle of passing out followed by coming round with a raging thirst and a tongue like Ghandi's flip-flop. I remember nothing about the flight other than being poked and prodded every now and then until finally I woke again as I was being wheeled off the back of the plane. I was home.

CHAPTER 13
RECOVERY

People were wrapping blankets around me. I could hear a low-pitched drone as the huge tailgate at the back of the plane opened. The air that rushed in was cold and damp. Something about it smelled familiar. It wasn't the foreign dusty air that I'd been breathing. I was wheeled down the ramp, out into the night. Blue lights flashed. It took a while for me to understand where I was.

'Welcome back to England, mate!' The cheery face of a burly ambulance man in green overalls beamed down as the gurney I was in was placed in position at the rear of his vehicle. Anna was still with us.

'Sorry about the landing, David. It gave everyone quite a shock in the back.'

I had no idea what she was talking about, and the blank look on my face must have said so.

'Do you not remember the landing? I don't know what was happening at the front of the plane – the pilot must have dropped coffee on his lap at the wrong moment or something as that was the roughest landing I've ever experienced,' she explained.

I thanked the morphine in my system for the blissful ignorance it had allowed me.

'Where are we?' I asked.

'Birmingham. You're being taken to Selly Oak. You'll be able to see your family soon.'

Selly Oak Hospital was the home of the Royal Centre for Defence Medicine. It was renowned for the trauma care it provided and had one of the best burns units in the country. It was the first place most of the severely injured servicemen and women from conflicts in Iraq and Afghanistan woke up in. Many of them had no knowledge that they had been evacuated from the battlefield. The last memory many had before regaining consciousness was of war, and countless patients awoke asking for their rifles, believing they were still in battle.

Because of the nature of the injuries the unit treated, many of patients did not even remember being there as they were sedated or unconscious throughout their stay.

Landing in the UK was hugely disorienting. It was too much to comprehend. One day I was lying bleeding in a shitty ditch in Helmand, the next I was in the Midlands. Since my injury I had drifted in and out of consciousness and when I was awake my mind was clouded in a drug-induced fug.

On the way to Selly Oak I could see out of the ambulance window that I was in a convoy of other ambulances and police cars. All had their blue lights flashing. The C17's macabre cargo had been unloaded and was being taken en mass to the next part of the process. Lucy explained later that she was there to see the convoy and was shocked by the sheer number of vehicles involved. The medical flights from Afghanistan were a regular occurrence, which gives an indication of the magnitude of the conflict that was taking place and the price our men and women paid.

'Rock star treatment for you, lads,' the ambulance man said when he saw me looking at the string of flashing lights.

It was too much for me: to be somewhere clean, to have normal people wearing normal clothes and not carrying weapons. My brain struggled to take it in. There were roads and cars on the roads. There were streetlights and brick-built houses. I passed shops and pizza takeaways. My senses were overwhelmed. It all seemed familiar, yet totally alien at the same time.

I don't remember getting to Selly Oak or being hooked up to machines in the intensive care unit.

When I next awoke everything was calm. A machine was bleeping softly somewhere in the room I was in and bright green LEDs blinked out in the soft, dim lighting. It was a room set permanently in twilight with no windows. It had the hushed atmosphere of a library. Anna was at the end of my bed, talking quietly to a couple of other nurses. She turned to look at me and noticed I was awake.

'I've got to go now,' she said and grabbed my blanketed foot, giving it a friendly shake. 'See ya!'

Later I read my medical report which she had filled in. On it she wrote: 'Thanks for the fantastic plane ride. Get yourself better soon. You'll be a fabulous daddy. Take care and look after yourself. PS Aren't you glad we put the catheter in!'

Another nurse was at my side – the next in the procession of people who were there to care for me and monitor me.

'Hi David, I'm Sam. I'm going to have to move your arm, but we've given you a big old dose of morphine, so it should be okay.'

I nodded. The morphine had me in its warm, fuzzy cloak. Sam slowly took hold of my arm and immediately pain shuddered through the whole limb and shot down my right side. I moaned. In a single gentle yet purposeful movement she stretched the arm up above my head and slipped it into a blue Styrofoam sling which she hooked on a metal bar above my bed. The pain subsided, and the morphine wrapped me up again in its relaxing grip.

'It's called a Bradley sling and it will help with the swelling,' Sam explained.

Up until that point I hadn't been aware enough to think about my injury, and it was the first time I'd had a good look at my arm. I was shocked at its size and colour. The bruising extended up from my elbow joint to as far as I could see, into my armpit and round to my back. It was black and vile, with a sickening swelling that seemed to throb and pulse as I looked at it. I couldn't move it, and it constantly felt like my fingers were uncomfortably crossed.

As the nurse adjusted my arm in the position it would remain in for the next week, she explained that my family were waiting to see me and asked whether or not I felt up to seeing them.

'They're here? Now?'

A mixture of shock, the drugs and the sensory overload of being back in the UK combined to produce a confusion that would not leave me for several days. I was totally disorientated. My head hadn't left Helmand. I truly could not comprehend that my loved ones were just on the other side of the door.

Minutes later my wife and parents were at my bedside. There are lucky soldiers who are fully aware of where they are and what has happened to them, and they have emotional reunions with their loved ones. I was too numb to feel much beyond the happiness of seeing them. To me it felt as if I'd been away for a while and come back to meet up with them in a pub. I wasn't tearful or overcome with emotion. I was amazed at the size of my wife's belly. It had swollen with my son inside her over the previous two months. She was six months pregnant and had the most perfect and neat bump that a woman had ever sported. Everybody commented that from any other angle other than the front and side she didn't look pregnant. It hadn't affected any other part of her. All she had to show for it was a beautiful little bump.

My mum and dad, Anne and Tony, were with Lucy. They didn't stay long, but Lucy stayed with me throughout as more and more visitors came through in pairs. Only so many people were allowed at my bedside at any one time so it was like a relay. I don't recall much about any of them. My younger brother Chris and his girlfriend at the time, Annabel, came through, then my Aunty Liz, then my sister-in-law and her boyfriend and finally Lucy's parents. As this parade went on in front of me, I felt more and more fatigued. I couldn't figure out what all the fuss was about.

My arm remained uncomfortable for days. The nerves in it were damaged, and I was convinced that my fingers were permanently crossed into an uncomfortable claw. For several days, whenever family visited, I asked them to help and uncross my digits. In the beginning they tried to tell me that I was mistaken and that my fingers were straight, but I didn't believe them, and eventually they reached into my sling and moved my fingers for me just to keep me happy, even though the frustrating sensation would remain. I had a nerve block in my neck, a line like an epidural that stops the messages from the brain to the nerves and helps with the pain.

As the weeks went by, more people came to visit. I couldn't fathom why they were so upset or so glad to see me. I'd only been away for a couple of months. People that I hadn't seen in years were travelling from all over the country to sit with me for an hour. All my friends from school, from university, from training and from the battalion appeared at my bedside. I couldn't believe it and at first, as I lay there in the Intensive Care Unit, I honestly couldn't imagine why they bothered to make the effort. I'd only been shot after all. I had no concept of how close to death I had come or of the extent and consequences of the injury I'd sustained.

In my head, I hadn't moved on from Afghanistan. My brain was not able to fathom the shift in reality and the shift in values. Afghanistan and the UK were so totally different. I had been immersed in a place where people got shot every day and where, if you were shot, others shrugged and asked 'Is he alive? Has he got all his limbs?' If the answer to both questions was yes, the inevitable conclusion would be 'Then it could've been worse'. I was alive, I had all four limbs and I wasn't disfigured, so taking a bullet really wasn't that much of a big deal. It was just nice to see my friends again.

While I was almost nonchalant about my situation, many of the people who visited me found that the experience of going somewhere like Selly Oak had a profound effect on them.

Walking through the rows of beds, each one occupied by a wounded soldier and most of them missing at least one limb, was harrowing. The average age of patients was 23.

Unconscious or under heavy sedation in their beds, some of the soldiers were still psychologically trapped in Afghanistan, suffering flashbacks of the moment of their attack. They could be heard shouting and tossing about in their sleep.

It made for uncomfortable visiting, and there were not many friends who visited twice. Later, a couple of them explained to me that they couldn't bring themselves to go back and put on a cheery face in what, to them, was a charnel house. A place of carnage and suffering, where the scars of war were openly displayed for all to see, hear and smell.

The true reality of war was writ large in those wards. For people unaware of what weapons of war do to a man, the hospital provided a stark education. Thankfully, the closest most people come to conflict are violent films where a man is shot and doesn't even fall; he clutches his shoulder and carries on with the battle. Or where a grenade goes off in the room and someone takes cover behind a piece of soft furnishing and then reaps his revenge on the enemy when the dust clears. Visitors to Selly Oak witnessed the true devastation weapons bring and had their eyes opened to the horror of warfare. An explosion will literally rip a man's limbs from his body. A bullet can tear open a man's belly and break his bones. Shrapnel will tear flesh and disfigure beyond comprehension or recognition. The unprepared friends and family who came to see me had received that education as they saw the boys' stumps, heard the groans and smelt the square yards of open flesh awaiting skin grafts.

I wasn't aware of any of this. I couldn't understand anything from my visitors' points of view. I even remember telling my Aunty Liz off for looking so glum when she first came to see me! I simply could not understand the seriousness of the situation.

It was so hard to gauge time in the ICU. I was there for nearly a week but didn't realise it at the time. I was constantly falling asleep, and whilst awake my brain was confused with copious amounts of drugs. The large room was kept in a constant state of dull lighting with no windows to the outside world so there was no way of knowing whether it was night or day. Not that it mattered. It was quiet except for the sounds of beeping, moaning, crying and the whispers of visitors and nurses.

I remember my progress there in snatches. At one point I was offered food, and I realised that I hadn't eaten since the morning I was shot. By my reckoning, that was three days previous; it could have been more or less, as time had little meaning. I realised I was hungry and a small plate of sandwiches was brought to my bedside. I attacked them like an animal. I hadn't even got onto the second before the inevitable occurred. It was too much for my frail insides, and I doubled over, retching. My chest was covered in regurgitated bread and ham but it didn't stop there. I continued to retch, and vile black lumps of slime projected from my mouth. I heaved and more of this disgusting substance was brought up in streaks, like dirty crude oil spilling over my blankets. I looked on in helpless shame and repulsion at the mess I had made all over myself as the nurses cleaned me up. It would not be the last time. I was still bleeding inside, and this putrid slime was made up of partially digested blood clots that were sitting in my stomach. It happened when I coughed as well. My lung was frantically trying to repair itself, but the bleeding inside was irritating the tissue, making me splutter up black clots with red streaks from deep inside my chest. It would be several days before this unpleasant episode would run its course.

My problems, however, were small in comparison to the other patients in the ICU. In Selly Oak, no matter how bad you were, there was always someone worse off than yourself. The guy in the bed next to me was in a wretched state. He was still stuck in Afghanistan and still stuck in the moment he was hurt. In his waking moments between the sedated unconsciousness he was kept in, his brain repeatedly replayed the horror he had suffered. Whenever he awoke he would moan and groan and cry out for someone to help him. During my first few hours in the ICU, I couldn't stand it. Why was no one helping him? He was obviously in pain.

I called the nurse, who explained: 'He's not in any physical pain. We've made him comfortable, but he thinks he's somewhere he's not.'

It was heart-breaking to hear him crying out pitifully, and I tried to reassure him as best I could when he was shouting. Neither of us could move very much but we could make eye contact, and I spoke to him, telling him he was okay and that I was with him. The reassurance never lasted long, and soon enough he was back to his pleading.

His dad was a great bloke. He bought every soldier on the ward an advent calendar for Christmas; it must have cost him a good couple of hundred quid but it brought a few smiles to everyone.

I'd arrived at Selly Oak on 16 November. I was heavily drugged and tired all the time. Outside the hospital the run up to Christmas was in full swing but there were no trees or decorations in ICU. It was a big room with around 20 people in. I only realised later when I started to come round that some of the injured from the police station were also there.

I was gradually becoming aware of my injuries but didn't comprehend the extent of them. I didn't think it was a big deal. I was desensitised to violence and the consequences of combat. During the two months of my tour I had been in close contact with several people who had been shot or blown up. I had witnessed the horror in the police station. Every day was alive with threat. And I had loved it. I had loved getting shot at and so I had no dramas with getting shot. It was not a big deal for me. I had been bloodied in battle and I was alive. I would recover, I would have some good stories to tell my fellow officers and I would continue my career in the army. This was the level of naivety to which I stubbornly clung.

At some point it was explained to me that I needed further surgery. The operations that I'd had at Bastion were purely life-saving. I was patched up and stabilised by the incredible medics there, then sent back to the UK for longer-term reconstruction. An artery running parallel to my collarbone had been badly damaged by the round and was being held together with stitches. The surgeon in Birmingham needed to perform a plumbing job to make the repair permanent and would take tissue from a vein in my forearm and graft it to the artery to form a proper seal over the wound.

When I woke from the operation I was back in the ICU with Lucy at my side. My right arm was back in its Bradley sling and I tried to move my uncomfortable body. Something felt wrong. I was still paralysed down my right side and I couldn't feel or move my left arm either. What the hell had they done to me?

Lucy called the nurse, who called the doctor, and no one could tell me what had happened. The doctor's only explanation was that I must have been lying on the left arm during the extensive operation and I had, in effect, a dead arm that would come back in due course.

Both arms were strung up in Bradley slings, both sides paralysed and I looked a proper Muppet.

As I lay immobile, my mate Gary walked in. He had given my family time and space to come and visit but now he wanted to see me for himself.

'What do you look like?' he laughed, trying to make light of the situation.

He was joking around, but there was no humour in his voice. I made light of the fact that I was inexplicably paralysed in both my arms, but there was very little to find funny.

I was on a range of different meds. All had different effects on me. The bullet that penetrated me had ripped apart my lung, which had been stitched back together. The bullet had also grazed my brachial plexus, the nerve and artery bundle which ran from my neck and branched out down from a junction in my armpit down my right arm and side. The artery was bleeding into the tube and putting pressure on the nerves. The pain and discomfort I felt was very specific nerve pain. It was different to the other pain caused by the broken bones and shredded tissue. It was an intense, jumpy, electric, stinging pain. It was horrendous. It was sharp and instant and came without warning in agonising jolts and could not be sedated by morphine, hence the nerve block in my neck.

The procession of old friends and colleagues continued. One of them was an old university pal, Martin Hewitt, who I hadn't seen for five years. Martin was largely to blame for me joining the army. My dad was an RAF pilot, and I hadn't been interested in joining the army one bit when I was a teenager. However, once enrolled at Manchester University I joined the Officer Training Corps because it looked like quite good fun, I could play rugby for them and it was a good drinking club. I originally wanted to be a pilot like my father but then I grew too tall. One day in 2004, Martin took me to one side and explained that he was doing something called Exercise Cambrian Patrol, an annual international military patrolling exercise over a 50 mile course. Participating teams are tasked with a number of challenging military exercises, testing skills such as shooting, casualty evacuation and strategic river crossing. The exercise takes place within the rugged Welsh terrain, and each team of eight is given a narrative to follow which often involves having to escape and evade capture and interact with friendly and not so friendly civilians or resistant groups. Martin had entered the competition and said he wanted me on his team.

'You are a good soldier,' he told me.

I accepted the invite and I loved the gruelling challenge. I also discovered I was quite good at it. The seed had been planted which eventually led to me becoming an infantryman.

I hadn't seen Martin for years when he appeared at the foot of my bed. I was asleep and when I woke he was sitting there.

'What are you doing here?' I asked groggily.

'You've been shot you fool. I've come to see you.'

Over the years we've had a strange relationship. I have the upmost respect for Martin and I love him to bits, but we don't always get on and we can rub each other up the wrong way. He can be quite arrogant and he can wind me up, but I think he's mega, and although it can appear he is sometimes all mouth, he genuinely isn't. He always follows things up.

Martin was in 1 Para. He had been shot the year before me, leading an assault against the Taliban. We had both received similar injuries, but he wasn't as lucky; his wound was nastier than mine. Whereas my brachial plexus was damaged, his was severed and his right arm was permanently paralysed. That hadn't stopped him, and since his injury he had developed an interest in adaptive sport. He took up skiing and was one of the first members of the Combined Services Disabled Ski Team. When he left, we vowed to stay in touch.

Soon after Martin's visit, I was well enough to leave the ICU and was taken upstairs to the trauma ward, S4, where bay upon bay was filled with dozens of young men returned from Afghan.

A few weeks before I was shot, a friend of mine from Sandhurst, Nick, had been blown up and lost both his legs. When I was released from ICU and placed in the trauma ward, Nick was in the bay next to mine. I wasn't well enough to get out of bed for a few days but when I was I got in a wheelchair and was wheeled round to see him. I'll never forget the smell. It was like walking into a butcher's shop. The surgeons had taken grafts of skin and muscle from his stomach, leaving him with strips of open flesh.

'You stink, mate,' I said. 'You smell like a butcher's shop.' In hindsight it probably wasn't the most diplomatic thing to say, but in my defence I was pumped with drugs and was barely coherent. Nick went on to come fourth in the mixed doubles sculls in the 2012 Paralympics.

A while later I was talking to another patient, a young man who had lost a leg. For those of us who were conscious, time was spent swapping injury stories.

'What happened to you, mate?' I asked.

'IED, Nad-e Ali,' he explained.

'I was in Nad-e Ali. Whereabouts?'

'Shin Kalay.'

'So was I,' I told him. When he told me where and when he sustained his injury, I realised he was one of the casualties whose HLS my unit had helped secure soon after we moved into PB Zoo.

He was a Grenadier Guard and was allowed out a few days later to go to the funeral of one of his mates, a victim from the police station. It was hard watching him go. When he returned, I spoke to him.

'I was there, mate,' I explained. 'I got there within seven minutes and he hadn't suffered. He died quickly.'

One of the injured from the roof was also there and came over one day to thank me, as was the first casualty I found, Liam Culverhouse. He, too, came to speak to me.

'Sir, can you have a word with the doctors for me?'

'Why,' I asked.

'They think I was fucking around in the PB, unscrewing rounds from their casing and swallowing them. I had a scan and they found a round in my stomach. I was never shot in the abdomen, so I'm being accused of swallowing it.'

I didn't know what to make of the conversation. I'd had some weird ones in hospital but that was one of the oddest. As it transpired, when Liam had been shot in the eye, the bullet had not exited. Instead it had pinged around in his head, striking his jaw and teeth, and had come to rest on the back of his tongue, from where he had swallowed it. This was the round that the doctors had identified during a scan that was now sitting pretty in his stomach.

Another guy next to me, Rob, was an explosives guy and had been on an operation deep inside the FLET where he was dropped and picked up by a helicopter. He had a bunch of detonators in his pocket and when he ran off the Chinook they went off and stripped the muscle off his thigh. When the Chinook had taken off to deliver Rob on his fated mission, it had blown over a brick wall which fell on the guy who had loaded the helicopter and crushed his back. He was in the bed opposite Rob.

After a few short weeks I was released and went to stay with my parents, where I spent Christmas Day with them and Lucy. However, our home was in Germany and I was eager to get back there, as that was where Lucy was due to give birth. Her pregnancy had not been straightforward and her notes and birth plan were there.

When I was released from Selly Oak it was recommended that I go to the rehabilitation centre at Headley Court in Surrey, where I was supposed to spend three-week stints, but I was too anxious to get to Germany, where I planned to recover and get back to work.

I was still on a range of heavy duty medication, including morphine, pregabalin and amitriptyline for pain. Each messes with your head in one form or another, and although I was there physically, my mind and spirit were elsewhere. On New Year's Eve we went to a dinner party at a friend's house. It was one of the first times I'd drunk alcohol since before I deployed, and it had a big impact on me. I was in bits. I couldn't hold back the emotions and went nuts. I cried in front of my mates, unable to explain to them why.

Lucy and I stayed at my parents until the middle of January, when we finally returned home. I was still very unwell and on lots of drugs. I slept all the time and couldn't get out of bed before midday. As I'd refused to attend Headley Court I was referred to a regional rehab unit in Gütersloh. There was a decent physio department there but it was mainly set up to deal with sports injuries. There were no other war wounded there. It was not ideal but it was my decision and was what best suited my family at the time. I was still experiencing chest pains and nerve pain down my arm, which would twitch involuntarily, a situation that would not die down until I had another operation a year later.

Luke was born on 27 February. Lucy was late and was induced, which was ideal, since I don't think I was in a fit state to be driving at break-neck speed through the night. I was there at the birth, and he was perfect.

In May I went back to work. I asked to go back as I felt like a malingerer sitting at home. I was given a desk job in the training wing responsible for training policy for the battalion. I had come off morphine, diclofenac and amitriptyline because I couldn't think straight, but I was still taking pregabalin for the nerve pain and would do for around 14 months.

I convinced myself that life was progressing as it should and that I was getting better. The physical wounds were healing, but under the surface there was a much bigger issue that I was trying my best to ignore.

CHAPTER 14
FLASHBACK

I'm back at the police station but I'm on my own and it's night time. I'm standing at the side door. As I am drawn inside the building, a small fire crackles at my feet to the right hand side of the door; it provides the only noise and the only light as I edge inside the building.

Bloody hand prints provide gruesome décor to the white washed walls, and my boots splash in the blood on the ground. My weapon is on my shoulder and I swing it first to the right and then the left to investigate the gaping blackness around me.

I move down the corridor with slow, creeping steps. I'm drawn into the darkness by something. Every fibre in my body fights the impulse to advance. My heart is in my throat. My breathing quickens as I reach the final door of the corridor.

I'm dreaming and I fight to wake up. I can't breathe. I try to scream and to thrash about, but no sound comes out and I can't move.

The door is just up on my right. I turn to face it, but it's not empty. The door frame is filled with a blackness darker than the night surrounding it. A figure fills the open space and it reaches for me. It has no form, it makes no noise and I know if I empty my magazine at it, it will do no good.

It's the devil. He's here.

I woke, bathed in sweat with my heart racing. I couldn't calm the panic and fear. The dreams happened almost every night. Eight months after being shot I was supposed to be on the road to recovery but I wasn't doing well. My emotions were all over the place. I was jumpy. I was anxious. I couldn't sleep and when I did I was having terrible dreams. I saw dead people at the end of the fucking bed. I couldn't talk about anything without crying, feeling like my emotions were bound together by the thinnest of eggshells that could be broken through at any point.

Physically my wounds were healing, but my injuries went deeper than flesh and tissue. To begin with I thought the dreams were just my mind's way of dealing with the police station and what happened there. I assumed I would put that to bed and everything would be okay. But other behaviours started to worry me. I was paranoid. I obsessed over what people were saying about me and what they thought about me. I was convinced I had failed.

To keep the dreams away, I laid awake trying not to think. But thoughts would snowball. I would end up arguing with myself into the small hours, exhausted and angry.

The episodes would be sparked by events that linked to Afghan. Half dream, half flashback, they would set a loop running. A dog would bark in the distance. There were lots of dogs barking in the night in Afghan. I'd be transported there. Dark thoughts would creep in and my internal dialogue would begin irrational arguments. I tried to fight against the thoughts that were spinning through my head.

SHUT UP, SHUT UP, SHUT UP!

I tried to think of positive things.

'What about holidays? I like holidays. Where would I like to go next?' I'd ask myself.

My internal dialogue always had a rebuttal. BUT YOU WILL BE FORCED OUT OF THE ARMY. WHO'S GOING TO PAY FOR IT? YOU'VE FAILED.

'No I haven't; I did well. I served my country.' It was futile trying to argue against myself.

FUCK OFF! YOU FUCKING CRUMBLED OUT THERE. WHEN YOUR MEN NEEDED AN EXAMPLE YOU WERE FUCKING WEAK AND YOU'RE FUCKING WEAK NOW. YOU'RE A JOKE.

'Forget it. What about that holiday?'

YOU DO KNOW WHAT THEY ARE SAYING ABOUT YOU IN BATTALION? WHY AREN'T YOU SOLDIERING ON? YOU'RE FINE NOW. THEY'VE ALL SEEN YOU PASS THE FITNESS TESTS.

More dogs would bark.

WHAT ABOUT SHOOTING THAT DOG? NICE ONE, DICKHEAD. BEST BIT OF COMBAT YOU DID.

'No, what about the CASEVACs I coordinated? They would've died if not for us.'

SOME DIED THOUGH…

Then the horror started; the deep sense of dread.

SOMEONE'S IN THE ROOM. SOMEONE'S HERE AND THEY'RE NOT ALIVE.

'No. No. It's not real.' I'd close my eyes tight. 'Don't look.'

BUT YOU HAVE TO LOOK.

My heart would race, and I would start to hyperventilate.

'Control your breathing. Just control it. Think about something. Anything. You don't need to look. You don't need to…'

But I would always look and descend into a deep panic. Thrashing around, ripping the bed covers off me and scrambling to get away from the thing at the foot of the bed. Punching for the light switch, recoiling from Lucy's touch and so hypersensitive that her voice, intended to calm, sounded like she was shouting in my ear.

At the worst times I could feel myself back in the police station. I would see the dead. I could feel them there in the room with me. I could feel the slippery blood on my hands and the feeling of a cold stubbly face next to mine.

I couldn't admit to myself that I was struggling, let alone to the people around me. But they all knew. Lucy tried to get me to acknowledge it and get help. She could see I was falling apart. I ignored her. One day I was sitting having a beer with a neighbour, Scott.

'Wisey, you're not yourself. You need to get it squared for the sake of your family.'

It took a friend to break through to me.

I did report it. I went and saw the Doc in battalion, who was a good friend, and explained what was happening. The army mental health provision in Germany was shocking. There were only a small number of psychiatric nurses, and the one I was referred too only ran a clinic in my area once every two weeks. Sometimes that was moved or cancelled because the nurse was having to drive from nearly two hours south of Munster to make the clinic.

By August, administrators at Headley Court had noticed I had not been in and called my medical officer in Germany to ask where I was. I had dropped off the radar because I returned to Germany instead of moving straight from Selly Oak to Headley Court as per usual. They called me in and I flew back to the UK and attended an appointment in the Surrey centre. There I was told in no uncertain term that I was staying. I had a big work project to finish and managed to persuade them to let me complete that. I finally went in for my first period of rehab in October, almost a year after my injury.

Headley Court fills two buildings on a site in the middle of the Surrey countryside. One building, a stately home, houses the wards and the administrative and living quarters and the other is where the business happens. There are a number of gyms there and a pool.

In contrast to the provision in Germany, Headley Court was excellent. It was easy to see how it had gained its international reputation as the gold standard provider of rehabilitation for injured service personnel.

There was no rank between instructors and patients. Sergeants called me by my first name which took me aback at first, but it made total sense in order to build the necessary rapport with the staff, who were there to help you. The centre was split into treatment areas, such as spinal complex trauma, upper limbs and lower limbs, and dealt with physical injuries, mental health issues and welfare.

I was placed in upper limbs and initially went there for three and half weeks. After my assessment I was given a tailored programme of focussed individual exercises specific to my injury. Days began at 8.30am and finished at 4.30pm and were devoted to physical activity.

While my physical injuries were being dealt with, the experts at Headley Court also assessed me psychologically. My diagnosis was 'symptomatic of PTSD'. I saw someone every other day for counselling and treatment sessions, which helped me to understand what was going on inside my head and helped me to realise that what I was going through was both normal and treatable.

There are three impacts to any injury: physical, psychological and social. In war wounded these three impacts are often much more acutely felt than in most other injuries. The psychological ramifications are complex and often lazily labelled as post-traumatic stress disorder, however, you don't have to have PTSD to be affected by war and I believe this label provides a barrier to those who might need to access assistance. I certainly feared receiving that label and was shocked when I heard those four letters. PTSD creates a one-size fits all rubber stamp but in reality it is a range of different conditions which sit on a spectrum. A soldier might not have PTSD; he might have adjustment disorder or anxiety disorder and will not ask for help in fear that he will be pigeon holed as some unstable loon that can't cope.

The MoD stands by figures that state the levels of psychological injury in the military are equivalent to those in civilian life. However, I believe that many people carry on suffering without ever reporting their decreased mental health to a professional. Out of the 15 or so men that I have remained close friends with from my commissioning platoon at Sandhurst, five of them have informed me that they are now struggling with the experiences they had in Afghanistan.

Many others deny to themselves that they have any sort of problem. A close friend has told me how he sees dead people in crowds on a regular basis, but in the next breath tells me he doesn't have a problem. Another has told me how he sometimes doesn't trust himself around loaded weapons, but yet won't seek help, thinking that time will work some kind of magic on the scars he carries in his head.

Socially, the impacts of traumatic war wounded are huge. My injury messed with my own definition of who and what I was. For a long time I had been able to define myself; I was a soldier, I was an infantryman. After being wounded, what was I? I was still defining myself on what I used to be – an ex-soldier – or using labels with negative connotations, such as wounded, injured, broken.

I was in a bad place when I first started my sessions at Headley Court. I made a lot of friends there and in the bar in the evenings we would drink and talk about our war stories, which helped us to understand what other people were going through and to develop a kind of trauma bond with others who had had similar experiences.

I couldn't watch movies or television programmes with shooting in the storyline. If someone got shot on screen, I felt it. The paranoia persisted. I was constantly preoccupied with what people in battalion thought of me. I was convinced they thought I was a bad soldier. At one point I became convinced for a while that one of my own boys had shot me. I got maps out and started to work out trajectories. I measured the diameter of the round from my X-rays to try and prove to myself what the sane part of my brain knew could not be true.

I was arguing in my head. It was frustrating and scary and it made me angry. My head was like a washing machine; thoughts would tumble over and over on themselves. There was massive self-loathing, paranoia and anxiety. It placed thoughts in my head about what other people were thinking of me, and those thoughts became true for me. I would get anxious and upset. It was such a huge mental effort. I spent days in emotional turmoil. I was tired all the time. Even after my injuries had healed, I was spending a lot of time sleeping in the day. I was knackered through thinking so much, and it took a huge amount of energy. When I was back in Germany between in patient stays at Headley Court, I would regularly come home and collapse and wake several hours later not knowing what had happening. I was still healing, and that was taking a lot out of me.

I was still on fairly high doses of pregabalin, which can have a number of side effects including dizziness and headaches. It can cause abnormal thoughts and feelings, confusion, irritability and, less commonly, depression, mood swings and panic attacks. In hindsight, it may not have been the best medication for someone in my position. I was on it for 14 months, and the chemicals in my brain were being messed up.

I felt like an egg with a fragile shell that would crack at any point. When it did, everything spilled out. I was constantly vulnerable and unstable, feeling like I was held together with baling twine and sticky tape. When I wasn't busy doing something, my mind was like a wrestling match, with the police station fighting for my head space. It was always there, waiting in the back of my mind. On occasions I would be having an innocuous conversation with someone and somehow, without even realising, I would find a way of bringing the subject to Afghanistan. I couldn't help it.

I became anxious about any scenario that would trigger a panic, mainly in the hour or so before bedtime, where I'd find myself anxious and twitchy and actively trying to think about other things rather than let my mind drift onto its default setting – Afghanistan. It was a vicious circle. By thinking about avoiding triggers, I was inadvertently thinking about those triggers. I had already started the process that would inevitably lead to anxiety, sleeplessness and, frequently, panic attacks.

I was in and out of Headley Court and trying to manage my career going forward. It was time for me to progress, and the natural progression from my rank and period of service was a staff officer job, perhaps at brigade level, but despite a string of excellent annual reports, with all the time off I'd accumulated and the requirement for ongoing treatment, I was not regarded as a shining prospect. Instead of a decent job, I was posted out of battalion back to Catterick in the spring of 2011 to do a job that was effectively a demotion, but symptomatic of the situation I was in at the time. I was posted to the Infantry Training Centre at Catterick Garrison, where I was to command a team of instructors and together we would mould new recruits into infantry soldiers in 24 week batches. Given my state of mind at the time, it was not healthy for me at all. Regular jobs in battalion do not involve practising war; most of the time you are at a desk, typing. Sure, you have to be the big man, but at a training facility you have to multiply that bravado by ten. You have to constantly portray the epitome of an infantryman to those you are instructing so that they understand what it is they are aspiring to become. As well as team work, high levels of fitness and self-discipline, this inevitably includes the ability to harness and deliver aggression and a passion for closing with and engaging the enemy at close quarters. The recruits were just taking their first steps on this journey and so were understandably interested in hearing about the experiences of their instructors and what it is like to fight in Iraq and Afghanistan, and it had the effect of constantly triggering memories and giving the intrusive thoughts a legitimate platform to be expressed openly, thereby feeding them and making them stronger.

Each day I went to work and piled in, I was making myself unwell. I would return home exhausted, sit on the floor, say 'hi' to Luke and Lucy and the next thing I would be aware of was Lucy poking me to tell me my tea was ready. It was like being a narcoleptic. There was no warning. I would crash into a deep sleep. It happened three nights out of five. There were many things I ignored. I didn't see anything wrong with driving along in a car and bursting into tears. It happened frequently. Other times I had to pull over as my mind had wandered and I would find myself shaking and unable to proceed until I'd had several cigarettes.

On a few occasions I had drunk myself into oblivion and was using drink as a coping mechanism. It wasn't healthy. I drunk to sleep and calm down and realised that I needed to stop. In 2011 I decided to give up entirely and went most of the year without alcohol.

The flashbacks became increasingly vivid. They would be sparked by the smallest things.

When Luke was around 18 months old, we were out shopping as a family. It was a beautiful sunny day. Everything had been normal. I squinted in the bright sunlight as I lifted my little boy out of his car seat and set him down on the tarmac.

'Car park, Luke. Stand still,' I told him.

He craned his neck so his little face could look into mine four feet above him. I laughed at him standing in front of me in his Union Jack cap, Disney Cars sunglasses and dinosaur t-shirt. I moved round to the boot of the car to get out the buggy out and saw a group of guys working on the roof of the building next to the car park. I unfolded the buggy but Luke refused to get in. He took every opportunity he could to use his newly developed walking skills. I called over to Lucy as I led Luke across the car park by the hand.

'Luce! You grab the buggy and I'll meet you in the bank.'

Suddenly, CRACK!

I instantly ducked and started running.

Then again. CRACK!

My heart was racing. I needed to get to safety and assess where the danger was coming from. Luke was tucked under my arm as I sprinted across the open car park looking for cover. He started to squirm and scream as I squeezed him tight. He bounced up and down in my grip. I was in a crouch. I didn't stop until I slipped us both in between two cars. My heart was pounding and my breath ragged. I heard Lucy shouting, but it was as if she was not there. She was really far away.

'David, it's all right. It's okay.'

My mind started to refocus. I was bought back to the present. To the car park in Catterick. People were looking at me as Lucy ran towards me.

Luke stood in front of me. I was sitting on the hot concrete floor. His cap was in the middle of the car park and his glasses were hanging off one ear. Tears streamed from his eyes and his mouth was wide open, but I couldn't hear him crying.

I was confused. I wanted Lucy to get down. What the fuck was she doing? Don't come over here, I thought. Don't fucking come over!

Everything was slow and I couldn't understand why Luke was there with me. Why would Luke be there? Why was he crying? I was in Afghan … wasn't I?

'David, it was the work men. It was just the tiles. They were throwing tiles off the roof.' Lucy tried to show me reason and reality.

The world sped up again, the sound returned to normal and I had a toddler screaming in my face.

CHAPTER 15
WALKING WITH THE WOUNDED

Lucy fell pregnant again as we were moving back to Catterick, and we were both overjoyed. Fatherhood had helped. I was very serious about my responsibilities to my family. Luke was the main reason I had given up drinking. I didn't want to be a pissed-up loser dad.

The time I spent in Headley Court made me realise that despite the severity of the injury I had suffered, I was one of the lucky ones. I'd escaped with my life, and although I had sustained long term damage, I still had my limbs. There were guys in Headley Court whose bodies had been torn apart, and for them recovery was a mammoth task. The nature of the conflict in Afghanistan and also in Iraq meant that blast injuries and amputations were common. The figures were grim; in the year after I was injured, 75 British servicemen sustained injuries requiring amputations. While places such as Selly Oak and Headley Court provided the expertise to rehabilitate them physically, the biggest challenge for many was finding a way back into civilian life after their injuries had healed. There were so many issues that these men had to deal with. Most of them had been fiercely independent, and suddenly much of that independence had been taken away. Being treated as a patient is a passive process. You are controlled by the people looking after you. You have to go along with the process and it can be frustrating. You have lots of stuff done to you and all control and any leadership or command abilities you had previously are stripped away by a system that wants to make you better.

Many of the injured from Afghanistan have injuries they will have to deal with for the rest of their lives. Some will suffer mental health issues much later down the road and do not realise they are injured. The lag between a traumatic event and PTSD presenting itself can be up to 14 years, so those who are not ill now may become ill many years in the future, many once they have left the military, and therefore the links will not be made or the figures recorded with MoD data.

For long term care there are several injured servicemen charities, such as Combat Stress and Help For Heroes. I knew all about these organisations and the important work they did before my tour. But like most of the troops I never considered that I would ever need them. I was an infantryman; I was invulnerable. I was bullet-proof!

One of the charities that wasn't around when I went to Helmand was Walking With The Wounded. It was set up in 2010 by two men: Ed Parker and Simon Daglish. Ed was in the Royal Green Jackets in the eighties and nineties and served in Northern Ireland. Simon was at Sandhurst with Ed but chose to progress with a career in the media. The charity came about when Ed was planning to attempt a trek the North Pole with Simon in a crazy mid-life review, a final clutch at their youth. They had planned to raise money for charity on the expedition. However, fate intervened, and in 2009 Ed's nephew and a friend of mine from training, Harry Parker, was serving as a captain with the Rifles in Afghanistan when he was horrifically injured by an IED, losing both his legs. His father was General Sir Nick Parker, a well-respected senior officer who commanded British forces in the country in the same year Harry was injured. Seeing the challenges Harry faced, Ed decided to use the North Pole expedition as a way of raising money for wounded servicemen and to increase awareness of the skills they have. He decided that part of the expedition team would comprise wounded soldiers. Walking With The Wounded was born and, as well as raising much-needed funds for a range of projects that supported the transition of wounded service personnel into the civilian work place, it also served to raise awareness for the war wounded through the North Pole expedition, which attracted huge media interest.

When I first heard about Walking With The Wounded and what they were attempting, it seemed too ambitious to realise. The wounded personnel were attempting to reach the North Pole, on foot with no support. They were going to man-haul sledges in the most hostile environment on earth in temperatures as low as -60°C.

Each one had been seriously wounded in Afghanistan. Steve Young was a platoon sergeant in the Welsh Guards who broke his back during Operation *Panther's Claw* in 2009 when an IED exploded under the Mastiff he was in. Guy Disney lost his right leg below the knee when an RPG pierced the hull of the Spartan he was in, tragically killing the trooper next to him, also during *Panther's Claw*. Jaco Van Gass was a private in the Paras and lost his left arm and suffered extensive tissue loss and internal injuries down his left side when he was hit in an RPG attack in 2009. The fourth member of the team happened to be my old mate from university and the man who had taken the time to visit me in ICU, Martin Hewitt.

This was truly an amazing and inspirational story of resolve and dedication and the refusal of its participants to give up despite the injuries they had sustained. I followed the expedition's progress with interest. It captured the nation's imagination, not least because a certain HRH Prince Henry of Wales, or Captain Harry Wales as he was known in his military role, joined the team for a section of the trek. I was truly captivated and inspired by their endeavour. They gave all injured servicemen a huge morale boost and showed what could be with will and determination. It made me feel that I wanted to do something myself, to give something back. I had been very badly hurt but I was all too aware of the fact that I had been extremely lucky and that there were many, many souls out there that hadn't been as fortunate.

Martin and I had kept in touch, and soon after his return from the Arctic I noticed a post on his Facebook page. It was inviting applicants for the next Walking With The Wounded adventure, an attempt on Everest. I knew nothing about mountaineering. I'd never climbed in my life. But, inspired by the earlier expedition, I knew I had to apply.

Over the following days I thought about whether it was a good idea and discussed it with Lucy. Potentially it would mean I would be away from home for long periods of time while she was left with the new baby. I mentioned it to the CO at work and thankfully they were encouraging; this is typical of the Armed Forces, as it is an employer that supports its employees to undertake adventurous training, understanding the benefits that these activities have on the individual and what they are then able to bring back to the organisation.

Lucy and I discussed it for a couple of evenings. At the time I was still in and out of Headley Court, travelling down for several weeks at a time. Physically and mentally I was progressing and getting stronger.

After carefully considering everything, we decided it would probably be a good thing. The guys on the Arctic expedition looked like they'd had a really good experience and I felt I needed to do it. It would give me a positive focus for my recovery, an aiming marker and a reason to double my efforts in physio and in the gym, and would give my brain something else to think about.

At that point I was looking selfishly at what I could get out of the experience. Only later did it become more altruistic and about what we were doing for others; I understood what inspiration I had drawn from the Arctic expedition and the effect that this had had on my own recovery pathway. I wanted to bottle that feeling and pass it on to the next guy who needed a shove in the right direction.

I filled out the application form and submitted it.

A few weeks later I got an email back inviting me to London for an interview on 6 June 2011. The expedition was due to leave in March 2012 and there would be several training trips in between. They were obviously anxious to capitalise on the interest generated by the North Pole expedition.

The interviews were held at The Rifles Club in London. I got the train down from York and arrived far too early. Dressed in a suit, I spent a good 45 minutes killing time in a coffee shop over the road.

I finally crossed over the road to the imposing address just off Oxford Street and was led up a steep flight of stairs and ushered into large open hall. The polished wood floor shone, and my shoes clopped loudly as I strode across the large room to greet the grinning face belonging to the scruffy bloke leaning against the far wall, his mug framed by outrageous sideburns akin to Wolverine from the *X-Men*.

'Wisey! What's with the suit?' Martin Hewitt chuckled as he shook my hand and patted my back.

'It's an interview, Martin. I know you're from Liverpool, mate, but surely you realise you can wear a suit even if you're not going to court? What did you expect me to wear?'

He beckoned to his attire: trekking trousers, a polo shirt and cross trainers.

'That's why you're a Para officer!' I laughed.

Martin continued to grin. We chatted and his Merseyside accent bounced around the empty hall.

'Good to see you, mate. You look a lot better than last time.'

My memory took me back to when I had seen him last. It had been the middle of November 2009, nearly two years previously, with me flat on my back, arm paralysed and my head thick with morphine.

'Yeah? You look worse!' I pointed out.

It wasn't just banter. The time he'd spent in the Arctic had taken a lot out of his body. He looked thin and tired and he'd aged, which made sense as I remembered him in his early twenties at university, nearly ten years before. It had been a busy decade for both of us. Martin's paralysed right arm was tucked in his pocket, but one couldn't fail to see how frail it looked – incongruous with the rest of his body, which, despite being thin, still looked strong.

Martin showed me over to a table where two older men were waiting. As they stood up and held out their hands, a boom microphone appeared out of nowhere and dangled just above my head. Simultaneously, a cameraman was at my shoulder capturing the handshakes.

I surmised that this was part of the interview process. The North Pole team had received a great deal of media coverage and their exploits were to be shown in two BBC documentaries in the coming months, *Harry's Arctic Heroes*. I assumed the camera was there to see how I reacted and therefore decided to ignore the crew as best as I could.

'Wisey, this is Ed Parker, co-founder of the charity.' Martin made the introductions.

I shook hands with a very tall chap in his late forties. He was nearly as big as me and had obviously been a powerful bloke in his time. He wore a pair of spectacles which sat on top of his balding head, and he shook my hand with his own shovel-sized grip. I liked him immediately; he gave me a sincere welcome and his public school accented voice and personality matched the size of his frame – large!

Martin continued.

'And this is Russell Brice. His company have put more people on top of Everest than any other.'

I was suitably impressed and shook hands with a gentleman in his late fifties. His hair was white and his face looked tanned and weathered. He spoke with a quiet, serious New Zealand accent as he explained that he had flown back from Nepal after another successful season on Everest that day.

Ed was wearing a polo shirt and Russell was in a fleece, so maybe I was a bit over dressed for the meeting but it hadn't crossed my mind to wear anything else.

The interview progressed and I was asked about my injury and my motivations for volunteering for the expedition. I told the panel about a collage of photographs that hung in the smallest room in my house, which had been taken during my final exercise at the Infantry Battle School. There was a group of us and we were in Kenya. One particular photo showed six members of my training syndicate. We were standing in the middle of nowhere underneath a scrubby thorny tree. The sun was starting to set so it was difficult to see our faces, but having spent so much time with the guys cutting about in the darkness, I could distinguish them as easily as if it was day. Of those six, three had been wounded in Afghanistan. Obviously, I was shot; one of the others received minor shrapnel wounds when an RPG exploded nearby. The third lost both his legs, one above the knee and the other at the hip. He was the most capable officer in our syndicate, widely reputed to have been the best officer cadet during our time at Sandhurst. His name was Harry Parker: Ed's nephew.

I explained how important I believed it was to raise finances for projects that helped wounded personnel back into the workplace and to integrate back into society following discharge from the army. WWTW also ran a scholarship scheme whereby wounded soldiers could apply for funds for retraining directly.

WWTW recognised that once the tremendous public fervour inevitably died down following our withdrawal from Afghanistan, there would still be a requirement for help for our veterans long into the future, and that there was no quick fix solution. It was a tragic fact proven in history that in every conflict the guys who spilt their own blood or gave their minds to conflict had been forgotten in the years after the rounds had stopped flying. It was only down to the great work by our forces charities, The Poppy Appeal being the most prevalent, that people were reminded of the fact that sometimes we need to give a little something to those who have given so much for us.

I explained how WWTW had personally given me hope and inspiration after returning from combat with my injuries. I drew encouragement from seeing other wounded soldiers getting on with their lives, setting challenges and reaching goals, and hoped, in my darker days, that a little further down the road I would be in a position to achieve something. I wanted to be part of it.

It did occur to me that altitude might affect my lung. I spoke to a doctor for advice, and the message that came back didn't instil me with confidence.

'I don't know,' he said. 'Give it a go and see what happens.'

I was fairly confident, however, that my lung could cope with the thin oxygen at high altitude as the real danger for me was rapid changes of pressure. For that reason I could never go scuba diving after sustaining the injury. Everest would be a slow, gradual acclimatisation. I was philosophical. I had never climbed a mountain without a round in my chest, so although my lung was badly scarred inside and it was likely climbing would have some sort of effect, I'd never know what as I'd never experience altitude with an undamaged organ.

A week after the interview I was called and told I had made the next stage of the selection process, so in July I headed to Wales. There was no mention of what criteria candidates needed to display. Obviously to get to the top of Everest you needed a certain level of fitness, and I was confident that I would pass on that ground. However, the other qualities remained a mystery. Over the following months, as I was increasingly tested in different locations and challenges, trying to work out what it was I was supposed to be doing became an obsession. I surmised that personality would be just as important as fitness. The organisers would be looking for team players, people who dealt well with pressure, quick thinkers, people who could cope with media attention and a range of other qualities.

Around 12 potential mountaineers spent three days cutting around North Wales and Snowdonia. We met on the train on the way there. At different stations, different people got on. At the station I saw Dan Majid, a mate from Headley Court who had been blown up whilst serving with the Paras, and as we were chatting a guy with long ginger hair, a beard, a skin full of tattoos and a biker jacket walked over.

'Check out this guy?' I whispered to Dan as he bowled over.

'Are you guys here for the mountaineering?' he asked.

He stuck his hand out as a greeting, and I could see it was deformed and covered in scars.

The man was Karl Hinett, or Burns as he became affectionately known over the next few months. He became one of my best friends. He had been injured whilst serving in Basra, Iraq in September 2005 when he was involved in a riot that resulted in his Warrior armoured vehicle receiving a direct hit from a petrol bomb. Karl struggled to escape as he was down in the turret where he was charged with operating the main armaments, and therefore suffered the worst from the fire that spread instantly around interior of the vehicle. As a result, he received 37 per cent burns to his hands, legs, arms and face and had to have 16 separate operations on his hands alone.

Over the following days we ran up and down Snowdon several times and also did some rock climbing. I'd not done any before, and it was a challenging, fun few days. They were a good bunch of lads, and we a laugh.

During that time I met a chap called Henry Chaplin, an older grizzly guy in his late forties who was involved with WWTW. He was an ex Royal Green Jacket who had done a couple of tours of Ireland in the bad old days when it was seriously punchy over there and therefore was an old friend of Ed Parker. After leaving the army, he went into finance and made a lot of money in the City before setting up his own company in Edinburgh. He was also an adventure sports enthusiast and a good rock climber. He was to become an important role model and mentor to some of the guys, myself included. The whole point of WWTW was transition: getting soldiers into employment whether through retraining or re-skilling. A lot of the guys on the team were officers with degrees. What retraining would they need? The reality was that anyone who had to make the jump from the services to civilian employment needed loads. WWTW arranged for people like Henry to go along and talk about entrepreneurship and setting up businesses or generally about the civilian work environment, to help open the narrow minds of those of us who thought that the infantry was the world. Henry was, and remains, a good friend and respected role model.

After those few days in Wales the group was reduced. One guy had a paralysed right arm and just wasn't fit enough at that point. It was harsh, but eminently more sensible than taking people on more dangerous training exercises and having to deal with the fallout of them not being able to cope. A couple of others just didn't make the team for other, unspecified reasons. It was not enough to have the ability to climb mountains. To get on the Everest expedition candidates needed to be the full package; unfortunately none of us knew what the package was.

Three weeks after Wales, the selection and training process shifted to the Alps. I found myself in the French mountain resort of Chamonix with the remainder of the team. There we met some of the guides who were coming with us. There was Monica: a gloriously inappropriate, specialist high altitude doctor who worked for HimEx, the commercial expedition organiser we were due to climb with. She was a real character, always quick with an innuendo and an outrageous flirt – she fitted in just fine. She looked like she shopped in charity shops, but in a cool way: a fact the boys delighted in telling her repeatedly. She was Spanish but raised in Scotland and she gave as good as she got.

We also met Adrian Ballinger, a world famous mountaineer who was sponsored by adventure wear firm Marmot and took loads of opportunities to take selfies of himself on mountains referencing what he was wearing so he could upload them and keep his sponsors happy. Whenever Adrian stopped to film himself we made sure we were pissing around in the background, swearing or getting naked in the vain hope that our ball bags would accidently end up on a sportswear commercial. He was raised in the US and was an awesome climber, like a goat. He was so skinny I reckoned he had to run around in the shower to get wet. He was a top bloke, and you could forgive his ego as I was soon to learn that mountaineers all tended to be very egocentric in order to survive in a very bitchy industry that was based entirely on reputation and claims of who's climbed what. I started out thinking that mountaineering was a team sport but learnt soon this wasn't the case; it was very much an individual sport and it was weird for our team as we were all about being in it as unit. At the end of the day, though, you climb on your own.

On our first day in Chamonix we learnt the basics of rock climbing before we went up into the mountains and started to learn about real mountaineering, which I soon discovered doesn't involve that much technical climbing. High-altitude mountain climbing it is a lot of plodding. Different mountains have different features, but getting up most of them is a long, very hard slog, for which one needs to be supremely fit.

On the Alpine glacier we learnt the fundamentals: how to use the right equipment, how to put on a pair of crampons, how to pull someone out of a crevasse and, one of the most important lessons, how to self-arrest while falling down an ice face using an ice axe. The correct technique is to jump on your ice axe with the shovel end into your chest and the spike end into the ice. You put all your weight on it as you fall, and dig it in, keeping your crampons up in the air to prevent them catching on the ice and flipping you over in a cartwheel. It is important to get the sharp tool the right way round!

We climbed a few mountains and we stayed in the huts spread out in remote parts of the range. Being up on the glaciers with the space and freedom and amazing scenery was incredible. The aim of the week was to get up Mont Blanc, the highest peak in Western Europe. However, mountaineering is hugely weather dependent and conditions while we were there were too dangerous, so instead we crossed the border and climbed to over 4,000 metres on the highest mountain in Italy, Gran Paradiso. The climb was challenging, but I had plenty left in the tank and at that altitude my lung gave me no problems.

At that stage I had given up drinking for eight months, which may well have been one of the reasons I was fit as fire. On the last night in Chamonix the guys were all going out on the piss. I was a right boring bastard and I needed to have a drink to have fun. In the luxury chalet we were staying in there was an honesty fridge which was full of beer but which we hadn't taken too much advantage of because everyone wanted to make the cut. On the last night the owner of the lodge came by to see if we wanted anything and joined in the banter.

'By the way, I think what you are doing is great, so everything in the fridge is yours,' he mentioned as he left.

Free beer? That was it; I crumbled like a wet Kit Kat. The first can, I hardly tasted. Then second was glorious. After that the floodgates opened and the pin came out as we smashed out on the piss into Chamonix.

Injuries were not an out-of-bounds subject of conversation; in fact we talked about them all the time. There was no getting around it. Each man bore the very obvious scars of battle. Martin's arm was paralysed, Jaco was missing an arm and Karl had his face burnt off. At first this helped to build a bond between us, but after a while I felt as if it was just become a bit too normal to talk about being shot or losing limbs; I began to feel like these conversations weren't healthy. It shouldn't be normal to talk frequently and openly about injuries that make the average person baulk.

The last boozy evening in Chamonix bonded us. We were becoming a team. There were nine of us, and after the Alpine exercise we were supposed to be cut down to six. As far as I could tell there was nothing to distinguish us.

CHAPTER 16
THE ROAD TO EVEREST

The selection seemed to be a rapid succession of increasingly challenging mini-expeditions and the leap between the Alps and the following stage was immense. Just a month after the luxury of Chamonix we were set to tackle the eighth highest peak in the world; Manaslu in the Himalayas which at 8,163 metres was over twice the height of Gran Paradiso and only 700 metres lower than Everest.

Along with Henry, nine of us were on the team to travel to Nepal; the mysterious selection process had not trimmed the numbers. Along with Martin, Karl, Jaco, Dan and me were Manindra Rai, a Gurkha who had joined the 1 Mercians and was shot in the buttock and through the groin in Afghan in 2010 (missing everything vital); Francis Atkinson, a doctor patrolling on the ground in Helmand, where he received a gunshot wound to his upper right arm in 2010 which rendered his hand semi-paralysed; Chris Gwilt, a reservist with 2 Rifles who was mobilised to Afghanistan in 2008 and survived an RPG attack which left him deaf in both ears; and Andy Hawkins, a sergeant in The Mercian Regiment who had received injuries to his leg, arm and hand when an IED exploded near him in Afghanistan. Andy also had extensive burns across his body from a terrible car accident in Cyprus years before. He was a constant joker and could always be counted upon to say something wildly inappropriate in any situation.

We didn't really have much interaction between Chamonix and Nepal except for one day when we all got together in Ambleside in the Lake District to pick up kit.

Apart from Francis, who was a doc, we were all infantrymen which meant we loved kit. It's fair to say that possibly the most common subject of conversation in the army is kit. Getting your kit sorted is good, almost therapeutic. I could fiddle with kit for hours. There are lots of guns, knives and hi-tech gadgets such as night vision binos and laser range finders that look like they've come off the set of a *Star Wars* movie, as well as more mundane equipment such as belt kit, but getting this just right is seen by many as something crossed between a science and an art form.

We picked up the equipment for Manaslu from a shop called Adventure Peaks in the Lake District which specialises in kitting out high altitude climbers. The team went in and practically bought the whole shop. Getting to over 8,000 metres requires a lot of kit, and since none of us were mountaineers, we had been advised what to get. There were essentials without which no climber would get far, the main thing being boots. There were 6,000 metre boots, which were heavy, beefed-up walking boots over which you can fit crampons, and then there were 8,000 metre boots, which were really cool, like astronaut shit. They were two boots in one with a soft, silver liner like a slipper which pulled up above the ankle. This sat inside the outer boot, which was huge and thermal-lined with loads of padding right up the wearer's calf, but was meant to be more worn loose due to the fact that your feet swell at altitude. I wore size 14, which is unusually large for mountaineering – a sport where it helps to be small – so I called round everywhere to find a pair the correct size, and there were only two shops in the UK which sold 8,000 metre boots that would fit me and each of those only had 1 pair: I had to move quickly to secure them.

Gloves were also vital and again they came in stages depending on the height of the peak they were to be used on. The first layer was a liner, then a liner and a gauntlet, then a mitt, then a high altitude mitt. Everything was layered; trekking trousers were worn under climbing trousers, which were worn under waterproof trousers, over which was pulled a down suit.

I drove to Ambleside with Karl who had stayed at ours the night previously after flying in from running a marathon in Finland. We'd become good mates. I had a crappy courtesy car because the previous week a lorry had drifted into the lane I was in and smashed the family car, so I ragged it all the way across the Dales in the Granny-mobile I was driving. I was excited about the kit-fest, and when we got to the shop most of the lads were already there and deeply engrossed in buying thousands of pounds worth of kit, thankfully being provided through generous commercial sponsorship. The kit list was long and it was all top of the range stuff – not through unnecessary flamboyance. We could not cut corners. Sub-standard kit at 8,000 metres would be a death sentence; it was simple as that.

In the store there were piles of equipment dotted around the floor. The lads all had grins on their faces as they added more to their piles, and I was soon among them making my own pile.

After dropping Karl off I took my haul home and filled the living room with it to show Lucy and Luke, before spending a happy afternoon in the study unpacking my new goodies, labelling it all up and repacking it for the trip. I felt the same excitement I felt before a tour when one is issued with new kit.

I left for Heathrow Airport and the journey to Kathmandu on 26 August. As ever, Lucy, who was pregnant with our second child, was very understanding, despite the fact that the last time I had disappeared for any considerable length of time while she was pregnant I had returned home with a hole in my chest.

Dan and I drove down from Yorkshire as he lived in Leeds and it made sense to share a ride. We'd left plenty of time, but the journey to the airport became increasingly stressful after we were forced to divert onto A roads because of heavy traffic. Towards the end of what should have been a casual drive, it began to look like we would miss the flight. By the time we got to the terminal we were sprinting with all our kit on. Check in for the flight had closed, but Martin knew we were running late and had squared it with the airline. As our bags were being weighed I wedged my toe under the scales to lift them slightly and save hefty charges!

'Gate 28: they are ready to board. Don't look right or left, just run,' advised the man on the desk as he handed us our boarding passes.

We passed through security and jogged out into the departure lounge.

'I need to change some money,' said Dan, looking around for a Bureau De Change.

'Didn't you hear what the bloke said? We haven't got time,' I fussed.

Dan grinned.

'Our bags are on the flight now. They're not going to leave without us.'

I thought about it for a second and then smiled.

'Oh yeah. Good, coz I'm dying for a piss.'

We flew Omani Air with a seven hour stop in Muscat, Oman, before a three hour onward flight to Kathmandu, which was already 1.5km above sea level.

We arrived there in the middle of the afternoon, and after some normal developing world bureaucracy which held us up for several hours filling out forms and getting them stamped, we left the airport and were immediately surrounded by dozens of small chattering taxi drivers and porters, all vying with each other to win our business. The scene was bewildering, exotic and exciting. We were thankfully approached by a man with a HimEx sign who drove us to the hotel.

During the journey I took in the sights and sounds of the city. It had the same kind of chaotic bustle as Baghdad but with much more charm and much friendlier people. It was dusty and smelt bad in the same way as most big cities in developing countries do; there were dogs and monkeys living wild in the streets and crazy drivers or moped riders cutting about everywhere on roads filled with huge potholes. As far as I could tell there were no rules of the road. Generally people drove on the left but that appeared to be a good idea rather than the law. The streets were lined with traders selling everything from fruit and meat to televisions and furniture. We drove past a stall where a goat was being butchered right there on the roadside. The national grid was a series of poles with a wire running along it, to which everyone else hooked on their own connections which then ran into their homes. I had to duck everywhere I went because the wires were all at Ghurkha head height; Nepal is a country where few people are 6' 6'.

Kathmandu was a mad old place with mopeds and monkeys everywhere. It was raw, intense and buzzing. Chaos reigned; the streets were snarled up with people and vehicles and lined with piles of rubbish, and there were paramilitary police everywhere trying to look hard as nails.

But it was friendly. Everyone seemed chilled, and no one was out to screw you over.

We stayed in the Hyatt Regency Hotel, which, in contrast to the surroundings, was an oasis of calm and luxury. We were met by a smartly dressed concierge and handed chilled melon juice drinks by a beautiful waitress in a sari. There was a quartet playing in the lobby, and, outside, the extensive gardens were well-manicured and decorated with statues and water features, with butterflies fluttering about the place. It was a complete reversal of what was just yards outside the front gates and not the type of accommodation I was expecting. I could tell by the gobsmacked faces of the other lads that they were just as surprised.

Russell, Adrian and Monica were there to meet us along with a contingent of Nepalese wounded soldiers who had been bussed in for a welcome drinks reception. We all chatted in the bar and swapped injury stories. Most of them had been wounded during domestic conflicts with Maoist rebels and had suffered a mix of mine blasts and gunshot wounds. I asked one of the men how he had been injured.

'I was gored by a rhino,' he answered. He'd been on patrol and was attacked by a beast which injured his spine. It was certainly one of the most unusual war stories I'd heard.

For the next two days we stayed in Kathmandu sorting out the final details and picking up more kit, which included ice axes and crampons, and being briefed on the mountain we were heading to. There are only 14 mountains in the world above 8,000 metres, so it was clear that Manaslu was not going to be a stroll in the park; it was a testing ground for Everest. Russell explained to us that it gets harder and harder the higher you go. 500 metre gaps, which are nothing at ground level, get increasingly harder and more noticeable the higher you climb. There is bollocks-all oxygen to begin with and the air gets even thinner; one could even feel a dramatic difference when swimming in the pool in Kathmandu. Above 7,200 metres is the Death Zone where nothing can survive. Most humans can adapt by gradual acclimatisation, with the body producing extra red blood cells to make the most of the little oxygen there is. For some, however, no amount of acclimatisation will allow them to cope at altitude, as their bodies aren't able to produce the amount of cells needed. It's believed there are genetic variants in populations which give people innate abilities to adapt to altitude; most people carry these genes, but some do not. If you don't carry these genes, no amount of acclimatisation will allow you to climb above just a few thousand metres and any attempt will result in the quick onset of some nasty and life-threatening conditions that are normally associated with those climbing at greater altitudes. There are a family of interrelated pulmonary, cerebral, haematological and cardiovascular medical conditions associated with the diminished oxygen at high altitudes. The acute forms of these debilitating and potentially fatal conditions, which include acute mountain sickness, high altitude pulmonary oedema and high altitude cerebral oedema, often develop in incompletely acclimatised climbers shortly after ascent.

The night before we caught a chopper to the mountain base I hardly slept. We'd been out for a few beers and I was reminded why I'd given up alcohol. I went slightly loco as the flood gates opened and I spent the night in tears talking about Afghan. I was sharing a room with Francis, and he was a good lad who talked to me and understood. It was still hard to keep a lid on the issues that were bubbling under the surface. Swapping war stories often led to difficulties and tipped me over the edge.

We flew from Kathmandu airport up into the valleys, and the weather was clear all the way. It was one of the most unforgettable flights of my life, despite nursing a terrible hangover. It was beautiful. We soared over the chaos of the city towards the mountains that tower over the edges of the sprawl. We followed a lush valley for an hour where at points we were just a few hundred feet above the ground, which would then drop away thousands of feet in an instant as we flew over deep ridges and gorges. The views were breath taking; however, after a while the combination of a bad night and the throbbing of the blades sent me into a deep sleep. When I woke we were descending to a village of bright yellow tents that would be our home for the following days.

We settled in, and after checking out the rudimentary toilet facilities – a shared hole in the ground – a few of us decided we'd make our own, and so Doc, as Francis was named, Henry and I set off with shovels into the countryside.

The first morning in camp I was woken in my tent by a Sherpa with a cup of tea and a hot towel: a little bit of luxury which went a long way.

We were at 3,500 metres and I was feeling fine. The only effect I noticed was slight breathlessness when walking. There were around 30 other HimEx climbers in the expedition, and the whole group set out for a hike as part of the acclimatisation process. We walked to a large glacial lake around 45 minutes away. On seeing the water all the lads immediately ripped off their clothes and dived in. The water was freezing; there were icebergs in it! I'm a strong swimmer and tried a width of the bay but had to turn back after 40 metres as I could feel my muscles seizing up. The civvies on the walk looked on open mouthed at the stupidity of these soldiers who thought it fun to take a dip in such inhospitable water. When we got out Adrian explained that the lake was a sacred Buddhist site and that the Gods of the mountains may not take too kindly to a group of hairy-arsed soldiers taking a dip it.

We spent the following days exploring the area and getting used to walking at altitude. I found myself missing Lucy and Luke, especially when we went into the village where there were several kids Luke's age running around.

The scenery was awesome. Within walking distance of the village were a range of waterfalls and holy sites strung with prayer flags. Manaslu stood sentinel over it all, snow-capped and glowering in the distance. I couldn't quite fathom that, if all went to plan, I would be standing on top of it in the following weeks.

Before we struck out to base camp we were given a medical brief by Monica and advice about pacing by Adrian. We weren't fully acclimatised to 3,500 metres and would be climbing a further 1,300 metres, which would be a lot to take in one day, so we were all expecting some form of sickness. Martin explained that it wouldn't necessarily be the fastest people up the mountain who would be selected for the Everest attempt. I didn't entirely believe him. None of us knew the criteria we were being tested on, which was frustrating, and I decided to take the mountain as it came. It was a big enough challenge in itself without having to worry about what was potentially coming next.

We set out for base camp on 2 September and were up and walking by 8am. I set off slowly, as advised. The trail steepened very quickly and wound up through a forest for several hours until it emerged from the treeline. Below I could see the blue lake we had swum in a few days before, and all around the mountains provided a staggering backdrop. I could see an ice fall on the flank of the mountain we were climbing. It was a vast expanse of jagged ice slowly moving down the side of the mountain. Occasionally I could hear the deep rumble of an avalanche far above as the sun warmed the ice fields above us and made them unstable.

The climb took us over several rickety bridges and into the clouds, where I couldn't see further than 25 metres and where I really started to feel the effects of the altitude. We seemed to be making good time, and I purposely slowed and took more breaks because I didn't want to develop altitude sickness through making too quick of an ascent. I started to feel dizzy and nauseous; not ideal as the narrow rocky pathway I was following was cut perilously into sheer slopes that dropped away suddenly. Plodding along, I was teased by false summit after false summit. The chill had started to set in too. I pushed on until I could see a huddle of yellow HimEx tents in the distance. Base camp had been set up by Sherpas, and when I walked in to the communal tent in the middle, there were six people inside who had made it before me. I was chuffed with myself, as we had been briefed that it would be a four-to-seven-hour climb. I did it in three and a half. Over the following hours the rest of group arrived in various conditions. Dan was suffering, as was Martin, but on the whole it was surprising how well most of us were doing.

We stayed at base camp for a few days to acclimatise, chatting, playing cards and practicing climbing techniques. Initially, as my body struggled to adjust, I felt awful and had a pounding headache for a while but after three days I felt strong and fit, ready for the next stage to Camp 1 at 5,500 metres.

It was a beast of a climb and hard work right from the start. We began by picking our way through a crevasse field. Sherpas had set fixed ropes in it to alleviate risk, but we still had to leap over gaping chasms and were carrying extra kit.

The views almost made up for the effort. The sky was clearer and bluer than I had ever seen, and the sunlight reflected off the pristine snow so radiantly that too look at it without sunglasses was blinding. Halfway up, the cameraman who was with the party stopped me for an interview. I had to catch my breath halfway through each sentence.

'I can't believe I am here,' I told him. 'Less than two years ago I was nearly dead, lying in intensive care with a paralysed right side, thinking that my life was over. Now I am here on the other side of the world, climbing over 5,000 metres.'

By the time I reached Camp 1 I was having to stop every 10 metres to rest. I passed Chris, who was totally fucked, and stopped to chat with him. A few yards further I passed Karl, who was completely blown out. I walked with him for a while and tried to encourage him, but he was too far gone to notice. Then I reached my own nemesis: a 100-metre steep slope of slushy snow. At the top of it a HimEx tent shone like a beacon. It took me 20 minutes of slog and guts to get up that hill, and when I did my legs were screaming and I was dry retching. Around ten climbers were already there and clapped me in. I dropped my pack and fell on it, heaving in great lungfuls of air in an attempt to catch my breath.

After several aching minutes my breathing felt more regulated and I stayed there for a while as the other guys came in before the next stage – descent. Once we'd reached Camp 1 we were to climb back down to base camp. It was part of the acclimatisation process and also a test to make sure our bodies were capable of adapting to the next stage of the climb. I went down with Henry and Doc and after a while started to feel all the effects of being pissed: dizziness, nausea, light-headedness. At one stage my right leg dropped over the track into nothingness and I had to scramble to regain my balance. I was glad to reach base camp and felt sick and dizzy as I sat at the table in the communal tent. I forced myself to down several hot drinks of screech: pineapple flavoured powder added to hot water, which replaces minerals and rehydrates. After four cups in the space of ten minutes I felt completely better. The additive laden drink was a miracle cure! A few of the other lads looked pretty bad as well, but we had a good laugh when Martin threw up in his tent.

A rest day later and I found myself back at Camp 1 on the way to Camp 2. In the interim it had snowed heavily, and we had to wait for better conditions before setting off. The scenery was amazing, and the climb took us through a crazy section of tumbling ice blocks. It looked like

Superman's crystal home. There were overhanging blocks and columns of ice, or seracs, and I scrambled through them quickly onto a plateau above the cloud line, which spread out before me like a rippling white carpet. I sat for a while and rested. A few jagged peaks poked through, giving the impression of archipelago in a sea of white. Just as I was gathering my things together to carry on, Adrian came over the radio.

The sun was too intense and was causing the ice to melt dangerously on the route. The area I had just traversed was in the drop zone. Everyone was being called back to base camp. I was disappointed as I was making good progress but knew safety was paramount. The group of Sherpas who passed me from Camp 2 confirmed the seriousness of the situation. They knew the mountains better than anyone.

I turned and headed back through the perilous section quickly. Further on we had a long abseil down to the next section of the descent, and after a quick bit of rope work I was back on the main line and continuing back to base camp. Barely a minute after the abseil, I was unwittingly walking over a snow bridge: a sheet of snow that has blown over a crevasse to hide the drop below. Several climbers had walked over it before me, but with the hot sun ever decreasing the stability of the frozen structures around us, and the added factor of a 100kg Yorkshireman stomping over the bridge, the ground suddenly and without warning gave way beneath me. I fell into the chasm and thumped down hard on an ice ledge. I lay still for a second. I didn't want to disturb anything in case it gave way again. I was hooked to the line and unhurt and so I glanced over the edge of the ledge I was on. All I could see was darkness. The crevasse was deep, so deep that I couldn't see where the blue tinged icy walls met the bottom.

We'd been told to be calm over the radio, so as I requested help I tried to sound matter-of-fact, but the tension and urgency in my voice was evident.

'This is Wisey. I've fallen into a crevasse.'

'I'll be with you in a minute,' one of the other climbers answered.

'No, I'm actually in a crevasse; I'd like you to come now please.'

Another mistaken voice came over the net.

'It's alright, Wisey, I can see you.'

I snapped.

'No you fucking can't. I'm 6 metres underground.'

Adrian came on to the radio and told me to secure myself further to the line with more karabiners and my jumar, a mechanical device that allows rope through its metal gate but metal teeth grip it and prevent the rope slipping backward. One of the other climbers in the group, Brian, was nearby and radioed to say he was on his way. While I waited, Jaco came on line to take the piss, and we had a bit of banter before Brian arrived, looked over the edge of the hole I was in and advised that I could climb out. I hadn't attempted to previously because I was unsure how secure the ledge I was on was. My concerns proved valid when I turned to get in a position to climb and the shelf crumbled away.

'Shit. Shit. SHIT!' I started to slip further below the surface. I was hanging from the fixed rope like a fish dangling on a line. I kicked around to try and get some purchase on the ice walls all around me and felt the sharp point of one of the crampons pierce my calf before I managed to stop my fall. My ice axe was sticking in the wall four feet above my head, and as I pulled on the rope it went slack. It had been ripped from the nearest anchor point by the force of my fall and was useless. I managed to get my crampons to grip further, reached my axe and eventually climbed out. Thankfully, the rest of the descent was uneventful and Monica sealed the hole in my leg with steri-strips after it had leaked blood all over my trousers.

Days later we pushed on to Camp 2 at 6,200 metres. The trickiest part of the climb was the hour glass, a near vertical climb that sapped energy and spirit. It seemed to go on forever and was tackled with crampons, an ice axe and a mix of poor technique and pure aggression – certainly not the most efficient way to climb. I was spent after the punishing climb and continued on feeling terrible. I felt sick and my spirit was at an all-time low. I honestly did not know if I could carry on and then I started passing out. The dizzy spells came from nowhere, and the next thing I knew I was sprawled in the snow. It happened several times over the following hour and I worried that I was having a brain oedema. I radioed down to Monica at base camp, who assured me that it was symptomatic of exhaustion. A kind Sherpa took my pack for me, and I pushed on. I collapsed five more times over the following few hours. I'm not sure how I made it but I got to Camp 2 and I was a wreck, physically and emotionally. It took everything

I had, and I was convinced that this was it, that I had ruined my chances of getting on to the Everest team. It didn't help that many of the other lads were in equally ragged states of exhaustion. Even Jaco, one of the strongest, said he would rather do P-Company, the tough Para selection process, five times back to back than repeat the climb. It was horrific and ruined my confidence. Every 500-metre vertical assent was like a marathon, and to cover the heights we were tackling was like several marathons a day. At Camp 2 my oxygen saturation level was 63 per cent; in comparison, at one point in Selly Oak it had dropped to 80 per cent, and I was subsequently hooked to an oxygen cylinder for several days and had a couple of pints of blood put in my veins.

However, I recovered after a rest day and adjusted to the new height. A few days later I made it to Camp 3 at 6,850 metres without too many effects. And that's how it continued as we inched up the mountain over the following days. We rested, ascended, rested and descended, up and down between camps, gradually climbing higher. I got stronger as we went. Some days were soul sapping; others were glorious. The weather was changeable and could close in within minutes. Days were spent in tents, playing cards and shooting the shit. Others were spent trudging through stunning scenery, lost in thought. We were a group and relied on each other to keep morale high, but ultimately you climb alone for most of the time, and we were ever conscious that these were the people with whom we were completing for a slot on the next expedition; however, many of us were having second thoughts about whether or not we wanted the place.

The push from Camp 3 to 4 was tough, but the trickle of oxygen at just 1 or 2 litres a minute was all I needed. I felt strong as I tackled an extremely steep ice face and a dangerous traverse. The winds were terrifying when we bedded down for the night, and no one slept. It sounded like a rugby team was outside rattling the tent and giving it a good kick in.

On the day of the summit attempt we used oxygen at 4 litres a minute and that provided the boost I needed. It was like rocket fuel. There was a tangible sense of excitement on the day of the climb and there was no doubt in my mind that I would get to the summit. We made our attempt in small groups and kept our pace. On this final day, we had Sherpas climbing with us to keep us safe and guide us to the summit. Conditions were still poor, with high winds and low temperatures, so we delayed our summit attempt, sitting in our tents on a trickle of oxygen, wearing every item of clothing we had and tucked deep in our sleeping bags. After an hour, the wind was still high but the sun had kissed our side of the mountain and it was time to climb.

It was the morning of 5 October and I set off from our tiny camp nestled in a col (the lowest point on a ridge between two peaks, sometimes known as a pass at lower altitudes) at 7,400 metres above sea level. My Sherpa set a good pace, and although the wind cut through me like cold daggers and hampered my progress, I was more determined than ever to get to the peak. It had been a long hard six weeks of climbing, and I was proud of the progress I had made. Not so long ago I could only focus on the negatives. I was convinced my life was over and that the challenges and excitement I had lived for were gone. Yet within the space of a few short months I had scaled the highest peak in Italy and was on course to reach the top of the eighth highest mountain in the world, on route, hopefully, to the highest.

A pain began to develop under my right eye in the only patch of exposed skin on my face, under my goggles and above the mask I wore over my mouth and nose. It developed into numbness and concerned me; the last thing I wanted was frostbite on my face and for my cheek to drop off. I tapped it and it felt hard and painful. There was no way I was turning back, and I mentioned it to a Sherpa who was on route with me. He helped cover the skin and I ploughed on.

Many in the other groups who had set off before us were struggling. I passed several people who looked like they were close to collapse. One had actually fallen; an older European chap, who was sitting, spent, at the base of a steep face of ice. A group had gathered around him, holding the other climbers back and causing a jam. He looked in a very bad way.

I learned a lot about mountaineering in a short space of time and I realised that, on the whole, it is a single sport driven by ego. Russell gave some advice before we set off on the expedition. He explained that we were in a great position because ultimately mountaineering is a lone pursuit and the people involved in it are bitchy and backstabbing. It is not a team sport at all. It is full of accusations, lies and counter-lies. Your standing as a climber was based on reputation because most of the time no one was around to witness your achievements and so it pays to doubt peoples' reputations. The European bloke that was in trouble was in the process of trying to set a climbing record. I know he was pulled down off Manaslu; I passed him, and the bloke looked like he was about to die. He did get down the mountain, but not without help from other company's Sherpas, which he later denied that he'd received.

It is also a selfish sport. Rescues put people in danger, especially the Sherpas who pick up the pieces when climbs go wrong, often with tragic consequences. In Nepal the top Sherpas are treated like rock stars. Comparatively they earn a decent living, but it is still far below anything people earn in the developed world, and they place themselves in mortal danger for that money.

While most climbed as individuals to fulfil their own goals and ambitions, we climbed as a team. We helped and supported each other. We weren't out to set records or expand our egos. We hadn't bought a ticket so we weren't motivated to reach the peak to justify the money we'd spent. I only took $300 for the entire trip! For everyone else it costs a hell of a lot of money to climb a mountain. If you want to climb Everest you need £100,000 in the bank in order to have the funds to climb a practice peak like Manaslu first; to pay for all the equipment, the flights and permits; and to pay someone like Russell for the logistics to get you there. Plus, you need to take a year out of work to do it. If you have invested that amount of money you won't give a damn what others are up to; if you only have one day, one chance, one weather window, you are getting to the top no matter what. We, on the other hand, were a bunch of mates having a laugh. We didn't know what we were doing and had a 'grizz-it' attitude and a team mentality. We were not going to tramp over each other in our crampons to get to the top. Although we cared, we didn't have £100,000 of care. I knew if I was 100 metres from the summit and I had to turn back for one of my buddies I would do so without thinking about it, because that would be more important to me than getting to the top. It also helped that I had cut my teeth in shitty habitats like Helmand and Baghdad, as it's always good to have a healthy gallows humour when things get tough.

'You okay?' the Sherpa I was with asked after we passed the struggling group.

'Yeah. Strong,' I shouted back at him through the wind.

'Follow me,' he beckoned.

We broke out of the tracks and overtook the jam of climbers. I was breathing hard and my legs were burning with the extra effort, but it was good to have no one in front of us and a clear run.

I saw a peak up ahead.

'Is that it?' I asked the Sherpa.

'False summit,' he answered.

We crested the peak a few minutes later and broke through the cloud into glorious sunshine. Everything changed within a few metres. The scenery was heavenly and we rounded a bend into the shelter of the actual summit. The wind dropped and the views were sublime. I was on top of the world. We crested another false summit, and the Sherpa pointed. The summit was within easy reach with just a small traverse to complete. I stood to get my breath, and Jaco appeared beside me. We whooped behind our masks and high-fived.

As I made the careful sunlit traverse I said a prayer of thanks into my mask. On the final section we passed a Japanese climber on his hands and knees who had collapsed and was being dragged down on a rope like a dog on a lead. He, too, was stretchered off the mountain.

The summit was a tiny platform as big as a pulpit, and there were other climbers there. I waited my turn to stand on it and looked out over the world. Francis was there too with the cameraman. I made a video and said hi to Lucy and Luke from my platform at 8,163 metres up.

When my turn came, it felt unbelievable to stand on top of Manaslu. I had been totally focussed on that one goal for so long that it was almost indescribable to reach it. I felt a mix of great joy and massive relief. I had done what I set out to do and I could go home proud. Mission accomplished.

After a very brief rest, Jaco and I practically raced down the mountain. On the way down to Camp 4 we passed Andy, who was only halfway up and struggling. I wasn't sure that he would make it, but the stubborn bastard did!

At the Camp 4 I took off my daysack and oxygen and started to clear up my belongings from the tent, ready to carry it all back down the mountain. I kneeled down inside the tent and tried to roll up my Thermarest mattress and simply couldn't; without my mask on I was useless, my head spinning, and gulping for air. It took three attempts and a huge gulp of oxygen from my mask before I found the co-ordination to do it. At that level my oxygen saturation level was between 53 and 65 per cent, seriously dangerous levels, and after any length of time at that altitude, one would soon learn why it is called the Death Zone.

Jaco and I carried on down. We were running low on water and planned to boil some up when we got to Camp 2, but were advised that if we stopped we probably wouldn't be able to get going again. Most people stayed overnight at Camp 2 before finishing the descent, but we just wanted to crack on all way to the base camp and to join the celebrations that would undoubtable ensue to mark our successful summit of the eighth highest mountain on the planet. We shoved snow into a water bottle, and by the time we got to the hour glass it had melted enough to give us a few desperate mouthfuls. We continued on and just after Camp 1 we heard Manny on the radio saying he was right behind us. The Ghurkha had flown up the mountain with no problems and was flying back down. We redoubled our efforts to try and beat him, maintaining friendly rivalry and competition to the end, but he caught up and we all reached base camp together.

It had been an epic climb and an epic six weeks full of physical, emotional and literal highs and lows. It was the hardest thing I had ever done and, apart from marriage and fatherhood, was one of the most rewarding. When I arrived home I was knackered. I had given everything. I had no preconceptions to begin with, but the infantryman in me was blasé. It was a big hill, that's all. I thought, yeah, I can put one foot in front of the other. I've done some hard tabs and carried a lot of weight. But you add altitude to the equation and it changes the game. It wiped me out. I was surprised at how hard it was.

I returned home and had lost two stone of weight in the time I was away. It was amazing to see Lucy and Luke, but for a month after getting back I had no energy and couldn't go a day without needed to take a nap.

THE ROAD TO EVEREST

Normally it takes six months for climbers to recover, but we were looking at starting the process again in the spring. I had stressed my body to stupid degrees; I felt like crap and looked like I had been through the wringer with a skinny body and a shit beard.

Some aspects, however, were advantageous. Back at sea level my cardiovascular system was super beefed up. My heart and lungs were massive. My resting heart rate was 30 to 40 beats a minutes and really strong. It would keep me awake at night, as all I heard was boom, boom, boom as my huge heart beat powerfully and slowly. I was advised to take it easy when exercising, as although my CV levels were through the roof, my joints were worn because climbing was like being on a stepper for hours and hours at a time on maximum effort level. I ignored the advice one day and went for a run while I was staying with my in-laws. I absolutely flew. It was awesome. I powered up and down hills for miles without tiring but when I stopped I paid the price. My knees, ankles and hips swelled right up and ached for days after; I could barely walk without pain.

Thoughts of the selection process started to niggle me. Before I left I was taking each stage at a time and enjoying the process. But Manaslu had been life changing. I loved the guys and the banter and I loved the challenge and feeling of accomplishment. I wanted more. I wanted a shot at Everest. Nine of us went, and only five were going on the final expedition. There were faster and stronger people than me on the team, better mountaineers, and I had doubts that I would be picked. I was competitive by nature and I wanted a place; all the doubts that I had had during the hard days on Manaslu were forgotten and I knew I would be gutted if it I wasn't chosen.

November arrived and my mood darkened. I always found that time of year difficult, as 3 November was the anniversary of the police station massacre, then there was Remembrance Sunday and finally the anniversary of me getting shot. It was a difficult month filled with a lot of very difficult memories.

On the 3rd I was due to attend a civic function in London to talk about the Manaslu climb. It was being held at Chelsea FC's ground, Stamford Bridge. The Mayor of Hammersmith and Fulham Council had chosen Walking With The Wounded as one of the charities she would support for her mayoral term. There was a black tie fundraising dinner, and I was due to give a talk after along with a couple of the other guys, including Ed Parker.

I really didn't want to go and tried to wriggle out of it, but Dan had pulled out as he was still unrecovered from some fresh surgery. Somehow he'd managed to break one of the plates that held together the bones in his arm on Manaslu and so was back in hospital getting it fixed. After a long journey to London I met with Ed at the venue. We chatted and I started to drink. I was getting drunk, and while everyone else was having a good time I was finding it difficult. I wanted to say what I had to say and leave. Eventually my turn came. The MC introduced me and polite ripple of applause went round the room. I got up to speak, and Ed reached out and shook my hand as I was walking to the stage.

He leaned in to say something.

'Wisey, you've made the team.' There was a smile on his face.

It took a split second for his words to register. My jaw dropped.

Jesus, I thought. I'm going to climb Everest. My mood immediately lifted. Ed had turned a very bad day into an amazing day. I was buzzing.

I'd like to say that after that I started to carefully consider the task at hand with the due respect and reverence it deserves. It's the highest place on Earth after all. But I didn't. The good old infantryman mentality kicked in. Of course I deserved the place, I told myself. I had no doubts, and from that point it was instant; it was only 700 metres higher than Manaslu. Fuck it, I could do that.

CHAPTER 17
BASE CAMP

My daughter, Jessica, was born in February. It was snowing in Catterick, and she came quickly, so quickly we needed to call an ambulance. Lucy woke me in the middle of the night. She didn't feel well, and we soon realised the baby was coming.

I called my parents to come round and look after Luke then called the hospital to tell them we were going in. When I explained Lucy's condition they told me she was in advanced labour. I called an ambulance, and when it arrived the driver explained that Lucy would have to give birth in the house.

I picked her up and carried her out to the ambulance.

'Where are you going?' asked the driver.

'We're going to the hospital and you are driving us there,' I told him and I wasn't in the mood to negotiate.

Luke loved having a little sister, and things were good. The Everest team was announced. Jaco, Martin, Karl, Francis and I were the summit team, Henry was coming too and Harry Taylor, an ex-soldier with considerable mountain experience, was to be our guide, working under Russell and the HimEx banner. I was really pleased to discover that Dan would be joining us to act as a media liaison with the press back home. Dan had been unlucky on Manaslu, as, despite being as fit as a butcher's dog, he was one of those that didn't possess the required gene that allowed people to acclimatise properly at altitude. They were a good bunch of lads.

Jaco really was the poster boy of the charity. He was a good looking guy with an accent – it drove the women mad! Luckily I could provoke a bit of jealousy among his female admirers by laying claim to a moment of passion with the Afrikaner in a nightclub. It's a long story which involved a silly drinking game and a series of dares which culminated in Jaco attempting to snog me on the dance floor, gripping my head from behind in his one-handed vice-like embrace while his stump uselessly tried to grab my face!

The final team was announced at a press launch in London which was attended by Prince Harry. I had been at Sandhurst at the same time as Harry and in the same intake as Prince William, but this was the first time I'd had a chat with the younger prince. We talked about the expedition and he was very keen. Because he was bouncing back to Afghan he couldn't come, but I got the impression if he hadn't have been going he would have enjoyed the mountaineering challenge.

In preparation we spent a week at Henry's riverside house in the Lake District where we did a lot of walking to build up fitness. It had only been a few months since Manaslu and most of us had recovered and were still fit from the climb. We also spent ten days in Morzine in the French Alps, where in just a few days we climbed over 10,000 metres and covered over 100kms. We were all fit as fire and we needed to be, because although Everest isn't technically difficult, the altitude and terrain you have to cover to reach its peak make it monumentally difficult. There are two technically hard parts: the Hilary Step, which if you were attempting at ground level would be negotiable without a rope but at 8,500 feet with various kit and crampons plus fatigue and altitude sickness presents all sorts of challenges, and the Khumbu ice fall. The Khumbu glacier overhangs a wide valley area just above Everest base camp and constantly sheds blocks of ice into the area known as the ice fall. The blocks can be as big as cars, houses or even cathedrals. The whole area is unstable and criss-crossed by deep crevasses and moving ground that can open into chasms at any point. Avalanches sweep through it regularly. In 2014 one of the blocks of ice broke loose and tumbled onto the ice fall, causing a huge avalanche that tore down Everest's southern flank with unstoppable force and wiped out a group of 13 Sherpas who were hauling equipment up the mountain for other climbers. They didn't stand a chance.

I did my last stint at Headley Court a month before leaving for Everest, where climbing season takes place in spring or autumn. In summer the heat makes the whole area too unstable, and in winter it is too cold.

I left for Kathmandu. It was hard to say goodbye to my growing family as I had missed them terribly last time and there was a new addition to bid farewell to. Luke was growing into a lovely boy – he loved his daddy, and I loved spending time with him – and Jessica was just a baby of just a few weeks.

At Heathrow Airport we had a final meeting with Prince Harry in the first class lounge where we were unwisely given access to free cocktails before being upgraded on the aircraft with more alcohol. It wasn't long before we were fast asleep and waking up in Muscat where we changed aircraft for the rest of the trip to Nepal.

It was good to get back to Kathmandu where we stayed for a few days to get our stuff together and to sort out the climbing permits and visas. However, soon after arriving I had picked up one of the common local ailments: the shits. And they got progressively worse. I was sharing a room with Francis in the hotel and woke several times each night literally running to the bathroom. I began to worry that my summit attempt would be thwarted. Shitting in such volumes ruins your body. Climbing is dehydrating work at the best of times, but when you're losing so much fluid out your arse as well it's a recipe for disaster. We bussed to Kathmandu Airport for choppers to the Tenzing-Hillary Airport in Lukla, and when we arrived I didn't want to get on the helo as I was convinced I wouldn't last a 45-minute flight.

I couldn't eat anything and my stomach was churning as the helicopter rose over the bustling city, which seemed to be half built and half held together with bamboo scaffolding.

By the grace of God and some Imodium I managed to survive the flight intact and was relieved to be on a chopper rather than a plane. Tenzing-Hillary Airport is often cited as the most dangerous airport in the world for aeroplanes. The approach to it is either awe-inspiring or terrifying, depending on whether you are on the ground having landed or in the in the air making an approach. The runway is on the edge of a cliff and there are sheer drops on both sides, so planes cannot abort landings.

The runway is short and on an incline, helping landing aircraft to slow down quickly in the short space, or, alternatively, aiding planes to build up the necessary speed to produce lift in the thin mountain air. Helicopters are much more sensible.

Lukla itself is a bustling little town that thrives on the tourist industry and therefore gets busy with climbers and trekkers. There are a lot of teahouses and hostels and lots of tourist shops selling Everest inspired tat: cuddly yaks and local pots.

It was breakfast when we arrived but I had no appetite. I tried to force some porridge down but threw up. We were not due to stay in the town and pushed out after everyone else had eaten.

The day was a killer. I had nothing in me, I was dehydrated, I had no nutrients and no energy. It was a relatively easy walk, but I only just made it to the next village.

The next day I was utterly chin-strapped and wobbling all over the place. I was dehydrated and had minor effects of the altitude sickness. Luckily the ascent up to base camp was very gradual. And after a few days my stomach problems began to get more manageable. We went slowly on purpose. It took us ten days walking through beautiful scenery to get to our destination. Each day we climbed gradually higher. We only climbed up to 500 metres a day, to give ourselves time to adapt. For several days the diarrhoea hampered my enjoyment of what should have been a nice amble up into the mountains. Some days we were only walking for three hours, and it was the slow pace and short walks that saved me from dropping out of the expedition before I'd even reached the slopes of Everest.

The route to base camp was well worn. It was like an A road for trekkers and hippies. There were thousands of people walking it, which made things awkward, as at times it was only a little mountain trail. There was a procession of people walking backwards and forwards along it. Most seasons the average is 10,000 people, and there was little effort to keep the numbers down as trekking is a big money-spinner for the Nepalese government. Along the route we went through several army checkpoints at which we were required to show our permits. The mountain had created a whole industry, from the teahouses and trailside sellers to the porters who carry gear up and down the trail; the permit to climb above base camp alone is £10,000. The gap between rich westerners and locals was obvious to see. While we had top of the range kit, most of the porters wore flip flops. We had one big duffle bag each and a day sack to carry. The rest of the equipment was carried up by porter or by a beast of burden. At lower altitudes, the porters use mules or large cattle called Zopkio; higher up only the Yak can be used with its huge lungs and ability to acclimatise.

We went through little villages and large towns, one of which was Namche Bazaar, a horseshoe-shaped town built into a deep and steep re-entrant. It was a two day hike from Lukla and is the capital of the region and the main hub for trekkers and tourists. It's the gateway to the High Himalaya region and a further eight days from base camp. As we progressed further the scenery change was amazing. We set off through lush green valleys, rhododendron forests and rivers, and gradually the landscape became more barren with rock, snow and ice as the mountains began to bare their teeth.

Along the route we passed many memorial cairns dedicated to climbers and guides who had died on the mountains. We stopped in several small cosy teahouses which displayed items signed by famous climbers, some of whom had died on the slopes. One had memorabilia signed by American climber Scott Fischer, who was a mountaineering hero and one of the pioneers of commercial adventuring along with the New Zealander Rob Hall. Both men perished, along with six others, in a storm on Everest in 1996, as outlined in the famous book *Into Thin Air* by Jon Krakauer. Scott's body remains where he fell in accordance with his family's wishes. The prayer flags and memorials on route served as sobering reminders of the task we were undertaking.

After ten days, the lush green landscape gave way to rock and ice and our slow plod into the clouds bought us to base camp. At 5,364 metres, it's the staging post for all commercial assaults on the south side of Everest.

The mountain itself sneaked up on me. All the way in we had been surrounded by rugged peaks which blended into each other to such an extent that I had become blasé to the majesty of the surroundings. With so many of the world's tallest peaks in the vicinity, it was hard to see past whichever particular wall of rock and ice was in front of me. But from the vantage point of base camp at the south-western foot of the mountain, there was no mistaking the distinctive, imposing profile of the world's highest mountain. I could trace our path up it, along the glacier that flows through the valley between Everest and its neighbour, Nuptse, through the deadly Khumbu ice fall to Camp 1, then up the Western Cwm to Camp 2 with Lhotse, the world's third highest peak, right in front of you at every step. Halfway up the wall of ice that forms the wide front of Lhotse sits Camp 3; after that a climber cuts left up to the South Col and Camp 4, before scaling the Hilary Step and eventually the summit. It was all laid out in front of me. But that was a long way into the future; for the time being we had days to acclimatise and prepare. And that meant getting familiar with base camp.

Before I arrived I had no firm preconceptions about what the site would be like, but, judging by the numbers of trekkers we had encountered on the trails on the way in, I assumed it would consist of more than just a few tents, some yaks and some Sherpas. I wasn't wrong. Base camp was a vast collection of tents inhabited by around 1,500 people. Imagine Glastonbury on a glacier without sound stages and burger stalls and you are someway there. It was a sprawling, mad, ramshackle collection of adventure junkies, mountaineering celebrities, braggers, weirdoes and businessmen with more money than sense.

Each climbing season, in spring and autumn, the camp popped up on the Khumbu glacier as an exodus of people traipsed in from all over the world. For many it was a destination in itself, marking the end of a long trek through some of the most awesome scenery on the planet. For us it was a place to practice the skills we would need for our push to the summit. Although the ground that base camp is on is relatively flat in comparison to the terrain around it, it is still rugged and provides plenty of obstacles to train on.

Each commercial expedition outfit occupies its own section of the camp. HimEx, being the biggest operator, had the largest section. Our green tents dominated the far western fringe of the site, which stretched out towards the ascent for half a kilometre. In the middle of the HimEx area stood the infamous White Pod, a domed tent around 8 metres high that acted as a hub for everyone. The White Pod was party central; it was where the booze and the music was. It was our own little nightclub on top of the world. The big sound system in the tent was run from solar batteries, and lighting came from guests' head torches, which were strung from the vast interior frame of the structure. White Pod party rules were simple; the party lasted as long as the batteries did and no one went home until the power ran out. HimEx parties were famed among Everest climbers. They were attended by the big-name climbers and the top Sherpas. With so many egos involved, dick-swinging was inevitable. One game that climbers enjoyed challenging each other to was a beefed-up version of pin the tail on the donkey with a manky tiger rug, which took pride of place on the walls of the White Pod. During parties someone would detach the tail from it, climb high up the inside scaffold of the tent and attach the tail to a suitably inaccessible point. The challenge for the drunken revellers would be to retrieve the tail, Spiderman-style. Before we arrived one of the Sherpas had fallen and broken his arm trying: something I was keen to avoid.

We got our induction to the White Pod the first night we arrived. There were around 40 of us in the torch light, giving it big licks, dancing to cheesy music from Franco's iPod. We all got pissed and we all danced badly. During that first night we adopted our expedition theme tune, 'The Safety Dance' – a naff, eighties electropop tune by obscure Australian band Men Without Hats. When it came on the sound system we all got a bit naked and acted like dickheads dominating the dance floor. Karl climbed on my shoulders, and I jumped around like a lunatic. But at 5,300 metres it wasn't long before I was gasping for breath and nearly passed out. I managed to stagger to the end of the song and when the last bar finished I threw Karl off and collapsed in a heap on the floor, panting. I wondered how I was going to manage to get to the top of Everest if I couldn't get the end of 'The Safety Dance' with a Brummie on my shoulders.

After that night we soon got a reputation for being the mavericks of the camp. The practical jokes we had been playing on each other – but mainly on Martin – became increasingly extreme.

On the second day we drew up signs advertising fictitious Martin Hewitt book signings and placed them around the camp. 'North Pole Hero Martin Hewitt will be signing copies of his book for the next two days at the HimEx camp' we wrote.

Over the following days a constant procession of trekkers and climbers wandered into our compound looking for an increasingly bemused Martin, who had to repeatedly tell people he hadn't actually written a book and there was nothing for him to sign for them.

Although we thought this was fucking hilarious, Russell soon started to lose his sense of humour. He was very strict about bringing anything into camp that could jeopardise any of his client's chances of making the summit. A lot of people had parted with a lot of money to be there, and all it would take would be a stomach bug or a cold to infect the camp and the season could be lost. Having scores of strangers traipsing through our corner of Base Camp increased the chances of something going wrong, and Russell told us in no uncertain terms to stop pissing about.

Suitably admonished I formulated another plan, utilising one of the weird anomalies of base camp. Each year, oddly, given its remote, inhospitable location, the camp attracts a dog. It's always a stray that wanders up the trail, following the trekkers who feed it. Each year it's a different dog, and this year's camp mutt was a mangy, grey, feral thing that looked like it would chew your face off if you looked at it the wrong way. Not only was it theoretically the highest dog in the world, it must have been the hardest too. Conditions for humans with thousands of pounds worth of kit were hard enough; this thing just had a flea-bitten fur coat to protect it from the elements. It made the fighting dogs I had encountered in Afghanistan look like pampered Chihuahuas. I marvelled at how the dog could have survived in such extreme conditions. It got so cold at night, regularly dipping as low as -20°C, and this little mongrel was still padding around sniffing for scraps. God knows where it slept; it must have crawled into a tent somewhere. And that gave me an idea.

I started collecting bacon from breakfast for a couple of days until I had a tasty bag of scraps and then one night, when the other guys had gone off to the White Pod, I set off in search of the dog. I found it sniffing around one of the mess tents of another expedition operator and gradually lured it back to our section with the morsels I had been saving.

Dan had pitched his tent next to mine, and I generously sprinkled the last of the bacon rinds around his entrance and threw a handful inside. The dog lapped them up, and the minute it stuck its muzzle inside the opening, I lifted its back legs up and heaved it inside, zipping the cover over quickly before it could turn round and take a chunk out of my arm.

Satisfied that the animal was snugly trapped inside my climbing buddy's accommodation, I wandered over to the White Pod for a beer. I chose Dan as the victim of this practical joke knowing that he'd leave the White Pod early, being the least able to acclimatise and therefore the first to leave after a couple of beers. As he left I grabbed the other lads.

'You've got to come and see this.'

We sneaked along behind him in the dark, trying not to laugh. I heard the zip on his tent open, followed by scuffles, a scream and then a shout.

'What the fuck…!'

The dog started howling and yapping, and Dan shot back out the tent and started looking for something he could wave around at the angry hound he had just woken from a nice warm snooze nestled in his sleeping bag; unfortunately for him there are very few sticks to be found on a glacier.

I ran up behind him, full of mock concern.

'What's happening, mate?'

'There's a fucking dog in my tent!'

I feigned amazement.

'No way! How did he get in there; did you leave it unzipped?'

I tried my best to hide the laughter that was threatening to burst out of me and helped Dan remove the animal. I felt guilty chucking the poor thing back out into the cold.

I should really have known better. Stunts like that were declarations of war, and I should have been on my guard for a return salvo the following night when I got into my tent. I'm a big bloke and getting into a tent isn't that easy for me. I have to launch myself in head-first like a missile. As I did I came face-to-face with my partner in crime from the previous night. I looked at it, it looked at me, it snarled, and I grabbed it and tried to wrestle it out of my living quarters. I could hear Dan in stitches outside.

The messing around and the parties helped punctuate the long periods of inactivity and boredom. While we were acclimatising there was not much to keep us occupied other than reading, playing cards, listening to music and talking bollocks.

The best stunt we pulled took place after a few days in camp when Jaco and I dreamed up a scheme to conduct the world's highest streak.

We waited until first thing in the morning as everyone was waking and venturing outside to prepare breakfast. We walked right to the far end of camp and took Karl with us to carry our clothes. One of the climbers there that season was an American called Conrad Anker. He was the team leader who, in 1999, found George Mallory's body on the mountain. We found Conrad's tent at the far end of base camp, climbed below a low ridge behind it and undressed. Wearing just a climbing harness and 8,000 metre boots, I climbed on top of the ridge and called over to the legendary climber, who was drinking coffee and lost in his thoughts.

'Hey, Conrad, kiss my British arse!' I turned and slapped my butt cheeks in his general direction.

Coolly, he lifted the brim of the cowboy hat he was wearing, looked and me and burst out laughing, lifting up his cup of coffee in a mock salute. Jaco and I then jogged purposely across base camp from one end to the other in full view of the hundreds of climbers and their teams.

Later in the day, when we were in the White Pod playing backgammon and revelling in the glory of the audacious stunt, Russell came and found us.

'So you guys did a naked streak this morning?' he asked.

'Yeah, hilarious wasn't it?' Jaco giggled.

Russell was diplomatic.

'Personally I do think it was funny.'

There was a 'but' coming.

'But,' he continued, 'the Nepalese officials haven't seen the funny side.'

Trying his best not to sound like a schoolteacher admonishing naughty children, he explained that the Everest officials who patrol the camp had heard about our little escapade and were not amused.

'What's the worst they can do?' I shrugged.

'They will come round later and will most probably fine you, but they might even revoke your permit and chuck you off base camp.'

'What, for streaking?'

'They just don't find it funny, Wisey.'

So later in the afternoon an English-speaking guide strolled over to HimEx and picked out Jaco and I. By that time we already had a plan.

'We'll just deny it,' we agreed.

He sat us down and asked us why we had done it.

'How do you know it was us?' I asked defensively.

He looked at us, sighed and raised his eyebrows.

'He's got one arm,' he said pointing at Jaco, 'and you're massive and you have a tattoo across half your back; you weren't hard to track down.'

I slumped.

'Alright, it's a fair cop,' I said, holding up my hands for dramatic effect.

We apologised profusely and told the guy we didn't mean to cause offense and we really didn't know that people would get upset. Thankfully he let us off, but that was the end of the practical jokes as even we had to acknowledge that things had started to get out of hand. We hadn't even started climbing and had almost been thrown off the mountain.

While there was plenty of messing around at base camp, we were also becoming aware that it was a particularly difficult year for climbers. Conditions higher up the mountain were far from ideal. Avalanches were going off all the time. The soundtrack to days was distant rumbling as huge sheets of snow and ice thundered down the slopes around us. The avalanches came off Nuptse and ran through the Khumbu icefall. They also happened at night, which was worrying, as colder temperatures were supposed to keep the ice and snow stable.

Climbers have to wait until conditions are right, and rope had been laid in order to make a summit attempt. That season the rope laying was not going as planned, and progress was slow because the weather was so poor with high winds and warm temperatures.

We had heard rumours before we arrived at Base Camp that conditions were not ideal. Russell and his team had set up camp before we arrived and was putting up tents in a t-shirt. It was unseasonably warm, which meant the ice was more active.

After a few days, when we had acclimatised to base camp altitude, it was time to start pushing on. The process of gradual ascents to get bodies used to increased altitudes we had practised on Manaslu can be done on Everest – but isn't a good idea. There was one major feature of the mountain's topography that would make any regular trips past base camp towards the summit potential suicide missions: the Khumbu ice fall, which climbers had to negotiate between base camp and Camp 1.

Most climbers to the top of the mountain will only cross the ice fall during the night or early in the morning when it is frozen solid and is less susceptible to movement. Experienced, acclimatised climbers can ascend the ice fall in just a couple of hours, while rookies like us could take over double that time.

Tackling the ice fall is a gamble; you are never assured of a safe passage, and so it was not a good idea to repeatedly climb up and down through it in order to acclimatise to the altitudes we needed to get to. We had to look for peaks to climb elsewhere and headed instead to a neighbouring mountain to reach the heights we needed to hit in order for our bodies to adapt. Lobuche stands at 6,100 metres and was a perfect training ground to get us used to the sort of conditions we would encounter at Everest Camp 2.

We planned to climb half way up the mountain, spend the night in camp and touch the summit the following day, then come back down to base camp where we would rest for two days before climbing all the way to the summit again in a day. We would spend another two days right at the top and we were all looking forward to some decent climbing after the long trek we had accomplished over the previous couple of weeks.

The first day out was difficult. It was extremely cold and the snow was coming down hard. Conditions weren't ideal, but I loved being out in this wild environment. It helped that Lobuche is such a cool mountain; the views were fantastic. There are only 14 mountains in the world above 8,000 metres, and from the slopes of Lobuche we could see four of them.

On the first section we climbed through a blizzard. The terrain was all rock and the route was strewn with big boulders that we had to climb around and over. Stinging, wet, cold snow was blowing in sheets at our faces.

At one point early in the afternoon we reached a part of the climb where we needed to rope up. While we organised our equipment, I swapped layers, changing my top to a waterproof one in an effort to keep out the damp.

Eventually, sometime in the middle of the afternoon, we reached our temporary camp and hastily moved into our tents. It wasn't dark but there was nothing to do except climb into the relative warmth of the shelter, talk, drink screech and sleep. My tent buddy was Karl, who was no good at altitude at all. He could hardly speak. As I changed out of my waterproof top, my hand instinctively reached up to touch the gold crucifix I always wore.

I wore it with my dog tags, and it had been with me through some of the most difficult times of my life. It was well worn – you could barely see the bloke on the cross – but I always found comfort in it and I always made sure I was wearing it during times when I needed strength. Weeks after I had been shot I took it off and looked at it closely for the first time and realised that my blood was still dried in the nooks and crannies of the tiny cross and figure. Of everything I owned, that small piece of jewellery was probably the most symbolic and sentimental. So when I couldn't feel it in its usual place on my neck, I panicked.

I started scrabbling around the tent, pulling up clothes and rifling through my pack. I tried to get Karl to get out so I could have a proper look, but he was out of it.

In the end, much to his cries of protest, I dragged him out into the blizzard. I tore through the bags, scrabbling around in the snow, but it wasn't there. I retraced our route in my head. The only time it could have fallen off was when I changed before we attempted the roped section of the climb. I got my kit on and went down to Harry's tent.

'Harry, I've got to go down. I've lost my crucifix,' I told him.

'What do you mean? It's getting dark, there's a blizzard, what are you on about, have you seen the size of the mountain you are sitting on?' he answered, slightly incredulous.

'But I think I know where it is.'

Harry was adamant.

'You know you have piss-all chance of finding that.'

'If I sit here I have no chance at all. I'm going, with or without you.'

Harry didn't really have a choice and reluctantly kitted up to accompany me back down. I knew how selfish it was, risking my life and his for the sake of some jewellery, but I believed it would be bad news if I lost it.

It was easier going back down the mountain that up it, and we reached the area where I was certain I had dropped it in under 20 minutes. By that

225

time at least 3 inches of snow had fallen. Our footprints from earlier had disappeared. From memory I found the place I thought I had taken off my top, and started scrabbling around in the snow and rocks. After just a few minutes something caught my eye: a yellowy glint in the otherwise white background. I reached over, and there, poking out of the virgin snow, was the crucifix. I actually started to cry. I couldn't believe that in a snowstorm, 5,000 metres up a mountain, I had recovered something that was less than an inch long.

That piece of good luck ushered in an amazing couple of days. The weather cleared and the vista that opened up around us was magnificent with spectacular views of Everest. One morning we were awake to see the sun rise over her. The daylight hit it at such an angle that it turned the whole western flank pink. I'd never seen light like it.

We camped just below the summit of Lobuche and to reach the peak we had to negotiate a narrow ridge line with a 2 kilometre drop on each side. It was a hot day, with bright sunshine, and Adrian Ballinger went up first to fix the lines.

When he'd secured the route he came back down and gave me some advice.

'Wisey, do not fall. It's too hot, the ice is melting and those stakes will not hold you. They're fine for a little guy like me, but you'd have no chance.'

'OK,' I nodded. 'I wasn't planning to fall.'

I got to the top and looked around at the incredible landscape, taking time to reflect. Less than a year ago I'd wondered if I would ever do anything meaningful with my life again. My body and mind had been shattered. Since then I'd scaled one of the highest mountains in the world, and here I was again, on another peak, preparing to tackle the biggest of them all. I had an immense sense of achievement and couldn't wait to get down and start the ascent to the top of Everest.

CHAPTER 18
KHUMBU MADNESS

We returned from Lobuche and spent five days at base camp resting. We planned to climb from there up to Camp 2 and stay there for several days before coming down, then going back up and finally making a summit attempt.

When the time came for us to move onto the southern route and make our way through the ice fall, Harry called us in for a brief. He was as serious as I'd seen him.

'You are going through the Khumbu ice fall tomorrow,' he explained. He had drawn a schematic on a whiteboard. There was a huge skull and crossbones drawn on it with the words 'western shoulder AVALANCHES' written on it.

'As you can see, we are running the gauntlet,' he emphasised. 'You go from base camp, you get to crampon point,' he said, pointing at the bottom of the diagram. 'Enjoy it and radio in from there. Once you reach that, the steepness begins.'

He had divided the diagram up into sections. The first was 'mini popcorn'. This was an area where the ice had started bouldering up after it had fallen down along the route we were taking.

'The next area is monster popcorn,' he continued. This was the deadly zone, full of huge blocks of dense, unstable ice which were constantly moving. After monster popcorn there was a small area of safety the size of the football field.

'Everything before it is dangerous; don't stop, keep moving,' said Harry. To enforce the point, he had written 'keep moving', 'move fast', 'do not fall' and 'do not do anything other than move' all over the schematic.

'At the field you radio in again and take a breather; it takes between one and a half and three and half hours to get to the football field,' he said.

Then he pointed to a drawing at the top of the diagram. It represented a ladder crossing over a crevasse.

'This crossing has been named "blood and guts",' he pointed out. 'It's where a young Sherpa lad fell and died last week. When they dragged him out they made a mess of it so it's covered in claret. Once you get to that area you are out of the danger area of the Western Shoulder.'

Unfortunately that hadn't been the case for the young man who had died.

Everest is harsh. It is not a pristine, untouched environment. Thousands have tried to conquer it and have littered its slopes with debris, rope, broken ladders and broken people.

We made our way out of base camp in the dark at midnight. There were 24 of us plus Sherpas. It was silent. All you could hear was the sound of crampons in the ice. Every so often I heard someone curse in the dark.

'Fuck this!'

I could hear ice creaking and sliding in the distance. Every so often there was a crash as another lump of ice gave way and shattered as it fell in the vast ice field in front and above us. I clambered on through a series of prayer flags flapping in the wind, which signalled that, from that point on, we were now playing fast and loose with our safety to get to the top of a mountain.

To my left the western shoulder of Everest loomed out of the darkness. Three office block-sized columns of ice clung to the rocky face and constantly shed blocks down onto the path I was taking. It was as though the mountain was throwing deadly hazards in our path to test whether we were worthy enough to get to the top.

If you stilled your beating heart and slowed your accelerated breathing enough, you could hear ice, rocks and debris skittering down the vast slope. It was one of the most dangerous situations I had ever found myself in. In Afghan there were plans you could make to mitigate risk. There was kit you could use to give yourself an advantage. On the ice fall, survival was in the lap of the gods. Wild, primal nature was in control.

I was psyched up. My adrenaline levels were through the roof. It had been drilled into us to move and move fast without stopping, so I went off at a reckless pace and by the time I got halfway through I was damned near done. By the time I got to the really dangerous bit I almost didn't give a shit. I was climbing against the clock. I knew as soon as the sun appeared things would get very interesting. The dark also had the added advantage of masking the scale of the topography I was clambering through. I trudged on as quickly as I could, all the time aware that by the rule of percentages the longer I was in there, the more chance there was that something would fall on me. The ice fall was steep; you gain height very quickly and so the altitude affects you quickly. I was soon struggling for breath as I climbed through this insane obstacle course of ice.

For a while I climbed with Alexis, the expedition cameraman, and he kept me going with constant encouragement.

At one stage, further ahead, I heard that Jaco and Franko got caught in a sheet of ice and snow that came falling down around them. They ran for their lives and took shelter behind an ice column. Neither of them were the same after that. It completely spooked them, and Jaco said later that was the most scared he'd been since Afghan. It was compelling but utterly terrifying.

Eventually I reached the football field, exhausted. I had been so focussed on moving I hadn't realised my face had frozen. My lips were swollen and my mouth wouldn't move. I just slurred words over the radio to let control know I was in the safety zone. I doubt they understood, but I stood and dry retched in the darkness as the cold air hit my lungs and compounded the nausea caused by the rapid ascent.

After a brief rest I continued to Camp 1. It was soul destroying work. The simple effort of placing one foot in front of the other was immense. We weren't afforded that luxury of staying there as two days before our ascent the camp had been hit by a huge avalanche that bowled down the valley off the south-western flank of Everest's giant neighbour, Nuptse. The tents that remained were full of snow and others had been completely swallowed into the white ground, with only a few tent poles or scraps of sheet poking out through.

After four hours climbing through a giant assault course where everything was frozen, I reached Camp 1 and I felt as if I was absolutely spent.

There was a vantage point at the top and the morning light was beginning to filter through. I stood with Harry on the lip looking over the frozen ice fall. We both shook our heads. As if to confirm our sense of muted awe, a sheet of ice broke away to our right and fell down the western shoulder onto the area where we had been just minutes before.

'If this wasn't Everest and the highest mountain in the world, no one would go through that; it doesn't make any mountaineering sense,' said Harry.

People underestimate what madness climbing Everest is. It is outrageous. The exhaustion was indescribable. It zaps every ounce of energy from you and crushes your will. The climb to Camp 1 was like doing an army obstacle course for four hours with a wet flannel over your face. And that was just the first part.

At Camp 1 I had a hot brew of screech electrolyte powder and a chocolate bar and contemplated the next stage. I could see Camp 2 in the distance. It didn't look that far.

That looks okay, I thought.

I didn't see all the undulations between. It was a proper ball breaker. It broke me emotionally and mentally. There were times I would take five steps and then put my hands on hips to recover my breath, then take another five slow steps and sit down. It took hours, broken down into tiny pockets of agonising movement where my lungs burned and my head pounded. But I hadn't gone that far to give in. Pride kept me going. I was getting to the end; I had been given a task and I was going to see it through. That's how I saw it: it was a mission and I had to see it through to the end. Ultimately, what were the options? If I stopped I would freeze to death or an ice block would come and hit me on the head. Who would walk it for me? No one. Once I was there, stopping was not an option. I was committed to see it through and I did: every last bastard step. I could see Camp 2, but it seemed like it never got any closer.

By the time I got there my body was giving up. It took four hours from Camp 1 over what vertically was hardly any distance at all. I came in with

Alexis, who sat down next to me and burst into tears. I was welling up as well. We had given everything; all I could do was sit there and sulk quietly. The mountain had taken everything, physically, mentally and emotionally. I was done.

I tried to move but I couldn't get my crampons off so Adrian had to come and take them off for me. I couldn't take my rucksack off and my eyes were rolling into back of my head. Martin had got in before me and vomited everywhere, his body just saying 'Have this, you bastard.' Jaco and Franko came in and their bodies went into shock. They were wandering around not making any sense, shell shocked. It was outrageous. A Sherpa grabbed them and put them into a sleeping bag together. It took hours before they stopped shivering. It was like a scene from a zombie movie. The place gradually filled with the undead.

So we sat there in our own worlds, not talking to anyone. Everyone was in the same state. I sat in the main tent in my full kit for hours drinking screech, unable to move.

Karl was in a particularly bad way; for the days we sat there at Camp 2, he barely said a word, and people were genuinely concerned about him. Karl had run nearly 100 marathons and ultra-marathons in the previous year, some weekends he ran two. He was supremely fit but on the mountain he died a death; he was destroyed. I was put in a tent with him and the first night I was told to wake him up every two hours to ask him questions and make sure his brain was working. He was in a terrible state. He didn't move for a day and stayed in bed for two. We passed the time by laughing at each other's misery and playing cards; it was all we could do.

We stayed in Camp 2 for six days. It was a small village of tents set up like base camp into expedition areas. We rested there for two days and then kept climbing to acclimatise, taking short jaunts up to the Ice Wall and back to keep the blood flowing, the fitness up and to keep pushing the body to ever higher altitudes. The plan was to touch Camp 3, which was half way up the Lhotse ice wall, and then come back down to base camp, before attempting the summit in a single push. But the weather was closing in. The winds were harsh. Everest juts into the jet stream and the winds near the peak can gust at up to 200mph; the weather windows that all the climbers wait for are formed when an area of low pressure caused by a monsoon massing over India pushes the jet stream temporarily higher into the atmosphere. This window can last for just a couple of days, giving climbers a tiny opportunity to hit the summit that is normally battered by hurricane strength winds.

Conditions were deteriorating and people were getting hurt. There was a lot of debris from Lhotse skittering down the ice wall. There had been no snow, which would have helped to hold together the rock and ice. Instead, the exposed face was starting to fracture. Each day when temperatures lifted it melted a little, and the surface water seeped into cracks. At night the water froze and expanded, making the cracks bigger. Eventually chunks broke off.

A few days after we arrived at Camp 2 there was a disturbance outside and people shouting for a doctor. A Sherpa had been hit on the side of the head and shoulder by one of these fragments and was being stretchered down from the ice wall.

The Doc went and had a look. It wasn't good. The injured guy had a suspected bleed on the brain; there was pressure building up in his skull and he was paralysed. He needed to get off the mountain, and the quickest way to do it was to call in a chopper. However, at £25,000 a ride, the company the guy was climbing with floated the idea of leaving him overnight and seeing how he was in the morning.

'He'll be dead in the morning,' Doc warned.

A chopper was called and the poor bloke was lifted onto the aircraft. I have no idea how it managed to fly in the thin air, but eventually it struggled to take off and skidded across the ground before getting enough bite to rise.

While we were there another guy dislocated his shoulder, and several more were hit by ice and rocks falling from up high. One of Conrad's colleagues was hit in the head and knocked unconscious but luckily he was wearing a helmet that undoubtedly saved him from serious injury or death. The signs were not good. People were getting hurt and the wind was too high to lay more rope to lay a different track; Adrian went up and tried with a few Sherpas, but the wind was fierce. Initially we thought about waiting it out at Camp 2 but we only had food for six days and a resupply would mean a couple of teams of Sherpas risking their lives to come up unnecessarily through the ice fall in the hope that things might improve in a couple of days. So that wasn't a good plan. The only sensible option was to go back down. There was nothing else we could do.

We left at dawn, and the climb down was a breeze compared to what we'd endured on the way up. I trundled down as dawn broke through the serene and beautiful scenery. The mile-wide valley looked stunning as snow and ice crunched under my crampons.

When we reached the top of the ice fall we had an 'every man for himself' agreement; the Kiwi guide with me shook my hand and told me to keep up, if I could, before crossing blood and guts bridge and launching himself down through the deadliest part of Everest. It was daybreak and the temperature was lifting. We needed to get a move on and I set off at a quick pace, but there was no way I could keep up with the seasoned mountain man from New Zealand. It was really quite hairy clambering over boulders of ice that could have collapsed at any time. Sweating and fatigued after spending so long at Camp 2, we walked back to base camp from the foot of the ice fall in high spirits, knowing that a couple of beers would be in order that evening.

That night we had a big party in the White Pod. We didn't know what the plans were and so we were just going to make the most of the night. Our window of opportunity was closing as we only had a few weeks left in the season to make the summit: we had already been there for six. However, we were hopeful the weather would clear and we would be up the mountain again before too long. I woke up the next morning still in the White Pod with Martin. He had got so drunk I couldn't move him, so in the middle of the night I went to his tent and got his sleeping bag and tucked him in where he lay.

The next day, with bleary eyes, we were called back into the White Pod. Russell was there with his whole Sherpa team. He was visibly upset; he had tears in his eyes when he told us that for safety reasons the expedition was being cancelled. The weather was no good, the avalanches off Nupse were too unpredictable and the debris falling down the Lhotse face was too frequent, but chiefly the ice fall was just too damn unstable this year with the route pushing far to the west and under the mercy of seracs hanging off Everest's western shoulder. All these risks added up in Russell's brain, and his conclusion was HimEx was not climbing this year.

'I've been talking a lot with the Sherpas. This year we see that the guys are not happy. We are pretty shit scared about this whole ice fall. We are very concerned that there will be a big accident here. Sooner or later there will be a big avalanche. If that happens we can kill half of you people in this room.' Russell swept his arm and pointed to each person in the room to emphasis the seriousness of the message.

'I've made the decision to stop our expedition. It's too bloody dangerous. I don't want to be responsible for killing half of you guys.'

It was a hard call for Russ to make but one we all respected. It was not just his business, it was his passion and he realised how much it meant to us. He didn't make the decision lightly. He listened to the people who knew the mountains the best: the Sherpas. And that year they were spooked. When we were climbing through the ice fall we could all hear them chanting and praying. They were scared, and when those boys shit themselves you know there is something amiss. It didn't come as a complete surprise. The writing had been on the wall for several days.

Russell's head Sherpa and Everest veteran, Phurba Tashi, explained: 'You tell us to climb and we'll climb, no questions. It's our job and our duty, but the boys are not happy about it this year. The mountain is not good this year.' He had lost his brother-in-law the day before, and by that point several others had died. It was turning into a bad season, and by the end of it 11 people would be lost on the mountain.

I had mixed emotions. I knew what he was saying was right so I supported it completely; he was the professional. If he said don't climb, it was time to go home. And that was the silver lining: going home.

However, I couldn't help feeling we had let some people down and I would have climbed the next day if Russell had changed his mind because that was the goal we set ourselves. We hadn't set out to go halfway up the mountain. I worried that not summiting would affect the amount of donations the charity received. I worried that I had let friends and family down, especially Lucy, who had invested a lot of time and emotion into the project alongside me.

It took some time to realise that, ultimately, it wasn't our choice whether any of us got to the top or not; that decision was down to the mountain, and if Everest and its neighbours do not want you to climb them, you will not, and you would be foolhardy to try.

The Nepalese believe the mountains have spirits and different temperaments and that people only get to the top of them if the spirits allow them to. They hold pujas before a climb to ask for safe passage. These are religious ceremonies where a local monk comes up to the camp and blesses the climbers and equipment. They burn juniper bushes as offerings; they clang cymbals and bang drums. The ceremonies last for hours and are a way of asking the mountain spirits for passage. That year the locals believed the mountains were unhappy and they believed they knew why.

Nupse had only ever been climbed by 19 people, and never commercially. In the eyes of the Sherpas that was because only 19 people had ever been allowed up the mountain. It just so happened that HimEx was conducting a commercial climb on Nupse alongside our Everest attempt in 2012. Some Sherpas were saying that the god of the mountain was angry at this, that commercially climbing a mountain was a violation. If you wanted to climb individually and pit yourself against it, fair enough, but if you were sending teams to commercially climb it, laying rope for others, that was seen as unfair. Nupse was indeed acting strangely that year. For some reason it was avalanching on the Everest side all the way through into Camp 1 and smashing down into the ice fall, which never usually happened so frequently. These factors together seemed more than coincidence, and in the eerie, looming, oxygen-deprived Himalayas it was easy to start buying into that way of thinking. Perhaps we were never destined to reach the summit after all.

EPILOGUE

We pushed our heavily laden trollies through customs and out into Heathrow arrivals to a small welcoming party. There were banners, balloons and people clapping. Some of the other guys had lots of family members there, but my sole contingent in the party was Lucy on her own; it was late in the evening and the children had been left in York with grandparents. To be honest, Lucy was the only person I wanted to see right then.

After a final short bout of banter with the lads, plenty of back slapping and bear hugs, we all said our goodbyes and went our separate ways. We'd been living in each other's pockets for over two months and it was time to reconnect with our families.

But that wasn't the end of the Everest expedition. There was a lot of follow-up. There were interviews and after dinner speeches where the good work of Walking With The Wounded was presented and support for the charity increased. This was compounded by a TV documentary, watched by millions, and meant I was recognised in the street for a couple of weeks, which was rather odd! A high point of this time was acting as compère for the team's presentation to the Royal Geographical Society. It was a huge honour to stand on the stage and speak to an auditorium that had, over the centuries, welcomed world famous explorers and adventurers through its doors, including Darwin, Scott and Shackleton.

But the real highlight of this period was when I was asked to carry the Paralympic Torch through central London in the summer of 2012. I formed up at the top end of Whitehall in my shiny white tracksuit alongside Ed Parker, Simon Daglish, Dag's son Felix and my old friend Harry Parker. Walking together, but taking it in turns to carry the flame, we walked from Trafalgar Square, passed Downing Street right down to Westminster Cathedral.

I was leading the small group with the torch in my hand as we approached the Cenotaph. I slowed my pace and stopped in front of this most humbling monument. The other four members of the group came to join me as the thousands of people lining the road saw what was happening and came to a moment's quiet. Shoulder to shoulder, we paused with our heads bowed and remembered. I thought of those who had died that day in November 2009 at the police station, those that had suffered terrible wounds and those that struggled to live with what they had seen and done that day. I don't know where most of those men are now, but I hope to meet up with them again one day, perhaps when time has healed wounds enough that we can talk about what happened on that dreadful afternoon.

After our brief reflection, the crowd began to cheer once more, as a team we turned to the left, I held the torch aloft and carried on with this momentous walk.

We had arrived back from the Himalayas in May 2012, and in July I had my Medical Board, which was the formal assessment of all the medical evidence in my case notes up to that point. Three senior doctors assessed my records and, based on the evidence within, made a recommendation as to how my career in the army should proceed. Dressed in my uniform for the first time in months and for what would be one of the last times, I sat and listened to their findings. They recommended that, on two grounds, service in the army was unsuitable for me. Firstly, from a physical point of view I couldn't operate a weapon safely due to the nerve injuries to my hand and shoulder; secondly, it was deemed that, due to all the psychological trigger points, it would do me more harm than good to continue to stay in the army. Either factor alone was deemed serious enough for a medical discharge, but combined it was clear my time in the army was over.

I was expecting the decision, and although it was not what I wanted, I accepted that it was the right one. However, it still felt like someone had punched me in the stomach as I walked out of that office and right over the road for a couple of lonely pints to think through what I was leaving behind.

However, I'd walked out of Heathrow a changed man. Somewhere over the preceding year, there had been a fundamental shift in the way I viewed myself. I'd only ever been in the army; it was what defined me. Whereas before I had been able to define myself as a soldier, an infantry officer, and had carried with me all the connotations that surrounds that definition, post injury I could only think of myself as something I used to be: an ex-soldier, wounded soldier, broken. Climbing gave me a chance to move away from these negative labels, and I discovered that my time in the mountains gave me something I could be proud of achieving, post injury, and gave me the strength to build up a new definition of myself, based not on the past, but on the present.

Some people find the transition from military to civilian life very tough, especially wounded men, for whom the choice was not theirs and who have to deal with the physical and psychological elements of their conditions, as well as the social impact and upheaval of leaving your home, friends and a fully immersive work environment that creates a framework to one's social life.

By the time I was discharged I hadn't worn a uniform for a long time, and Everest had given me the opportunity to find a transition point between soldier and civilian. It made the process easier to deal with and acted like a full stop between the chapters of my life. If I hadn't made the networks and built the confidence I did through mountaineering it would have been much harder, and, what's more, the process of climbing itself was cathartic.

Just prior to being discharged, Ed Parker stepped in once again and nudged me onto a new set of tracks by telling me about an opportunity. Ed sat on the board of a brand new charitable organisation, The Endeavour Fund, that existed to support wounded, injured and sick service personnel and veterans in their ambitions to enhance their recovery through sporting or adventurous challenge. It was hoped that through their actions they would motivate others to take up inspirational activities of their own. The ethos fitted exactly with my own beliefs and values at the time, and I hoped that I had found something to which I could engage my passion and enthusiasm and my vested interest in improving recovery through sport. Ed told me the fund was looking for a project manager, I sent in my CV for consideration and after a couple of nerve wracking interviews I got the job.

I hoped this job would give me the chance to pass all that I had gained through my own adventures on to a greater number of people. As I write we have supported hundreds of wounded service personnel, and if only half of them have taken away what I took in terms of building confidence, understanding my position and gaining some perspective through power of sport, then I'm happy.

I am further honoured to be playing a role in running the inaugural Invictus Games that will see over 400 wounded, injured and sick service personnel and veterans from around the world take part in a sporting competition utilising iconic venues made famous by the 2012 Olympic Games. It truly is amazing to be involved in a project that will amplify the message across the globe that sport is an amazingly powerful accelerant to recovery.

I feel immensely privileged to have been involved in the Everest expedition. It truly was a rollercoaster year or so and I took a great deal away from the Himalayas. It would have been easy to jump onto the next expedition or the next opportunity, but I feel it's hugely important that these experiences are used as staging posts or spring boards to propel guys back into civvie street with a greater chance of success than they had previously. For guys that can move on, the activities presented to them should be used to bolster their chances of transition, not to hold them in a network that prevents them from moving on with their lives.

The bullet that changed the course of my life remains embedded deep in my chest, and I will carry it with me for life. To remove it would mean further bouts of chest surgery, and since it's sitting there not bothering anyone, the doctors have decided to keep their scalpels at bay for now.

It is part of who I am and a permanent reminder of the fragility of life and how things can change in an instant. For our team, Everest remained unconquered in 2012, but that round acts as my reminder that adversity is there to be conquered and that conversely I, and my comrades, remain and will remain unconquered.

GLOSSARY

2iC	second in command
A-COG	Advanced Combat Optical Gunsight
ally	slang for something particularly cool, pertaining to the military
ANA	Afghan National Army
ANP	Afghan National Police
AO	area of operations
arcs of fire	the points at which an individual rifleman or group of soldiers can safely engage the enemy without encroaching onto neighbouring friendly positions. Correct overlapping arcs ensure that a position has all round defence and further ensures that individuals are sure of their own area of responsibility and that all men are not focusing on a single area of threat. Given as fixed and prominent points to the left and right of the rifleman.
Babba	a term of respect and endearment in Pashtu, meaning Old Man or Grandfather
BATSUB	British Army Training Support Unit Belize
BIAP	Baghdad International Airport
bone	slang for boring or mundane, can also mean stupid or pointless depending on context

bundu	wilderness region
CASEVAC	casualty evacuation – from point of injury to medical post
CCAST	Critical Care Air Support Team
CO	Commanding Officer
Comd	commander
Coy	Company
Crab Air	derogatory name for the RAF, and those in the service are known as 'crabs'
CWS	Common Weapons Sight
dossing	slang for sleeping
EOD	Explosive Ordnance Disposal
ETA	estimated time of arrival
fighting season	the period of increased violence in Afghanistan witnessed annually throughout the summer months, around Easter until September
FLET	forward line of enemy troops
FOB SQT	Forward Operating Base Shawqat
GMG	grenade machine gun
GPMG	general purpose machine gun, also known as 'Gympy'
go firm	to go static on the ground during a patrol
Green Zone (IRAQ)	International Zone in Baghdad, Iraq, generally safe
Green Zone (AFG)	the irrigated area that runs parallel to the Helmand River as opposed to the desert that surrounds it. The most violent area in which to operate in Afghanistan.
ground truth	the information that presents at a certain time and place as opposed to what is assumed in intelligence reports
HE	high explosive
Head Shed	HQ – the building itself, but normally the term to describe the people who operate there. Can be used loosely to describe any commander.

Herrick	Operation *Herrick* was the codename given to British operations in Afghanistan
HMG	heavy machine gun – example DShK .50
IDF	indirect fire – any munition projected with an arc that allows it to be fired over obstacles. Including mortars and artillery shells. As opposed to bullets that fire in generally a straight line.
IED	improvised explosive device
int	intelligence
ISAF	International Security Assistance Force
JCCC	Joint Casualty and Compassionate Centre – provides information from theatre to loved ones back home when an individual has been killed or wounded
Lancs	Duke of Lancaster's Regiment
LMG	light machine gun – example minimi 5.56mm
MERT	Medical Emergency Response Team – a chinook helicopter fitted out with essential lifesaving equipment and medical specialists
MiTT	Military Transition Team, mentoring team in Iraq
MMG	medium machine gun – example GPMG 7.62mm
MoD	Ministry of Defence
MRS	Medical Reception Station, the Med Centre
NCO	non-commissioned officer
OC	Officer Commanding
OMLT	Operational Mentor and Liaison Team, a small team of British soldiers embedded within the Afghan National Security Force, typically the ANA
'one fist left of axis'	when talking a group of people onto a target, you use a reference point and the number of finger widths to the left or right of that point

	to guide their eyes. Four finger widths equates to one fist.
Ops	operations
PB	platoon base
PDT	pre-deployment training
PRR	Personal Role Radio
PTSD	post-traumatic stress disorder
R&R	rest & recuperation
Red Zone	anywhere outside the Green Zone in Baghdad, Iraq; potentially hostile
REMF	Rear Echelon Mother Fucker
ROE	rules of engagement
RPG	Rocket Propelled Grenade
Sanger	elevated sentry positions
SBMRI	Senior British Military Representative in Iraq
SOP	standard operating procedure
stag	sentry duty
terp	interpreter
TrIM	Trauma Incident Management
UGL	under-slung grenade launcher
WWTW	Walking With The Wounded
WMIK	Weapons Mount Installation Kit (a variant of a Land Rover Wolf armoured utility vehicle), a light vehicle fitted with various munitions, typically 2 x GPMG at the front and rear

ACKNOWLEDGEMENTS

Firstly I wish to acknowledge how difficult this story must be for survivors of the attack on Blue 25, 3 November 2009, and for the family members of those who were lost, those that returned with terrible wounds and for those who live with psychological injury as a result of what happened that day. I have made efforts to describe the incident in such a way that portrays the horror of the day, anything less I would count as a denial of the truth, whilst protecting the identities and dignity of those who died or suffered as a result of these actions.

To Coops, Barney, Tag, Endo, Cow Head, Clarky, Humph, Fong and Manny, it was a privilege to know you in Afghanistan, thank you for joining me in that place and for helping me to get back.

I must thank all those that were involved in my own CASEVAC, MEDEVAC and onward medical treatment. People who will remain nameless as I have no idea who they are, from a moustachioed paramedic in the back of a Black Hawk that was brave enough to land and pick me up, to an unknown surgeon at Bastion that repaired the artery that was pouring blood into my chest. To the wonderful team of doctors and nurses at the ICU and up in S4 at Selly Oak Hospital Birmingham (I'm sure many of you are now at the QE), you have my gratitude, especially Phil Caulderbank. I found DMRC Headley Court an amazing place brimming with enthusiastic, patient and motivational staff including JP Nevin, who accelerated my recovery no end. Mr Fox at the PNI Clinic,

Stanmore Hospital has performed amazing surgery that has helped me and many of my friends regain feeling, movement and relieve agonising pain.

Importantly, all the professionals that have helped and continue to help me give the premise of being remotely sane have my internal gratitude. Elton (Headley Court), Gillian (DCMH Catterick) and Kerry (Veterans Outreach – NHS) have all been particularly instrumental in giving me tools to overcome psychological injury. It was actually Gillian who first saw an early draft of this book (when it was too painful to discuss the details but easier to write them down) who suggested that the material might be helpful to other people who were suffering from psychological injury and therefore was a catalyst for the book you have in your hands.

Thank you to Ed Parker and Simon Daglish for founding Walking With The Wounded and continuing with your tireless work in helping wounded, injured and sick service personnel and veterans to retrain, reskill and reintegrate back into the civilian workplace post discharge. It is not an exaggeration to say that my involvement with your charity has been life changing for me and many others.

Thank you to Help For Heroes who gave me clothes in hospital when I arrived back to England wearing nothing but a wedding ring, a crucifix and dog tags. You do so much more helping thousands of wounded, injured and sick service personnel and veterans every year but this simple act had a huge impact on me.

Russell Brice and his team at Himalayan Experiences kept me and the team safe in some of the most hostile environments on the planet. Thank you for believing in a novice team of mountaineers who had no idea what they were letting themselves in for and thank you for making difficult decisions to keep us safe.

Some of the photos used in this book were taken by Petter Nyquist and David Cheskin. Thank you very much for allowing me to include these amazing images in this book.

I offer my thanks to Kate Moore, Emily Holmes and the team at Osprey for the kind support and advice you have given during the publishing of *Helmand to the Himalayas*.

This book would never have left my hard drive if it wasn't for a chance encounter over a beer with Nick Harding. Nick has been a huge ally of mine in taking my scribbles, diary entries and rough drafts and putting them into a format that could be converted into a book that a publisher might take seriously. He has become a trusted friend over the past year and he has my gratitude.

To Lucy, you have all my love and thanks for agreeing to 'in sickness and in health'!

INDEX

ABOUT THE AUTHORS

David Wiseman joined the British Army in 2006. He was commissioned from The Royal Military Academy Sandhurst into The Yorkshire Regiment with whom he served tours in Iraq and Afghanistan. In 2009 Captain Wiseman commanded a small team of British soldiers imbedded within Afghan Forces deep into the Nad-e Ali district of central Helmand Province. He was involved in vicious fighting and personally dealt with 25 casualties in just eight weeks before falling to a gunshot wound to the chest himself during an engagement with the Taliban. David flew home to a heavily pregnant wife and after extensive surgery and months of rehab at DMRC Headley Court he joined a team of wounded soldiers with Walking For The Wounded who climbed the highest mountain in Italy, the eighth highest mountain in the world and took on Mount Everest. David was medically discharged from the army in 2013 and continues his charitable work for other wounded personnel on a professional basis. He fulfils a number of public speaking engagements each year and lives at home in Yorkshire with his wife and young family.

Nick Harding is an author and award-winning journalist. He has written several Sunday Times Booklist top ten best-sellers and is a regular contributor to the national press.